English as a Second/Foreign Language

From Theory to Practice

FOURTH EDITION

Mary Finocchiaro, Ph.D.

Professor Emeritus
Hunter College of the City University of New York

PRENTICE HALL REGENTS
Englewood Cliffs, New Jersey 07632

Finocchiaro, Mary Bonomo, (date)
    English as a second/foreign language : from theory to practice /
Mary Finocchiaro. -- 4th ed.
        p.   cm.
    Bibliography: p.
    Includes index.
    ISBN 0-13-279738-0
    1. English language--Study and teaching--Foreign speakers.
I. Title.
PE1128.A2F495 1989
428'.007--dc19   89-30644
                                                                CIP

To Santo, Sal, and Rosemary

Editorial/production supervision: Linda Zuk
Cover design: Baldino Design
Manufacturing buyer: Laura Crossland

©1989, 1986 by Prentice-Hall, Inc.
A Division of Simon & Schuster
Englewood Cliffs, New Jersey 07632

Printed in the United States of America
10 9 8 7 6 5 4 3

ISBN 0-13-279738-0

Prentice-Hall International (UK) Limited, *London*
Prentice-Hall of Australia Pty. Limited, *Sydney*
Prentice-Hall Canada Inc., *Toronto*
Prentice-Hall Hispanoamericana, S.A., *Mexico*
Prentice-Hall of India Private Limited, *New Delhi*
Prentice-Hall of Japan, Inc., *Tokyo*
Simon & Schuster Asia Pte. Ltd., *Singapore*
Editora Prentice-Hall do Brasil, Ltda., *Rio de Janeiro*

Contents

87109

Introduction

My experience as a teacher and teacher trainer in the United States and my assignments in many parts of the world where I have had the good fortune to work with interested, devoted teachers and prospective teachers have reaffirmed my belief that teachers everywhere share the same concerns. With only slight variations because of factors which may prevail in a local situation, teachers voice similar doubts and hopes.

Teachers who are not native English speakers have misgivings about their linguistic competence. Native English speakers who do not know the language of their students wonder whether they can nevertheless teach effectively. Teachers everywhere are uneasy about controversies over current linguistic theories and about the realistic contributions linguistics, psycholinguistics, sociolinguistics, and other sciences can make to language learning and teaching. They are deeply concerned about keeping abreast of the best, most modern methods of teaching, about the attention being given in the literature to individualized instruction and to performance objectives, about tests and grades, about homework, about uninterested pupils, and about "gifted" or "slow" pupils.

All of them are strikingly similar in that they want to become more effective teachers. Nonnative and native English speakers alike express the hope that they can develop communicative competence in their pupils despite what some consider their own linguistic limitations. They want to motivate their students so that they will find language learning a pleasurable, successful activity. They are deeply aware of the fact that they can help their students, their community, and their country better fulfill their needs and aspirations by providing another medium for communicating with neighbors near and far.

This book is dedicated to all those devoted teachers and to my university students whose questions and concerns have forced me to focus attention on the multiplicity of elements involved in the process of teaching and learning a language. It is designed for prospective teachers of English and also for experienced teachers who may find pleasure in confirmation of some of the techniques they have undoubtedly been using. While bringing some current theories to the attention of teachers and other interested persons, the book states in as many ways as possible that the *real* issue is not modern versus traditional teaching, but more efficient, more effective, and more stimulating learning. Such learning will result not only from the knowledge of various, alternative theories which the teacher may bring to bear on the solution of learning problems. It will stem also from the teacher's conviction that successful language teaching is a judicious blend of science and art—art which only the teacher can provide through enthusiasm for the subject, interest in the students, and creative use of the environment and of the materials available.

This book has been written for use both where English must be learned as a second language—that is, as the major language spoken in the community or the language of instruction in the schools—or where English is taught as a foreign language. While such factors as motivation, pace, and priorities will differ, the principles underlying learning will bear understandable similarities. After all, in both situations we are attempting to add a new mode of communication to human beings who possess similar innate physical, mental, and even psychological capabilities. Adaptations for special situations are treated more fully in Chapter 6.

I have confined myself to what I call minimum essentials, written in language that lay people would understand. This has been done because increased interest in the English language throughout the world and special situations within the United States and Great Britain often make it necessary for teachers or even lay people without a special background in education and in related subjects to start teaching with little or no preparation or orientation.

It is my hope that many of you will pursue even further the facts or thoughts I will outline and that you will make use of the many excellent materials which were the source of much of my knowledge and which you will find mentioned at the end of the book. I regret that you cannot share with me the stimulating talks on language learning that I have had with such people (and how I wish it were possible to name them all!) as Virginia French Allen, of Temple University; Douglas Beakes, Education Advisor, United States Air Force; Helen Beko, USIS; Julia Burks, Deputy Director ELT, USIS, Washington; Denis Girard, Director of BEL in France; Dr. Charles Ferguson, former Director of the Center for Applied Linguistics; Prof. Albert Marckwardt of the University of Michigan; Prof. William R. Lee, Editor of *English Language Teaching;* Mme. Sczablowska of the Polish Ministry of Education; Prof. Ludwig Zabrocki and Prof. Alexander Sculz of the University of Poznan; Prof. Rudy Troike, Director of the Center for Applied Linguistics; Harold Urist, Ainslie Minor, and George McCready of the English Teaching Section of USIS; and Paul Weaver (Nigeria) and Donn Byrne (Italy) of the British Council. The list could fill many pages.

I am indebted to Dr. Jacek Fisiak of the University of Poznan in Poland and to Prof. Gerald Dykstra of the University of Hawaii for their careful reading of the first edition of the manuscript. Their comments, suggestions, and encouragement have been extremely valuable.

As you read, I hope you will keep constantly in mind the fact that all *any* book can do is recommend or suggest ideas or practices. *You,* and *only* you, can choose from among these suggestions those you know will work best for *you*, with *your* pupils, in *your* school, and in *your* community.

—*M.F.*

Introduction to the Fourth Edition

Among the many colleagues, associates, and friends who contributed to this edition, I would like to thank Helen Beko, Joseph Bertot, Julia Burks, Gloria Kreisher, George McCready, Ruth Montalvan, Anne Newton, and Lois Roth, all of the United States Information Agency. Virginia French Allen, William R. Lee, Betty W. Robinett, Peter Strevens, Rudi Troike, and Muriel Saville-Troike have each added to my sources of knowledge. British Council officers in Italy in the last twenty years have inspired and challenged me. Paul Weaver, George Preen, Donn Byrne, Kevin Flanagan, Shelagh Rixon, Harley Brooks, and James McCafferty have given me a feeling of belonging by inviting me to give lectures at the British Council and by speaking at United States Information Service and TESOL-Italy (Teachers of English to Speakers of Other Languages) functions.

I am indebted to Dr. Jacek Fisiak of the University of Poznan and to the late, dearly beloved linguist, also of Poznan, Dr. Ludwig Zabrocki, who encouraged me to give public demonstration lessons and to publish in the university journal.

It is with a feeling of deep gratitude and humility that I express my sincere thanks to Ms. Brenda White, the editor of this book, and to Prof. Joseph Virrilli who read the manuscript several times and made numerous excellent suggestions which I incorporated into the text. Many thanks, also, to two anonymous reviewers who made worthwhile comments, not all of which I could use because of the increasing length of the manuscript. I did, however—thanks to them—update the glossary (Appendix IV) and the bibliography (Appendix V). Recently published American, British, and Italian texts will be found in the Bibliography. Appendix VI, listing the names of language associations and language journals with their addresses, has been added.

—*M.F.*

1

Learning a Second Language

The Communicative Purposes of Language

The focus on language and language learning today centers primarily on what human beings do with language and how they use it in their lives. What, for example, do they want to clarify in their minds? What messages do they wish or need to communicate to their listeners? In other words, what functions of language do they want to convey?

In order to express a message so that it can be easily understood, speakers must make sure not only that their purpose in speaking is clear and coherent but also that the language they use—particularly in talking with others—is appropriate for the person or persons for whom it is intended. Appropriateness will entail a number of situational elements: (1) the person or persons to whom the communication is addressed, for example, their age, background, and the language they speak and understand; (2) where the communication is taking place; (3) when the communication is taking place (Is it, for example, a conversation that occurs regularly or frequently?); (4) the topic that is being discussed. More will be said about these elements later in this chapter. Here we will point out that these situational elements are subsumed under the term *pragmatics* and that the functions of language have been subdivided—for the sake of simplicity—into six major categories. While not all writers use the same terms, the communicative purposes intended under each function are similar.

What are these functions?

1. *Personal*. To express one's emotions, needs, thoughts, desires, or attitudes; to clarify or classify ideas in one's mind.

2. *Interpersonal*. To establish and maintain good social relations with individuals and groups; to express praise, sympathy, or joy at another's success; to inquire about health; to apologize; to invite.

3. *Directive*. To control the behavior of others through advice, warnings, requests, persuasion, suggestions, orders, or discussion.
4. *Referential*. To talk about objects or events in the immediate setting or environment or in the culture; to discuss the present, the past, and the future.
5. *Metalinguistic*. To talk about language, for example, "What does _____ mean?" "Is 'hand' a noun or a verb in the utterance 'Please hand me that book'?"
6. *Imaginative*. To use language creatively in rhyming, composing poetry, writing, or speaking.

Notions, specific vocabulary items, complete the functions; in other words, they clarify the communicative purpose of the speaker.

Second Language Acquisition: Some Hypotheses

The last twenty years have seen the publication of a wide range of books and articles on second/foreign language acquisition. A number of these have been based on in-class observation and research; others have been based on observations of those who acquired language through various out-of-class, informal experiences. Some have been longitudinal studies. These are process-oriented studies in which the researcher concentrates on the learner's state of knowledge, that is, the learner's linguistic competence and interaction with the linguistic environment in which he or she exists. Others have been cross-sectional studies. These are based on the product, that is, the language that the learner can produce at the time of the study. I have reread books by Ellis, Seliger and Long, Hatch, Dulay, Burt, and Krashen (see Appendix V) and numerous recent articles. I have found that a number of theories are still highly tentative. Moreover, the sampling of subjects in some studies is not large enough to really differentiate among the factors which are important in second/foreign language acquisition, for example, age, personality, first language, time in the English-speaking country, curriculum, method, and others.

There exist areas in which researchers are in agreement; there are others in which there are basic disagreements. I will outline both areas, as well as their teaching implications, briefly. Many of these implications are based on hypotheses and not on proven fact. Nevertheless, some of these hypotheses will be reflected in the competence and performance of the learners.

AREAS OF AGREEMENT

1. A natural order of language acquisition at a beginning level is the same across cultures and across ages. Both children and adults follow the same route of development.
2. The simplest speech to learn at beginning levels is formulaic speech, that is, utterances learned as wholes and not derived from creative rules. These are em-

ployed for particular occasions, for example, greeting, leave taking, apologizing, and requesting directions. Such formulaic speech helps ease processing difficulties.

3. Formulaic utterances are often termed prefabricated *routines*. They differ from prefabricated *patterns* in that the latter are partly memorized and partly creative (novel) utterances.

4. Every human being is born with a language acquisition device (LAD) which consists of two parts: (a) the general, universal "rules" of all natural languages, and (b) a set of lower-level rules for finding out how the universal rules (e.g., to form the interrogative or negative) are realized (expressed) in the language to be learned.

5. Second language acquisition (SLA) is a universal process which reflects the properties of the human mind. The innate mechanism operates (more or less) as a result of input (hearing normal, comprehensible, conversational language).

6. Learning is fairly regular in its development: imitation, intonation, routines, *wh* and yes-no questions, creative *wh* and yes-no questions, inversion rules (e.g., *Is that* a new story?).

7. Variables are found both in the rate and route of learning. For example, age, classroom environment, motivation, and personality affect both the rate and the route.

8. Interaction plays a role in the rate (not the route) of second language development, as does age. Adults tend to learn at a faster rate.

9. There is a natural order of acquisition, according to studies by Dulay, Burt, and Krashen. The order of acquisition of eleven morphemes has been tested on several populations and has been replicated. The natural order emerged primarily when the data were elicited through natural communicative tasks. The order is as follows: (a) nominative and accusative cases, word order of simple sentences; (b) singular copula, plural copula, singular auxiliary, *ing*; (c) past irregular tense forms, possessive forms, conditional auxiliary, *es* plural, *s* in third person singular present-tense verbs; (d) perfect auxiliary, past participle in *en*, possessive *s*. The acquisition sequence for children and adults has been found to be similar and holds for both the oral and written modes.

10. Burt and Dulay have prepared a working model for creative construction in second language (L2) acquisition. (See Figure 1.)

AREAS OF DISAGREEMENT

1. Hatch (1978) feels that the innate mechanism operates independently of the input factors. She posits that second language development depends on two-way conversations that learners engage in.

2. Hatch states also that (a) the frequency of syntactic forms heard influences the forms the learner produces, (b) conversation provides the learner with larger units which are incorporated into the sentences he or she constructs, and (c) conversations with different interlocutors provide a desirable variety of input.

3. Cooperative styles of pupil-pupil interaction may be better suited to SLA than teacher-dominated activity.

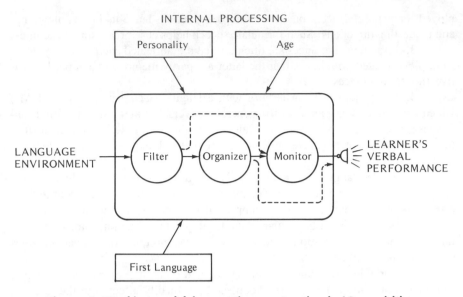

Figure 1. Working model for creative construction in L2 acquisition.

    4. Instruction does not appear to influence the order of acquisition of the morphemes studied. They appear early or late depending on the natural order.

    5. Krashen states that there is no transfer of knowledge from acquisition (subconscious language knowledge acquired through comprehensible input—natural listening and speaking activities) to learned knowledge, that is, material learned in a formal class situation. The interface hypothesis assumes that knowledge can be transferred from one source to the other. The noninterface hypothesis posits that knowledge cannot be transferred.

    6. Krashen states that acquired knowledge is stored by the learner and is therefore available for automatic processing and uninhibited performance. Learned knowledge, on the other hand, requires time for processing, focus on form, and knowledge of the rules.

THE MONITOR THEORY

Stephen Krashen's monitor theory, as well as others on SLA, created excitement in educational circles. His work with Dulay, Burt, and Terrell has given us some insights into novel hypotheses which have implications for teachers, though not everyone is in total accord with all their premises.

    1. The central hypothesis of Krashen and Terrell is that we acquire language when we obtain comprehensible input, that is, when we understand what we hear or read.

    2. The learning/acquisition distinction is primarily for adult learners. Learning (in a formal situation) is useful as an editor—as a monitor—to give the speaker feedback.

3. A lower affective filter, particularly in a formal learning environment, is crucial. The atmosphere must be one of positive attitudes, low anxiety, and self-confidence built on a base of successful achievement.

4. The $i + 1$ principle is important in acquiring language. The learner can move from i (his or her level of competence at the time of instruction) to $i + 1$ (where 1 is the stage immediately following in the natural order). A new word or expression is added to a familiar context. The new item need not be in the natural order.

5. Input should be *roughly* tuned. The teacher should use much known language in context so that there is constant recycling and review of known material.

6. The affective filter hypothesis is realistic: input → filter → LAD → acquired competence. Notice that input does not become intake when the filter rejects it.

7. The monitor is used by learners to obtain feedback on any errors made and to self-correct. Time is needed as well as (a) a knowledge of the rule, (b) a knowledge of first language (L1), and (c) a knowledge of the world.

TEACHING IMPLICATIONS

Implications for teaching culled from various sources of SLA hypotheses are briefly outlined below.

1. Teach a subject in English or use English as a medium of instruction (with bilingual teachers if at all possible).

2. Simplify lexical items through paraphrase, circumlocution, gestures, miming, and demonstrations.

3. Elaborate and expand a learner's response so that he or she is able to end a conversation with what is called a *vertical construction*, that is, an utterance that has been built up gradually by brief questions or comments made by the teacher in response to the learner's question, statement, or comment (cf. Ellis, 1985, 1986).

4. Expansion by the teacher will facilitate the rate of SLA.

5. At beginning levels (a) accept nonverbal or one-word responses; (b) use short, simple sentences; (c) repeat and expand the learner's response; (d) use the here-and-now principle (discuss what the learners can see and touch, not the outside world nor past or future events).

6. Interaction should be reciprocal, not one-way.

7. Make the learners aware of core goals (the activity and the topic) as well as framework goals; that is, (a) input must become intake through the performance of a wide variety of tasks or activities in pairs or small groups, and (b) the learner must be helped to feel the need to communicate. He or she must have control, where feasible, of the topic being discussed. The input must be rich in directives (instructions to be carried out). It must make continuous provision for extending and elaborating the learners' utterances. It must be uninhibited. Learners should not be interrupted when errors are made unless comprehension has come to a standstill.

8. In teaching grammar, in the formal operations stage (over about the age of twelve), allow for different degrees of explicitness, depending on the learners' developmental levels. Provide for enough time to elaborate rules and examples in context.

9. The learnability of a rule depends on formal and functional simplicity. For example, whereas definite and indefinite articles are formally simple, they are functionally difficult.

10. Remember the importance of a silent (nonverbal) period. The learner must have minimum competence in L2 before he or she can begin to communicate.

11. Ellis (1986) advocates a variable competence model. Encourage learners to use an alternative L2 rule (for either planned or unplanned discourse) at any point. Moreover, encourage them to use formulaic speech and routines which can be developed into patterns. He believes in teaching, first, reduced speech (lexicon only), then syntactic utterances, later marked morphemes, and at more advanced levels complex utterances (logical connectors, embedding, clefting). He believes, moreover, that expansion, paraphrasing, and repetition facilitate language learning.

Methodology Today

Many theories and methods favored at the turn of the century are still in use in classes today in many parts of the world. Moreover, and this is another truth about language teaching and learning, few theories and methods practiced in the past have disappeared completely.

We improve them, discard the nonproductive features in them, but much remains, which is then integrated into a succeeding approach. To take a fairly recent example, we still utilize some facets of the audio-lingual method with its emphasis on structural linguistics and behaviorist psychology. We have not done away with dialogues, but those found in texts today are shorter and more lifelike. Moreover, we now make certain that learners comprehend the meaning of all utterances through pictures, gestures, dramatization, or native language equivalents (in classes where all the learners understand the same language). We enable learners to remember dialogue utterances through role playing and other forms of dramatization but never through brute memorization. We still make time, where necessary, to engage in pattern drills, but utterances today are usually contextualized, leading to ease in habit formation and, therefore, to fluency. We still believe—and recent research does not disprove this—that a student response which is rewarded by the teacher is reinforced and learned, while negative, insensitive teacher reaction or feedback can be detrimental to learning since the affective filter will be raised and will thus reject the material.

It is very difficult to select from the plethora of hypotheses, theories, and methods or techniques in use in the twentieth century those which are significant. However, I shall mention those aspects of teaching theory and methods which I have used myself or have seen good teachers use in some fifty countries. Sometimes the results were gratifying; sometimes they were unsatisfactory. The following methods have made an impression on me for a variety of reasons.

1. *The Gouin method*. In this method, sequential actions are accompanied by utterances which describe the action being performed, first by the teacher and then by individual learners. This technique has been quite effective with the younger learners and is still in use today.

2. *The direct method*. In this method, chunks of language are taught in the target language. I loved it as a student of French because I had a superb teacher. However, learners, especially older ones, often find that the overweening preoccupation with pronunciation and intonation, the time often spent in getting a meaning across, and the tension caused by the exclusive use of the target language are frustrating to them.

3. *Basic English* (or other language). I was forced to use basic English for two years in the New York City schools. In this system, language is simplified to include only 16 verbs and 800 content words. The tasks students were asked to perform (e.g., Use these words to write a correct sentence: I/basket/with/go/the/to/park/a.) were time-wasting puzzles and did not lead to even the suspicion of interaction or communication. In basic English one is forced to render Churchill's famous words "blood, sweat, and tears" as "red water from the body, white water from the body, and white water from the eyes."

4. *The grammar-translation method*. This method has been with us through the centuries and is still with us. I hear it used all around me in my work assignments. Here again, there are excesses which are deplorable. Only the deductive approach to grammar learning is used. (In German, I memorized the rule, "Aus, bei, mit, nach, and so on, take the dative," but I never heard or produced an example with any of these prepositions!) Translations of meaningless sentences were found in texts, for example, "The pen of my grandfather is on the dresser of my grandmother" or "The ice is not hot." These exaggerations can be laid not only at the door of textbook writers but also at the door of teachers who are afraid to use their intuition and common sense to modify and adapt the presentation of material and practice activities in a method or text in fashion.

5. *The reading method* (used primarily in the United States and Canada). In the late 1920s, people concerned with education began to realize that few students spoke any foreign language correctly and fluently upon leaving high school or even college. A commission headed by Algernon Coleman prepared a report by American and Canadian educators in which they stated that research and observation indicated that no one could learn to understand or use a spoken language in the limited time for language study given in schools. They recommended that reading skill be given emphasis—both intensive and extensive reading—and that only the grammatical structures found in reading selections be presented, primarily to ensure recognition. Readers (instead of grammar texts) containing simplified and adapted or original stories were used. If the books selected were interesting and at the appropriate reading level, many students derived a positive feeling of achievement from the reading method. It is interesting to note that the market has recently begun to be flooded again with simplified readers at the 1000-word, 1500-word, and 2000-word levels and higher. In some instances, the words are simple, but the sentences in which they are embedded are quite complex and therefore difficult for students to decode.

6. *Structuralism, behaviorism, and the audio-lingual method.* In the United States, World War II brought with it the realization that military personnel who would be serving overseas could not understand or speak any foreign language. Intensive, total immersion language courses (Army Specialized Training Program) were launched to remedy the situation immediately. The work of Leonard Bloomfield in linguistics, Edward Sapir in cultural anthropology, and B. F. Skinner in psychology was used as the basis for materials preparation at the University of Michigan by such well-known names as Charles C. Fries, Robert Lado, Aileen T. Kitchin, Betty Wallace Robinett, Virginia French Allen, and Kenneth L. Pike, and by many others associated with the Army Specialized Training Program. The audio-lingual method dominated the American scene until about 1960, when the first complaints (which had been felt by many) were voiced aloud. The whispers soon became a roar, particularly after Noam Chomsky's two books on transformational grammar and his criticism of B. F. Skinner's work.

In the audio-lingual approach, the structuralists and, consequently, textbook writers emphasized the formal properties of language (the oral and written forms of nouns, verbs, etc.), which students had to learn in order to encode and decode speech whether or not they understood the meanings of the words or of the total message. These were the years when "The Jabberwocky" of Lewis Carroll was quoted ad infinitum to indicate that any student could understand structural meaning if he or she understood the formal signals of language, for example, the fact that *the* signaled a following noun or that *ed* attached to a word generally signaled the simple past or, with an auxiliary, the past participle or the passive voice. While this was true, learners were no closer to comprehending what was being said. The methodologists of those years underscored, too, the necessity for overlearning, a principle which led to endless mimicry and memorization.

The overlearning, the attention to form, and the exhaustion of classroom teachers after five or six daily classes using the audio-lingual method still did not produce large numbers of learners who could communicate with the teacher, their peers, or native English speakers.

7. *Transformational theory and cognitivism.* Despite the Chomskyan revolution and the attention to cognitive psychology which grew from it but which has gone far beyond it, no real method has emerged from the generative-transformational theory. This was, in part, Chomsky's own wish when he announced that his theory referred primarily to native speakers and not to second or foreign language learners and that it could make no contribution to language teaching. While his statements are true, there are several aspects of his theory which have been adopted by practicing teachers and researchers. One is the concept that a language makes infinite use of finite means. Depending on the language, ten phonemes enable its speakers to say anything they want to in that language. Incidentally, this principle had been recognized for many years but never stated in such definitive terms. Another is that to help learners interpret ambiguous sentences (e.g., "Flying planes can be dangerous''), they should be helped to recognize the kernel (deep or base) structures from which they are derived. By the same token, sentences that look alike on the surface but are derived from different kernel sentences should be practiced separately with appropriate words in the sentence slots as, for example, Chomsky's pair, ''John is eager to please'' and ''John is easy to please.''

On the other hand, Chomsky's notion of creativity has been unfortunately misunderstood by many teachers who sometimes expect imaginative ideas and utterances to spring full-blown from their learners' minds after one week of learning at the junior high school level. This may be ascribed also to his notions that all human beings are born with a language acquisition device in their brain and that all languages contain universal categories. These have led to the erroneous beliefs that learners can acquire language effortlessly and that we need to teach only what is not universal. The truth of the matter is different. Second or foreign language learning is a long, arduous process which depends on cognitive and affective factors as well as on stimulating, effective teaching. Whether or not all languages reflect universal categories is still disputed. The ''universal'' negative, for example, is expressed in different forms and positions in nearly all languages.

The cognitive code theory is nothing more than the old, well-known inductive approach in which learners are given examples (models) of language in a context or a situation and are then helped to discover the rules or generalizations which underlie the structure or communicative expression embodied in them. Despite the fact that this information has been available for centuries, many articles continue to speak endlessly about the cognitive code theory versus the habit formation theory.

Good teachers today, as in the past, follow the cognitive code theory to the extent that they present a linguistic item or category through tasks and activities which will lead to habit formation, which will in turn lead to fluency and accuracy in pronunciation, morphology, and syntax. By loosening direct control and encouraging the use of spontaneously emitted utterances from the repertoire of linguistic items they have stored in their memories, students have always been led by good teachers to in-class communication which duplicates communication in the real world. The difference today is that a larger percentage of teachers and texts focus on communication as the major objective of language teaching.

8. *Sociolinguistics, communication theory, and humanistic psychology.* While the United States was concerned about what to use in place of the audiolingual approach, France was using and exporting an audiovisual method, which made extensive use of filmstrips and tape recorders or cassettes. At the same time, many teachers and textbook writers in Great Britain were advocating the situational method. Both methods had their ardent followers and their denigrators. Again, however, both methods were used to good effect by teachers who had the courage to adapt and to transfer the newly learned material to social situations other than those for which it was initially presented and, above all, to follow their own intuition in modifying the methods to suit their teaching styles and their students' learning styles.

It was, however, at about the time that the audio-lingual method was declared nonviable that the eminent sociolinguists Hymes in the United States and Halliday in England began speaking and writing about the importance of semantics and of a theory of communication. These theories, humanistic theory in psychology, which underscored the importance of students as human beings, and a new cognizance of the affective factors and personality traits that influence learning gave rise to a gamut of hypotheses, methods, approaches, and techniques. Here I will make three brief statements about semantics, communicative theory, and humanistic psychology. Attention to semantics gives the learner a variety of behavioral, linguistic, and paralinguistic alternatives (gestures, sounds, stance, etc.) for conveying a message. Attention to communicative theory enables learners to realize that since every speech act takes place in a specific social situation, they must be aware of the people (number, age, sex, roles, status, personality, etc.), the place, the time, and the topic in order to determine whether they will need to use a colloquial, informal, or formal variety of English in communicating with their interlocutor(s). Moreover, appropriateness and acceptability of speech in the particular social situation are as important, if not more so, as accuracy of pronunciation or grammar. Humanistic psychology has brought back the pivotal importance of motivation and personality factors in language learning and the necessity for making the learner feel valued by teachers and peers in the classroom.

These theories have led to the development of a functional-notional or communicative approach, which is described in the next section.

In the United States, several methods have succeeded those previously described in influence, in use, and as topics of research. You may wish to incorporate features of one or more of them into your teaching procedures. Several of them contain techniques worth trying; others have weaknesses you may recognize. I shall list them alphabetically.

Community language learning, created by the late Charles A. Curran, is based on a humanistic theory of learning. At the very beginning, six to eight people sit in a circle or around a table. The teacher (called the knower) walks to each student in turn, stands behind him or her, and places a hand on his or her shoulder. The teacher invites the student to say any utterance, which the teacher translates in a low voice into the target language. Note that the teacher is required to know the language(s) of the students. The teacher repeats it as often as the student desires. When the student feels ready, he or she says the utterance into a tape recorder. The idea of a nonthreatening, one-to-one relationship with their teacher is comforting to adult learners.

The natural method of Terrell and Krashen is also based on a humanistic approach, along with hypotheses about second language acquisition (see the earlier discussion in this chapter). I have one important reservation: The teacher does most of the talking. Some of the positive points are the following:

1. It emphasizes the need for comprehensible language input to learners.
2. It recommends that utterances be expanded and elaborated using a spiral approach for continuous reentry of familiar language.

3. It advocates the $i + 1$ principle; that is, while giving the comprehensible input, teachers add one word or structure (to the familiar context) if they feel that the learners are ready for it. The new items are generally learned without difficulty.

4. It subscribes to the here-and-now principle. Learners talk about things that are part of the class environment and events that are happening at the time of the instruction.

The silent way of Caleb Gattegno contains several principles which you may wish to use: (a) color coding for the sounds of letters, (b) collaboration of learners to produce utterances, (c) silence of the teacher during peer collaboration, and (d) silence of students as they think about what they will produce.

Suggestopaedia, created by Georgi Lozanov, enjoyed a few years of fame but has now been set aside by Lozanov himself. Some of the principles on which the method was based hold some attraction. The course was for adults, who were given new names and professions. They sat on white velvet couches and listened to delightful background music. They learned many vocabulary words during a six-hour daily session but, to the best of my knowledge, not in any meaningful context. Communication and interaction did not seem to be an integral part of the program.

Total physical response, devised by James J. Asher, is a mixture of the Gouin method and the direct method. Asher uses imperatives and actions (jump, sit down, run, etc.) which the learners carry out. The sentences become longer and more complex, requiring that the students perform multiple actions (if they can remember the several parts of the utterance).

I'd like to mention two other methodological proposals. One is by Robert Lado, who believes in starting to teach reading early, that is, when a child is about three. He reports success with his experiments. The other innovative proposal is by Valerian A. Postovsky, who feels that there should be a silent period before students are asked to produce language. Learners start to produce utterances only when they are ready. He found that when learners did start to talk, they did so fluently and with good pronunciation. It should be noted that the experimental subjects were university students learning Russian.

To conclude this section on innovative approaches, the teaching of language through literature has assumed a tremendous importance at all levels of the school system. This trend has had three immediate results:

1. Numerous comprehensible books on stylistics and literature have been published.

2. Many simplified or adapted copies of classical literary works have appeared.

3. The order of teaching literary works has been reversed. We now start with modern texts with which learners can identify because they recognize the life experience and the language. We do not generally begin with *Beowulf*, the *Canterbury Tales*, or Shakespeare. This seems to be a step in the right direction. Literary appreciation on the part of students has become and will continue to be a real possibility instead of a seldom-gained hope of the harassed teacher of English.

THE FUNCTIONAL-NOTIONAL APPROACH

The objective of second language teaching has now become the development of communicative competence, which includes the central role of appropriateness and acceptability of the speech act in a particular sociocultural situation. While many teachers use an eclectic approach, presenting grammar, situation, and topic as they did in the past, but adding numerous communicative tasks and small-group or pair activities, others have decided to adopt a *functional-notional approach*, which is designed to lead to communicative competence from the first day of learning.

This approach was the work of representatives of all the countries with membership in the Council of Europe. They originally wished to prepare material for adult guest workers in their countries. The project is now being expanded to include all interested nations, all age levels, all levels of instruction, and a greater number of languages. The functional-notional approach integrates communication theory; attention to grammar, to semantics, and to situation; and humanistic psychology. In addition to the fact that the material has undergone wide experimentation, the project incorporates a unit credit system in its curricular plan: It is hoped that persons who have studied particular functions of language, structures, units, or specific notions (areas of meaning) will be given credit in participating school systems no matter which textbooks they have used. This plan has not as yet been accepted in all school systems.

The tremendous merit of the functional-notional approach is that its proponents have considered with great care (1) the probable student populations and their actual and foreseeable needs, (2) the preparation that teachers will require to make the most effective use of it, and (3) the available resources in schools and communities, before setting down a number of realistic and practical objectives, which can in fact be realized not only in Europe but anywhere in the world in which foreign languages are studied.

There are other cogent reasons for the wide interest engendered by this innovative approach. It sets realistic learning tasks in which full-class or individualized instruction may be utilized. It provides for the teaching of everyday, real-world language use in sociocultural situations in which items of phonology, lexicon, grammar, and culture are selected and graded and yet intermeshed meaningfully from the first lesson at the beginning level of learning to serve the learner's immediate communicative purposes. It emphasizes the need for numerous receptive activities before rushing learners into premature performance. It recognizes that, while the language used in any speech act should be based on the situation or setting in which it occurs and be grammatically correct and semantically appropriate, the speaker must, above all, have a real purpose for speaking and something to talk about. The act of communication, even at elementary levels, will be intrinsically motivating simply because it expresses basic universal communicative functions of language and because it makes use of notions (the term used for the semantic themes and

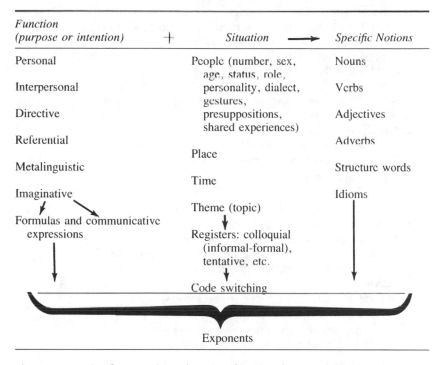

Figure 2. Basic elements in a (functional-notional) communicative approach.

language items) that are most appropriate to complete the specific function or functions being expressed.

The accompanying figures illustrate several aspects of the functional-notional approach. Figure 2 shows the basic elements that make up a particular speech act, or exponent. Figure 3 lists some typical exponents. Figures 4 and 5 illustrate two aspects of a spiral approach. Figure 4 shows how the same or similar functions are presented in different sociocultural situations, and Figure 5 indicates how a grammatical structure is presented in increasingly greater depth. Figure 6 is an example of a series of notional-functional units at one level. Only a few of the notions (vocabulary items) possible are illustrated.

The syllabus is divided into units, which are in turn divided into teaching lessons—the number depending on such factors as the learning level and the material to be covered. The functions the learners would need or wish to express within a social situation form the nucleus of each unit and serve as the fulcrum around which the dialogue or reading passage, the communicative formulas, the relevant structures and notions, and the learning activities are developed. The starting point is *always* the *communicative function* and the *social situation* in which the function or purpose is being expressed. The vocabulary and structural items—that is, the notions—are centered around one or more functions (e.g., complimenting someone), making immediate communication possible.

1. *Personal* (clarifying and classifying)
   I should (I ought to, I have to, I must) go shopping for food.
   I can swim; I can't swim (I've never been in the water).
   I like spinach, but I don't like peas.
   I'm cold. I'd better put on a sweater.
2. *Interpersonal*
   a. Greetings and leave takings: Good morning, Good evening, Hello, Hi (in-formal), Good night
   b. Introducing oneself and others:
      I'm. . . . What's your name?
      What's his name? He's Professor X. (He teaches English)
   c. Introducing people:
      May I present Mrs. X?
      How do you do? I'm happy (pleased) to meet you.
   d. Making or breaking an appointment:
      Can you meet me today at five at my house?
      I'm sorry. I can't come today. May I come tomorrow?
      Yes, of course; or No, I'm busy tomorrow.
3. *Directives*
   a. Making a suggestion: Let's go to the movies.
   b. Requesting someone to do something:
      Could (would) you go to the store for me?
      Would you mind going to the store for me?
   c. Ordering someone to do something: Come to my office at three.
4. *Referential*
   Where did you put the dictionary?
   Could you give us an example with the present perfect with *since*?
5. *Metalinguistics*
   Talking about language: collocations, tense, aspect, and so on.
6. *Imaginative*
   How would you end this dialogue (story)?
   Can you put Dialogues X and Y together? What did you like about the poem?
   Which character in the play did (didn't) you like? Why? (Why not?)
7. *Formulas*
   How do you do?
   I am pleased to meet you.
   How are you?
   Good morning.
   Good night.

Figure 3. Examples of exponents.

A spiral approach is used in presenting the same or similar functions in different sociocultural situations. Following is an example that encompasses a number of units at one level of work. Only a few of the notions (vocabulary items) possible are illustrated.

While the functional-notional approach has been accepted in the United States, the communicative approach has been drawing the attention of teachers and

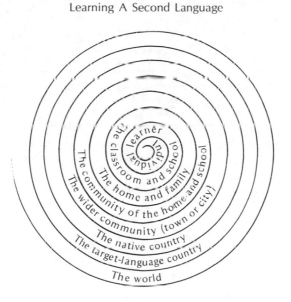

Figure 4. Sociocultural themes.

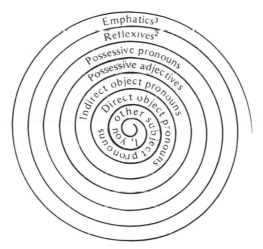

1. Starting with *I* and *you* makes possible immediate student-student and teacher-student communication in such activities as chain drills, questions and answers of all types, and paired practice.

Depending on the function and situation (Figure 5), possessive adjectives (*my*, *your*, etc.) may be presented before direct or indirect object pronouns (*me*, *him*, etc.).

2. For example, I washed *myself*.

3. For example, He did it *himself*.

Figure 5. A structural topic (personal pronouns).

Unit	Date	Title and Function	Situation	Communicative Expressions or Formulas	Structures
X	2/4	Apologizing	Cinema (asking someone to change seats)	Excuse me. Would you mind . . .? I'm very grateful.	V + *ing*
XI	2/11	Apologizing	Department store (returning something)	I'm sorry. Would it be possible . . . ?	Simple past, present perfect
XIV	3/15	Requesting directions	At the bus stop	I beg your pardon. Could you tell me . . . ?	Interrogatives (simple present) modal—*must*
XVI	3/25	Asking for information	In a post office	Excuse me. Where would I find . . . ?	Modal—*can*
XVIII	4/5	Expressing frustration	Home (dinner guests late)	How inconsiderate! Why couldn't they have telephoned?	*be* + V*ed* It's (time)
XX	4/25	Requesting directions	Gas station	I beg your pardon. How would I . . . ?	Imperatives (affirmative) (negative) *tell . . . to*

Figure 6. An outline of a series of units.
Some of the structures may be (1) taught for receptive use only, (2) presented for the first time, (3) reintroduced after having been taught earlier. It is desirable to indicate on the right side of the chart several of the major

writers in Europe and Great Britain. Early written reports contained some basic principles which were excellent; others were exaggerated. Of course, language use should receive priority over language usage. Grammatical structure, accuracy, and fluency should all play a role in language use without sacrificing the message we are trying to convey. An information gap is not absolutely necessary in an utterance or dialogue. If I say, "I like your tie," and the person to whom I say it responds, "Thank you," there is no information gap. Yet we have completed a speech (or communicative) act.

Crucial Factors in Learning

THE LEARNERS

Our consideration of sociolinguistics and psycholinguistics cannot help but underscore the fact that the student and the community in which he or she lives are central to the learning process. We have stated that individual learners restructure, in their

Nouns	Verbs	Adj.	Adv.	Misc.	Activity
seat place friend	move change				Dialogue study, role play, expanding sentences, paired practice
shirt	buy wear	small	too	Dates	Aural comprehension, indirect speech, changing register
Names of places	must get to get off take		how where	Numbers	Reading questions and answers, cloze procedures, dictation
stamps saving account	sell buy open				Expanding sentences of previous dialogues, role playing with these
food dessert roast	ruin spoil serve	late	so	Time and numbers	Any of the above, dicto-comp
auto route traffic light	reach get on turn off say tell			Ordinal numbers	Any of the above, reported speech (e.g., car passenger wants to know what attendant has said)

**learning activities the student can engage in within the unit. (You should
also list these activities under the dialogues in a separate notebook.)
Nearly every activity suggested can be engaged in within each unit.**

own way, the material we present—based on past experiences in acquiring knowledge and in solving problems. There are other factors, too, within the students
which need to be considered.

You will understand from your own reading and from your own experience
that chapters could be written about each factor. My intention, however, is not to
discuss any characteristic at length but, through questions, to make you more deeply
aware, perhaps, of the complexity of learning and teaching a language. I hope, too,
that you will bear in mind the answers to some of these questions as you prepare the
various parts of your lessons and as you gather together the appropriate materials of
instruction.

Age. Are your students young children who can imitate you easily? Will they
prefer to learn language through games, songs, and so on? Are they adults whose
native language habits are more deeply established? Are they adults who can be
helped to analyze the new language?

Ability. Are there wide differences among the students in your class? How can you use the abilities of the bright students? How can you help the weaker students? Can you appeal to the *ear* alone? Do you need to appeal to the *ear* and *eye*? Do you need much concrete, visual material?

Aspirations and needs. Particularly with adults, do they need to learn English to get a job, do further study, conduct a business, take a trip? Do they need to learn English quickly in order to be able to understand other subjects which are being taught in English? Do they need to learn English because they live in an English-speaking community?

Native language. Are there any similarities to English in *sounds, structure,* and *vocabulary*? (Some cognates have completely different meanings; e.g., in French *assister* means to be present at and *not* to assist.) What are the basic *phonemic* features of the sound system? How do these contrast with those of English? What devices does the language use to show meaning? (intonation, word order, inflection, function words, etc.) What writing system is used? (alphabet, pictures) How is the culture reflected in the language? (How many forms of address are used? What are these based on—sex, age, social status?)

Previous language experience. Have they studied any other foreign language? How much English do they already know? Did they study English in a school where you might reasonably expect the methods and materials to be the ones with which you are familiar?

An effective teacher needs answers to these and to other similar questions. How can a teacher find the answers? Some of them are easily recognizable. Age and ability usually need no special study. In some situations and with young learners, however, it may be important to obtain results of tests of ability (if these exist in your community) and also to find out the grades the students make in their native language studies, particularly in the language itself. These will offer some clues to explain a discouraging lack of progress. Is it due to poor ability on their part? No motivation? Poor previous teaching?

If you are teaching in an English-speaking community, it is clear that your students need to learn English as quickly as possible in order to participate in the life of the community. If your students are adults and are not living in an English-speaking community, it is very desirable to find out (through an interpreter if you do not know their native language) what their needs and aspirations are.

In order to learn about the native language of your students (I realize this may not be possible for all groups if you have more than two or three language groups in your class), you could:

1. Examine any studies that have been made comparing English and the native language of your students.
2. Ask someone (a teacher, perhaps) who speaks the native language of your students to tell you in broad terms what the language does about word order, and so on.

It may be desirable for *all* teachers of English to prepare charts of the vowels and consonants of the students' native language, as well as of other phonemic features to indicate the gross patterns of its structure and vocabulary, as in the section on the English sound system later in this chapter.

THE SCHOOL AND COMMUNITY

In this section as in the others which have preceded it, we cannot possibly explore the topic in depth. Again, I can only ask some questions hoping that you will seek their answers by asking questions yourselves, by observing, by studying, and by examining records and other materials.

1. How long is the English program? Is it an intensive program, for example? Is it a two-year or a three-year course?
2. Is the curriculum divided into various subjects *within* the English program? Does *one* teacher teach spoken English, written English, and reading to the same group of students, or do different teachers teach different aspects of the language?
3. What facilities exist in the school (language laboratory, library, television, video, computer)?
4. What instructional materials exist?
5. Is there a testing program?
6. How are records kept?
7. Are there provisions in the school for practice or reinforcing English (a newspaper, assembly programs, club)?
8. Does the community have large numbers of English speakers?
9. What facilities does the community have (library, museum, etc.)?
10. Is it an urban community or a rural community?
11. Are there people in the community whom you could invite to speak to your classes?
12. Are there English language newspapers, radio programs, television programs, or movies in the community?
13. Are people in the community interested in social mobility?
14. Are there opportunities for the language learners to feel that they can "enter" the English-speaking group?
15. Is there a tradition of education and instruction which will motivate the learners? Are they encouraged to acquire the language by their parents or their peers?

The accompanying variables chart on page 21 gives us some insight into the multiple factors that enter into a second language teaching situation. The age levels of the students necessitating a different curriculum for each age level, the types of programs available for learners over the age of sixteen, the curriculum which will be suitable for each level, and the numerous organizational components which cannot be ignored will determine the success or failure of the program. This chart is worthy of careful scrutiny.

YOU, THE TEACHER

Most important is *your* role in the learning process. In recent literature, the teacher has been called the "facilitator" or "mediator" of learning. To me, these terms imply that machines, books, school walls, or other people come between the teacher and the students. The truth is—as all of us know—that you could be sitting in a field with a group of students and still transmit to them not only your knowledge of English, but also—more especially—your interest in them as human beings, your desire for them to learn, and your enthusiasm.

You might wish to ask yourself these and many other similar questions:

1. Are you convinced that all normal students can learn?
2. Are you enthusiastic about your subject?
3. Do you plan your lesson carefully?
   a. Is it suitable for the age and ability levels of the students?
   b. Do you make provision for individualizing instruction so that pupils can work at their own pace or respond according to their present ability?
   c. Do you provide for a variety of activities which will have meaning for the students and which will foster their desire to communicate with each other?
   d. Do you vary your patterns of student participation in the classroom?
4. Do you evaluate your students' progress periodically?
5. Do you stop to judge yourself, your attitude, your choice of materials, your interest?
6. Do you make every effort to sustain the motivation of your students by giving them many small successes, by praising them, and by establishing and maintaining warm, friendly relations with them?
7. Do you make *judicious* use of audiovisual aids?
8. Do you, when absolutely necessary, when you know the language, and when the same language is spoken by everybody, use the native language of your students?
9. Do you use a system of "buddies" (student helpers from the same class) to help pupils who have fallen behind because of absence, inattention, poor comprehension of certain basic language elements on which others depend?
10. If there is a language laboratory, do you integrate the work done in the classroom with that done in the lab?

Teachers' Needs
There are many competences, many skills, and much knowledge you the teacher should possess if learners are to acquire a lifelong love for the English language and culture. All teachers should be expected to

Variables

In Second Language	Age Level				Type of Program		
	5-9	10-12	13-16	Continuing education program	16 and above	Illiterate or functionally illiterate	Special-purpose program (vocational, technical academic, etc.)
Types of organization available in the school or community for newcomers (e.g., integrated, pull-out, bilingual, ESL program)							
Numbers of learners involved in the school or community							
Variety of languages and cultural backgrounds in the same class							
Linguistic distance between L1 and L2*							
Background of learners (education, customs, e.g., in their country, students of both sexes in same class)							
Literacy in L1							
Previous schooling in native country (years, subjects, foreign language learned, if any)							
Schooling in host country (subjects taught in L1 and L3), bilingual, immersion,† maintenance‡							
Availability of bilingual personnel (training and qualifications)							
Community (resources, interest, involvement)							
Time of entry into special class (ESL)							
Age of entry into L2 program							

COMET

What do teachers do about

C Curriculum?
O Objectives?
M Methods and materials?
E Evaluation procedures?
T Teachers (preparation, attitudes, and skills), Techniques?

*Is there a major difference between L1 and L2 in pronunciation, syntax, morphology?

†Where everything is taught in English (subject areas, English).

‡Where classes are given in their L1 in order to give them a sense of identity and belonging.

1. Learn how the findings of linguistics, psychology, and other related disciplines can facilitate learning and teaching.

2. Acquire an awareness of the significant features of the linguistic and cultural backgrounds of their pupils as a bridge to an understanding and acceptance of linguistic interference and possible cultural conflict.

3. Find out everything they can about their educational backgrounds—of their older students particularly—as a springboard for the introduction of new concepts and skills and as a basis for providing group or individual instruction.

4. Gain conscious familiarity with the basic features of the English sound, grammar, lexical, and cultural systems. (Let me say in passing that the mere fact of being a native speaker of English does not qualify one to teach English as a second/foreign language without special training.)

5. Learn about and experiment with the methods and techniques of teaching English as a second/foreign language which would be most productive with their students, with their personalities, in their schools, and in the communities not only of the school but also, where pertinent, from which the learners have come and to which they plan to return.

6. Understand the dynamics and techniques of grouping, since these are crucial in teaching ESL and EFL. (Not only must the teacher provide for differences in abilities, learning levels, and interests among language learners but also, in some current organizational patterns, for the teaching of both language learners and native English speakers in the same classroom.)

7. Learn how to utilize and/or develop simple instructional materials in harmony with program objectives and students' goals, as well as for students with possible learning problems.

8. Know how and when to evaluate achievement and proficiency in order to make students aware of their progress, and to modify or discard nonmotivating and nonproductive teaching practices.

9. Make use of community resources—people and places—to enrich the students' learning experiences. (This is possible and happens daily in the most remote corners of the globe.)

10. Provide a classroom environment conducive to successful learning and especially to the retention of pride and hope.

11. Integrate the English program with the other school and community experiences and activities of the student using an interdisciplinary approach.

Qualities of Superior Teachers

Let us make no mistake about an important truth. The heart of any successful learning program is the classroom teacher. Let me, therefore, outline some of the characteristics of superior teachers. These hallmarks of the teachers I have had the privilege to know in over fifty countries will be given in no particular order, since they are of equal importance in the classroom.

1. Superior teachers are committed to the principle that all normal people can learn. They modify curriculum content, however, as they ascertain the strengths and weaknesses of learners and—with older students—their aspirations. They make every effort to help these students achieve their aspirations or redirect them into more attainable channels. In relation to aspiration, they realize that what one student may consider success may not be important for another.

2. While they do not neglect formal features of language, they know that other factors in learning are of greater or of supreme importance and that these elements should permeate the total classroom environment. Learners must feel loved, respected, and secure. They must be made to feel that they are important members of the group, that they can assume responsibilities, and that they can achieve success.

3. They keep the motivation of students at a high level by using *their interests, their lives*, and *their communities* as a starting point for the introduction of all material; by adapting procedures; by using a variety of instructional materials in addition to the basic text; and by reassuring students of the normalcy of reaching plateaus in learning.

4. They recognize that the correction of student errors is a matter requiring sensitivity and, above all, common sense. For example, when a student is expressing himself or herself creatively, the teacher does not correct each error unless the error impedes comprehension; in language activities the teacher never repeats a student's error but may say instead, "Listen," followed by the model or the correct answer. While the teacher praises a student for any sign of improvement, he or she does not say "Very good" to a student who responds incorrectly and then go on to another pupil with another question. The teacher never asks another student to correct an error, since this may create hostile relationships among class members.

5. Superior teachers provide for individual differences in class and in out-of-class tasks. They know that individuals learn in different ways and at different rates: Some learn by intensive repetition and overlearning; some learn best by trial and error; younger children learn through play activities, through tasting foods, through touching, and through hearing and identifying noises around them; older students generally learn best by applying generalizations to new situations and from hearing much comprehensible input.

6. They organize each learning experience carefully. They select, grade, present, and practice language items and communicative expressions in a systematic, logical manner which will facilitate the students' restructuring and subsequent acquisition of them.

7. They plan in advance the communication situations and meaningful contexts through which the communicative purposes of all material will be made clear.

8. They provide in each lesson not only for pronunciation practice leading to necessary habit formation but also to real-world use of the language. They also help older students to perceive the underlying rules that govern the use of language and, through pertinent questions, to arrive at a generalization or rule (always in descriptive terms) which they will be able to transfer to other appropriate communication situations.

9. They use the native language of the students sparingly in the classroom (if they are familiar with it and if all pupils speak the same language), but they do not hesitate to use it or ask bilingual teacher trainees or community assistants to do so in order to clarify instructions, to ensure that essential information has been understood, and, most important, to maintain the students' sense of security. In this regard, they may also (a) organize a buddy system in which more able students help those in need, or (b) plan for a few minutes at the end of each hour when students may ask them or each other questions in their native tongue. Moreover, they realize that it is perfectly natural for learners to speak among themselves in their native tongue until they acquire enough English to engage in normal communication in the new language.

10. They know that, although group recitation is desirable during many phases of the lesson, especially at beginning levels, because (a) it gives the learners a sense of initial security and (b) it enables all of them to produce speech much more frequently than would be possible otherwise, communication is essentially an activity conducted by individuals. They have learned, therefore, to plan language activities in pairs or small groups which duplicate or simulate those needed in actual communication.

11. They have become accustomed to preparing or to utilizing existing instructional materials which enable pairs of learners to practice together.

12. They have learned to supplement the basic text where necessary by preparing dialogues, drills, or reading selections in order to lend variety to a lesson or to reinforce—through their recombination in more extended communication activities—language or cultural items which have been presented.

13. They have become skillful in preparing scripts for tapes, in voicing them, and in integrating laboratory or computer practice (where these exist) with classroom activity.

14. They are aware of the fact that there are no passive language skills. Listening and reading are extremely complex and demand the active involvement of students. They therefore devote much more time in class to the development of listening comprehension. They realize that while it is possible to control what we say, we cannot control what other people say, especially in movies or on television, nor is it generally possible to listen again to something we may not have understood.

15. They plan reading lessons—story telling at the lowest levels—which will not only extend the pupils' knowledge of the language but will also foster discussion and thought. With older students they may decide that it is desirable and possible to introduce reading from the first day. They do not assign reading unless they have clarified linguistic items and cultural allusions in it. Moreover, they generally read aloud the material the students have been assigned, especially at beginning levels, in order to ensure correct grouping of structures, accurate word stress, and normal rhythm. They teach learners to use contextual clues, to use cognates where pertinent, and to make effective use of dictionaries. Since they do not know everyone's learning style, books should be open so that learners can look and hear at the same time. Some teachers also encourage students to repeat what they have heard during the pauses. Moreover, they constantly make students aware of redundancy clues in language by pointing these out in reading, giving dictation, and engaging them in cloze exercises.

16. They incorporate guided writing activities in lessons, which will lead gradually to more creative, "free" student composition. Through a gamut of experiences such as reading, listening, and discussion, they stimulate pupils to think of ideas, to put them in a logical, informational sequence through the use of cohesive devices, and to find the language most appropriate to express them.

17. They provide learners with cross-cultural insights both incidentally—as they explain allusions in dialogues or reading materials—and, later, in student-directed projects or in more formal discussions.

18. They make sure that students retain their sense of individual dignity and ethnic pride, while learning to appreciate aspects of English and other cultures. Both with relation to their culture and to that of others, they guide pupils not only in sensing the basic similarities of the human experience but also in realizing that "different from" does not mean "better than" or "worse than." One of their major objectives in the teaching of culture is to make students sensitive to their own values and to the values and customs of any cultural group with whom they will come into contact. It is not only the idea of biculturalism which we must foster, but also that of cultural pluralism and global understanding.

19. They learn to select and use only those audiovisual aids which will enable students to learn a particular communicative expression, specific notion, or cultural fact more efficiently and effectively.

20. They create an opportunity for learning resulting from incidental experiences the students may have had or happenings in the classroom, the school, or the community.

21. They utilize the strengths of the learners, while giving them the feeling that they are responsible human beings, by having them help in the numerous tasks of the classroom, such as preparing instructional materials; checking homework or test papers; assuming the role of group leader, recorder, or reporter at different times; serving as "teacher" in asking questions; correcting chalkboard work; putting up timely bulletin boards; helping fellow students who have been absent or have fallen behind in some aspect of the classwork.

22. Superior teachers use the same piece of material—a dialogue, a reading selection, a set of flash cards, or a group of pictures—for multiple purposes. For example, while a reading selection may be useful in expanding vocabulary, in teaching skills of comprehension, or in motivating the presentation of a grammatical structure or communicative function, they also use it as a source of listening comprehension.

The great majority of teachers the world over have been cognizant of their responsibilities and have continued to take in-service courses, attend international conferences offered at many learning centers, join language organizations and teacher resource centers, read avidly in their fields of interest, and write articles for publication.

A Teacher's Guide to Self-Evaluation

Where a school has no language department head or outside language inspector, the teacher will find a listing such as the accompanying one an invaluable reminder of the many facets needed to round out a lesson. (This listing was adapted from Finocchiaro, M., and M. Bonomo, *The Foreign Language Learner*, New York: Regents Publishing Company, 1973.)

Class:
Date:
Teaching emphasis (e.g., communicative functions, structures, peer interaction, reading, writing):
Teaching level:
Materials used (purpose, e.g., communication situations to be clarified):

A. Was my manner friendly, warm, and understanding?

B. Was I patient in eliciting information, engaging in language tasks and activities, and in correcting possible errors?

C. Did I praise students at every opportunity?

D. Was I sensitive to their problems (personal and school) and questions?

E. Was my voice clear and audible in all parts of the room?

F. Was my appearance pleasing? (Was I well groomed?)

G. Was I well prepared? For example,
  - Was the material I needed readily available?
  - Was my presentation orderly and sequential?
  - Had I "memorized" the steps of my lessons?
  - Did my lesson have balance and variety?
  - Was I able to answer questions related to culture?

H. Did I use gestures clearly to elicit different types of participation?

I. Did I let the students do most of the talking?

J. How was my questioning ability? Did I, for example,
  - Ask appropriate, logical questions?
  - Ask questions of all students and then call on one by name?
  - Avoid choral responses to questions?
  - Call on volunteers?
  - Call on nonvolunteers?
  - Provide opportunities for students to question me and to question each other?
  - Repeat answers unnecessarily?
  - Vary types of questions (yes-no, alternative, full answer, short answer, inferential, personal)?

K. Did I engage the learners in pair and group work?

L. Did I help students maintain pride in their native language and background? How?

M. Did I ascertain their aspirations and needs and those of the community?

N. Did I make every attempt to involve parents and community members in the program?

My Lesson in General

A. Were the method and communicative situations used appropriate? Suitable to the age and ability levels of the students? In accordance with communicative principles?

B. Was the content too much? Too little? Geared to the students' level? Geared to their language level? Varied?

C. Was the aim clear to the students? How did I make it clear (stated by me, written on blackboard)? Was it logical? Important? Was it adhered to during the entire lesson? Was it achieved?

D. Was the lesson development smooth? Sequential? Logical? For example, did I introduce each new step or activity with a transitional or introductory statement or comment?

E. Was there a variety of tasks (repetitive, pattern practice for functions and structures, question-answer, freer communication)?

F. Was there a summary? Given by whom? Was material left on the board for easy reference?

G. How did I evaluate whether my goals had been achieved?

H. How was the tempo of the lesson (too slow, too brisk, hurried, sustained)?

I. Did I use the native language judiciously (where necessary—when, why, how)?

J. Was there sufficient time given to the maintenance and/or development of listening and speaking skills?

K. Did I adhere slavishly to the textbook?

L. Did I individualize instruction?

M. Did the lesson look back on material covered and ahead to the next lesson?

N. Did I use audiovisual aids efficiently and effectively?

O. Did I develop both accuracy and fluency?

P. Did I integrate broad communication activities, for example, listening and writing, reading and speaking?

Lessons With Special Emphasis

A. Pronunciation

    1. Did I help students hear and distinguish sounds and contrasts before asking them to produce them orally?

    2. What aids were used (diagram of speech organs, explanation of points of articulation, arrows or dots for intonation, etc.)?

    3. Were all new sounds and other pronunciation features used in context in authentic situations after they were taught?

    4. Was I satisfied with reasonable progress?

B. Dialogue presentation

    1. Was the dialogue authentic, current speech?

    2. Was the dialogue situation made clear to the students? How?

    3. Were students made aware of the speaker for each utterance? How?

    4. Did I model the individual utterances several times before expecting the students to repeat them?

5. Did I move to various parts of the room so that all students could hear me and see me?

6. Did I have (in the early stages only) two large groups facing each other as they recited a dialogue role?

7. Did I break down long sentences into manageable segments?

8. Did I offer help to individuals who took roles in the dialogue?

9. Did I stop practicing the dialogue before boredom and a plateau set in?

10. Did I personalize the dialogue, vary utterances in it, ask questions about it?

11. Did I help students combine, create, and adapt dialogues?

12. Did I help learners engage in role playing?

C. Communicative functions and structures

1. Was there an obvious relationship to known material (familiar target language or native language function or structure)?

2. How was the meaning clarified? What situations did I use?

3. Were examples modeled by me? How many did I give? How many times was each example given? Was the language used in them authentic?

4. Was repetition done chorally first, then by subgroups, and then by individuals?

5. How was the recurring feature clarified, emphasized, and described (diagrammed on board, elicited)?

6. Practice activities:

   a. Were the most appropriate chosen?

   b. Was the type of activity varied, for example, substitution, replacement, question-answer, transformation; sequence sentences; brief dialogue; extended dialogue; role play; games?

   c. Was the type of pupil participation varied? (Did I cue pupils? Did pupils cue me or other pupils? Did I vary the types of chain drills?)

   d. How was the new structure or function used in authentic communication?

D. Reading and word study

1. How was motivation developed (related to students' lives, to a longer story)?

2. How were difficulties clarified (cognates, pictures, objects, paraphrases, dramatization, native language equivalent, other)?

3. How was my oral reading (tempo, phrasing, rhythm)?

4. Which techniques did I use to ensure comprehension (questioning to elicit the main thought and to note cause-and-effect relationships, completion exercises, true-false questions)?

5. Was a summary given? How did I elicit it?

6. Did I include time for word study [antonyms, synonyms, cognates (where feasible), words of same family, derivations]?

7. Was any oral reading done by students? Were able students called on first? How much class time was spent on it?

8. Was the homework assignment based on what had been done in class (answers to questions, outline, note taking, summary)?

E. Cultural appreciation
   1. How did I provide motivation for a particular aspect of culture?
   2. Did I relate the aspects of the target culture to ours?
   3. Do I feel that the presentation helped to reduce prejudice and to develop positive attitudes?
   4. What mode of presentation was used (lecture, demonstration, other)?
   5. What visual materials were available?
   6. Were any follow-up activities assigned to students (group projects, book reports, composition writing)?
F. Composition writing
   1. How did I motivate the topic?
   2. How did I elicit ideas related to the topic?
   3. What questions or techniques were used to place ideas in logical sequence?
   4. Were students given enough help with functions, structures, and vocabulary needed to express and expand each idea?
   5. Did I allow students enough time in class to write an introductory paragraph?
   6. Did I give them enough time to prepare the composition at home?
   7. Were my comments on their compositions tactful, clear, constructive?
   8. What correction techniques were used to simplify the work?

THE LEARNING ENVIRONMENT

The best prepared, most beautifully written lesson plan will have no real impact on the learners and their learning if it is presented slowly and haltingly, without spark and vigor. There are many simple procedures that a teacher can use in the classroom which will give learners the feeling that they are participating in a well-conducted lesson in which they are actively involved and in which learning is taking place.

In this section, I shall limit the discussion to the classroom, at all levels, and to the learners in a formal, but relaxed, atmosphere. The environment outside the school, where English may be the language of the majority group, of stores, clubs, places of worship, libraries, museums, and other places of interest, would of course be stimulating with its unlimited opportunities for natural language acquisition. But my experience in the United States, Great Britain, and other European countries has demonstrated over and over again that many foreign students in universities and children of guest workers or of permanent immigrants do not take advantage of the opportunities and, sad to say, are not often invited to do so.

Let me return, therefore, to the classroom with special emphasis on junior high (middle) schools and senior high schools where students generally change classrooms every forty-five to sixty minutes. One of the reasons I have decided to write about this topic is that, in forty years of classroom observation and in talks with teachers, the major complaint has been that they cannot possibly finish the lesson and/or the course book because it takes five to ten minutes to call the roll and twenty to thirty minutes to correct the students' homework unless they take it home or stay after the school day is over.

Let me outline some simple procedures which work and which will create a positive, warm, sharing relationship among the students and the teacher.

1. *Routines*. Routines should be kept to a minimum and not take precious class time away from learning.

a. *Greetings*. Greetings are not really a routine but a social courtesy. Greet the students cheerfully every day. Do not start by saying, "Open your books to page twenty."

b. *Taking attendance*. Taking attendance should take one minute. On the first day of class, ask the students to line up in alphabetical order and to sit in that order every day. An empty seat will indicate that the student is absent. On a sheet of graph paper, or paper on which you or a student has drawn lines before the class begins, indicate the seats. The name of the occupant will be written by you at the bottom. The small squares on the right side will be used to write in the date of the student's absence. The small squares on the left side will be used to write "V" for volunteer or "NV" for nonvolunteer.

This single sheet is attached to a piece of cardboard. An attendance volunteer will pick up the sheet from your desk at the beginning of each lesson, look for the empty seats, and write in the date. This has several purposes: (i) You will know that the student has missed the lesson and that he or she may need special help; (ii) you will not expect him or her to bring in homework on the following class day; and (iii) you will not ask him or her to take the thirty-second test which will be based on the missed lesson. Attendance monitors can be rotated every two weeks or as you desire.

As we know, in every class there are students who raise their hands contin-

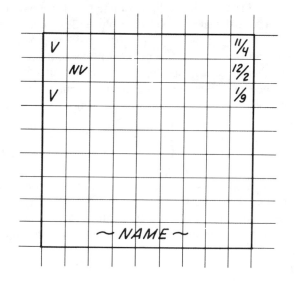

ually to answer questions or to make comments. When you call on them, put a "V" in their square. By the same token, there are those timid learners who are loath to volunteer. At least once a week, look at the sheets, make a note of students who have not offered comments or responses, and make sure to call on them during the following week. Remember that students who do not volunteer may know the answers very well but may be shy. Write "NV" in their square when you have called on them.

Three other comments should be made about our chart. If you know that a student has a vision or hearing problem, place him or her up front. Change the seating plan every three months, moving those who have been sitting in the back to the front. If possible, learn the names of the students as quickly as feasible. It is amazing how quickly possible discipline problems disappear when you say the name of the offender rather than "you in the brown shirt."

c. *Assigning homework.* In two minutes, while attendance is being taken, write the homework assignment for the next lesson in a small box in the upper left-hand corner of the board or on a piece of paper posted on the front wall on the left side. Write simply St (study) pp. 00–00, R (read) pp. 00–00, Wr (write) ex. 0–00. Give the students one or two minutes to copy the homework assignment. Tell them from the first day that the homework will be based on that day's class work. Remind them to tell you when they enter the room if they have not been able to do their homework, and this will avoid unnecessary problems.

d. *Correcting homework.* Correcting homework should take from five to seven minutes maximum. The procedure you use will depend on the chalkboard space you have available.

If you have a large board, ask your board assistant to divide the space into five sections, numbering each section. You will then give a board slip or card to a student, asking him or her to read the questions or statements aloud. You will ask a second student to answer the question or react to the statement, and a third to go to the board (preferably without his or her notebook) to write the answer. While the student is doing so, you are following the same procedure with Question 2. When all the answers are on the board, you will ask your homework assistant for that week to go to the board and ask a question such as, "Do you see any errors on the board?" If there is an error, he or she will put a line through it and ask the person who indicated the error to make the correction (to be written above the error). After all the sections are corrected, you may read the answers and have the students say them after you reading from their notebooks, particularly at beginning levels. While the homework is being corrected on the board, you may walk around the room and write a grade or comment (good, fine, etc.) in several student notebooks. Notice that sixteen learners are involved in the homework correction.

If you have no chalkboard, (1) ask individual students to read the answers from their notebooks while the other students make corrections in theirs, or (2) ask pairs of students to correct each other's work as you walk around the room glancing at their notebooks and answering any questions they may have. Students (volunteers or nonvolunteers) who have acquired reasonably good pronunciation may be asked to read aloud from their notebooks. Always ask, "Do you have any questions? Did you understand everything?" or whatever you normally would say.

e. *Distributing materials.* This should take no more than thirty seconds. When you are giving out paper, a picture, games, or whatever, do not walk to each student's place and put it on his or her desk. Ask a student assistant to put a pile of material on each desk at the head of a row. The material is then passed back to those in that row. Materials are collected in the same way.

Here are a few other reminders about routines.

- Have extra pencils available in case a student has forgotten one or has broken the point.
- Do not ask that a student have more than one notebook. (Some parents may not have the money to buy them.) Have the notebooks divided into clear, separate sections (e.g., assignments, homework, vocabulary, dialogues).
- Accept excuses when youngsters come in without their homework. Naturally, if it becomes a daily occurrence, look into the reasons.
- Never send a student to the principal's office for a misdeed. Learn to handle your own discipline problems, but I assure you that you will not have any if your students feel that you are being fair. The one trait of teachers that learners appreciate the most is a sense of fairness. Research in many parts of the world attests to this fact.
- Never ask embarrassing questions such as, "How many rooms do you live in?" or "What does your father (mother) do?"

If students are not paying attention, don't raise your voice. Stand quietly until there is silence. These and similar actions will usually lower the affective filters in your classroom and make you and your students look forward to class.

2. *Using the textbook.* Remember that the perfect textbook will never be written for you and for your students. Authors cannot see into your personality or those of your students. Authors cannot know your community or your school the way you do. However, there are several steps you can take to mitigate the problem.

a. Before the semester begins, read the author's preface and the teacher's guide (if any) to note whether you can use all the ideas and activities you will find in the text. Mark those you can or cannot use.

b. Divide the units into teaching lessons (unless they are already divided in the book).

c. Spread the learning of dialogues, communicative expressions, grammatical structures, vocabulary (lexical items), reading passages, and other tasks and activities evenly over the approximately six to ten lessons into which you divide each unit.

d. Add material you would like to use, for example, short dialogues or vocabulary which is relevant to your community.

e. Simplify or adapt reading passages you consider too advanced for your class.

f. Discard tasks or activities you consider inappropriate for your student population.

g. Before assigning homework, look carefully at the sentences in the exercise. Renumber them (using different-colored pencils) so that you can be sure that your students have learned about the communicative, structural, or lexical item during the lesson.

h. Clarify any difficult (unfamiliar) items in the text before asking the students to "go home and read the next three pages." It is not always possible to guess meanings by looking at the text, nor is the author there to explain meanings to the learner.

i. Make time to do one or two items of the homework assignment as examples.

   3. *Writing the daily lesson plan.*

a. School districts and principals may have different criteria and specific formats for the preparation of lesson plans. If they do, follow the required procedures. When I first started to teach, I would write nearly every word I planned to say on several pages of a notebook. Later, when I had gained some confidence, I wrote plans for the entire week on two facing pages of a notebook. I made duplicates of the plans and kept them in my desk for the substitute in the event of my absence. If I had a roving program, I gave the duplicate plans to the principal or to the school secretary to give to the substitute. The plan for six classes a day looked like this:

Eng2A Eng3A Eng4B Eng5A Eng5B Eng5C

Monday
   Aim:
   Pres (presentation):
   Mat (materials needed):
   PP (pages in text):
   HW (homework):
   Comments:
Tuesday
   Aim:
   Etc.
Wednesday
   Etc.

At the bottom of each lesson, note that there is a space for comments, such as *Exercise X not completed, presentation not grasped entirely, pictures not effective, lesson not completed (fire drill, visitor, etc.)*. Use abbreviations on the form.

b. Put the plan on a file card. An embarrassing situation may arise when you are teaching if you are near the back of the room and you forget the next instruction for a game, a cue word for the next sentence, a prereading question, or whatever. The fact of forgetting is not the real problem; what is a problem is that you may feel that you have to walk back to your desk to look through one or more pages of your plan book to find the missing item. The students may begin to lose confidence in you and to become restless. I found a solution for me which I hope will work for you. On a file card (so that it can be stored for future reference), jot down the aim of the lesson, the material you will need, the situation you will use to present a communication expression or structure, a list of cue words for drills or a game, and a brief list of one-word tasks or activities in which you plan to engage the class during the teaching hour.

Keep the card in your left hand so that you can glance at it when necessary. The card will not prevent you from pointing to individuals in pairs or groups and indicating through hand signals which half or section of the class is to participate in any activity.

4. *Group work.* Grouping students presents many advantages, but there should be a real purpose for doing so. Why, when, and how do we group? Are there any constraints of which we should be aware?

Bringing together groups of three to six learners for ten to fifteen minutes during a class period ensures wide communication and real interaction among the students. They become socially cohesive. They pay more attention to the messages in the discussion. They worry less about grammatical accuracy. On the other hand, in a foreign language situation where everybody speaks the same native language, they may express themselves in the native tongue.

We may group for a variety of reasons. Students may need help because they have been absent. They may not understand some of the uses of a structure, for example, the present perfect. Their pronunciation may need improvement (this group should work with the teacher or with another English native speaker). Moreover, the various groups can perform different tasks. They may work on a cloze passage. They can prepare a cultural project to be presented to the whole class. With a tape recorder and earphones they can listen to a passage which they will then tell the class about. They can play a communication game or perform many other tasks and activities relevant to the aims of the class program.

Before starting the group work at the beginning of the school year, you should place three words on the board: *leader, recorder*, and *reporter*. These are three positions to be filled by students during group work. The leader can be anyone in the class, preferably an introvert who would gain a feeling of security and status by being asked to serve as group leader. Under the word *leader*, write and explain utterances that the leader uses, such as "Do you agree with X?" "Why?" "Why not?" "Would someone like to add another idea?"

The recorder should be someone who writes reasonably well. He or she may need utterances like "Can you speak louder?" "Would you repeat the last word/sentence?" "What do you mean by X?"

The reporter should be someone who speaks comprehensibly. He or she informs the class as a whole about the group's work.

Here are several additional comments.

a. All the groups can work on the same task or on different ones, according to individual or class need.

b. Instructions should be clearly stated and written on the board where feasible.

c. Time limits should be clearly indicated and held to.

d. Students should stay with the same group only when they are working on a long-term project. They should be asked to join another group as often as feasible. This will widen their social and intellectual contacts with other learners, a particularly important advantage in an ESL situation.

e. You should walk around the classroom and listen in on discussions, making mental notes of possible conceptual or grammatical errors which you may want to talk about at some other time.

f. You should make time during the week to have the entire class listen to one or two reports. It will be impossible to hear all the reports, but when time permits, you can collect summaries of discussions, for example, and comment on Group A's report, which "was quite good." Never make uncomplimentary remarks about any group's report to the class at large.

    5. *Other interaction stimulators.* Despite the numerous books which advocate that the teacher move offstage to make room for a learner-centered classroom, the teacher has a central role to play in suggesting, initiating, and making possible extensive interaction in the classroom. At beginning levels, the teacher may model brief dialogues, pointing to stick figures on the board or to pictures in the text, and invite whole-class, half-class, large-group, small-group, and, finally, individual repetition from different parts of the room.

    This can be followed by chain drills which are moved to different sections of the room after six learners (maximum) have participated in the chain. Paired practice may follow, first with the words found in the brief dialogue, and later with the learners supplying other appropriate initial utterances and responses. Role playing can be the next step, followed by a simulated real-life activity in which similar utterances are used. In a class with fewer than thirty learners, you may ask students to move to other parts of the room frequently to communicate and interact with their classmates. They can ask each other about interests, hopes, and plans, and these can be reported to the whole class.

    At later levels, simple communication games can be played. For example, if indefinite articles and the position of adjectives have been learned, the game "The Minister's Cat" can be played briskly: The minister's cat is an angry cat, . . . is a beautiful (bad) cat, . . . is a cute (cunning, curious) cat, and so on.

    A basic principle to follow in interaction activities is that numerous recognition activities should precede productive activities. For example, after listening to the teacher or to a tape recording of a dialogue, learners can answer questions about the elements in the situation with either one or two words or gestures. How many people are there? Who are they? What time do you think it is? Is the language formal? What words indicate the message or communicative function?

Beginning, simple, planned production activities include (a) having the two halves of the class stand and face each other and take dialogue roles using varied intonation patterns to express different attitudes, (b) inviting students to come to the front of the room and take roles in a dialogue, and (c) giving a brief situation for students to improvise on. For example, you have an appointment with a friend, but you can't leave the house. What would you say to your friend?

6. *Testing and grading student performance.* I generally give a thirty-second written test on work done during the previous lesson. Here are some comments about testing which are relevant to the learning environment.

a. Tell the learners exactly what you will test (during the lesson before the test).

b. Give a test with only five items for ease of grading and in the interest of saving time.

c. Never give a test or homework when you know the students are going to have a major test in another subject, a sure way to raise affective filters. Never give homework over long, important holiday periods.

d. Let the learners themselves keep a record of their daily quiz grades in a notebook.

e. Collect the papers and ask a student to go to the board to ask, "What is the answer to number one?" (two, three, etc.). Then ask if there were any problems and engage in a brief discussion if necessary.

f. If you give longer unit or midyear tests, do *not* under any conditions read out the grades. Such a procedure may embarrass the learners unduly, causing serious emotional problems sometimes leading to disastrous results.

7. *Rapport with parents.* Any communications to the home should contain laudatory remarks with, if you feel it imperative, a suggestion for change in some relatively unimportant area. Junior and senior high school students generally have emotional, psychological, and generation-gap problems. We should do everything possible to show an awareness of such problems and, above all, not do anything which will worsen the situation.

Unless you are the friendly next-door neighbor, do not make home visits to complain about matters that parents and youngsters can do little or nothing about. In a second language situation, if a parent speaks no English, lives in one room with a large family, and is not expecting you, the humiliation to the parent and youngster will be indescribable.

As teachers, we must be aware of differences in cultural patterns, for example, the extended family concept in which it is normal for a youngster to have to stay home to help care for an ailing family member. Unless too many absences cause serious problems, do not tell the students they cannot stay home to take care of a sick grandmother or younger family member. Help them retain their cherished values. They can always learn an irregular past participle they may have missed as you reteach it using a spiral approach. Encourage students to get their peers to tell them about important work they may have missed.

8. *Rapport with the administration.*

a. Avoid problems by sending in your attendance reports on time, by preparing lesson plans as prescribed, by attending faculty meetings, by arriving on time to meet your first class in the morning, and by reporting for lunchroom or hall duty at the times you are scheduled.

b. Discuss problems with the principal or his or her assistants without expecting instant solutions. They may not be familiar with language-teaching practices.

c. As noted above, do not send minor discipline problems to the administrative office. Handle problems yourself. You know your students, your procedures, and the source or background of the problem. The principal may not.

d. If you are teaching in a poor school district, do not make demands for video recorders, computers, and other costly material. Until monies are available, make do with a record player, a tape recorder if possible, and yourself and the students.

You are probably wondering what this discussion has to do with teaching ESL or EFL. It has a great deal to do with it. You cannot enter your classroom and greet your learners with enthusiasm if you have just had an unfortunate encounter with the principal or the head of the department.

9. *Rapport with colleagues.* How important rapport with colleagues is! If you are striving to use an interdisciplinary approach in your classes, you will need the cooperation of teachers in all the other departments, such as music, art, and social studies. This is even more important if you are teaching ESL in pullout classes where pupils come to you from many different teachers for a brief period during the school day. In order to help these learners, you must (a word I generally do not use) find out what they need to know in order to survive in their regular class. Can you arrange to meet the regular teachers at lunch, over an afterschool cup of coffee, or for an hour during the weekend? You will avoid a feeling of frustration and the students will benefit immeasurably from this cooperative endeavor. Teachers with special talents can help your students with advice and sources of information.

10. *The classroom.* The classroom should have charts, games, bulletin boards, written papers, or drawings prepared by the learners themselves; a table with objects collected by the students; maps and/or a globe; a library corner with monolingual English or bilingual dictionaries, simple and simplified readers, tourist brochures representing, in an ESL setting, the countries from which the learners have come; a record player and a tape recorder where possible; and a file of pictures of single objects and of places in the community.

All the material should serve to stimulate communication and interaction. A shell may be the source of utterances like, ''It's beautiful,'' ''Its colors are lovely.'' ''Where did you find it?'' ''I didn't. My aunt brought it from Hawaii.''

Here are several comments to round out this section.

a. Have the bulletin board changed every few weeks, particularly if it is devoted to current events.

b. If you put up papers written by the students, make sure that every student's paper is displayed—in alphabetical order to avoid invidious comparisons.

c. Allow the students to borrow a book whenever they want to and to prepare a short resume of what they liked (or did not like) about it. Create an audience situation for them so that they can feel pride in what they have accomplished.

The classroom should be cheerful, stimulating, and functional. Charts that you use often may be hung on a clothesline with clothespins for easy access. Everything should be labeled so that no time will be wasted looking for a picture or for the vowel chart, for example.

To get back to my first thoughts on the learning environment, forty-five to sixty minutes is more than enough time to present and practice whatever language items you have planned to teach that hour, provided that you and the learners share the same enthusiasm and that the materials you need to create realistic situations are at your fingertips. Most important is that the students feel the love and warmth, the respect, and the empathy that only we, the teachers, can provide.

The Teacher's Skills

There can be no doubt that the single most important factor in the instructional process—the important variable—is the teacher. It is what the teacher does to create a desirable classroom climate, to plan a variety of learning activities, to use materials of instruction effectively, and, most important, to try to identify with the needs and aspirations of students. It is these things that will determine, in the final analysis, whether learning will take place. I do not believe that teachers are ''born''— although I would admit that genes and early environmental influences have an effect on personality and character—but I am convinced that anyone who is willing and interested can hope to become a skilled and effective teacher. In addition to attitude traits such as a sense of justice, an abiding desire to grow professionally, fairness, tact, humility, intellectual curiosity, and enthusiasm for teaching—either simulated, on occasion, or real—the teacher needs to develop certain knowledge, skills, and insights. He or she should, for example:

1. Study the educational backgrounds of the students as a springboard for planning varied group or individual activities.
2. Gain conscious familiarity with features of the English sound, grammar, vocabulary, and cultural systems. He or she should make an inventory of the pronunciation and grammatical items that cause difficulty for the students.
3. Learn methods and techniques of teaching English as a second language.
4. Integrate principles and/or procedures of related disciplines (linguistics, psychology, sociology, and anthropology) into the teaching of English.

Further Tips on Techniques

1. Make every effort to help the students listen carefully and produce only correct responses. The trial-and-error method of learning, especially in an intensive course, is basically nonproductive and psychologically unsound.

2. If a student makes an error during a drill period, however, you might simply say "Listen" and then give the correct form. It is undesirable to repeat the incorrect form, not only because the student who made the error will feel humiliated but also because your repetition of it might confirm the error in other students' minds.

3. Short daily quizzes on the previous day's presentation—which I highly recommend to you—should be corrected immediately. Since the new lesson is generally based on material learned during the preceding session, it is essential that you and the students be aware of any problem that may exist. There are two other immediate reasons for giving daily quizzes: a high score enhances the student's feeling of achievement, and the anxiety surrounding the taking of tests will diminish as students come to regard them as routine, nonthreatening activities.

4. Order all sentences within drills in such a way that they will provide practice in items that generally belong together and that are learned more quickly through association. I would drill together, for example, sentences with *be* or *have* or *can*, even though the sentences on the laboratory tape will appear in another order. I would first drill the utterances around a particular verb form or item. You can do this by marking the sentences in your text in colored pencil or by renumbering them for the first round of practice. Then, after the students have gained some confidence in performing drills, you can give the utterances in the order in which they will be heard on the tape.

Another point I would like to make regarding drill sequences is this: For questions requiring yes-no answers, I would conduct the drill so as to elicit first only responses beginning with *yes*. Then I would elicit all the *no* responses. Alternating *yes* and *no* is not only confusing to students, but it does not provide the kind of practice that reinforces realistic situations. A question such as *Are you a teacher?* answered alternately with *yes* and *no* violates basic principles of situational development. If the *no* responses are not authentic, you may introduce the drill by saying, "Now, let's pretend."

5. Before requiring students to engage in more complex transformation drills, we should give them extensive practice in making substitutions in already transformed sentences. For example, if our aim is to teach students to transform direct speech into indirect speech, we would not immediately expect them to combine *he asked* and *what's the girl's name?* Intermediate steps, in my experience, would call for substitution drills in sentences such as "He asked what the girl's name was," in which the students would substitute other pronouns or proper names for *he* and other words for *girl* and *name*. Several substitution drills, each with five or six examples, will help students internalize the word order and rhythm of the pattern and will reduce stumbling in the transformation exercise.

Another helpful drill for practicing indirect speech, and numerous other grammatical items, is the directed practice drill. You might want to engage in it in the three stages described in later chapters.

6. By the same token, you should not as a rule ask the students to prepare any work at home or in the language laboratory unless you have first presented it and clarified it in class. For example, if the students "learn" pronunciation or meaning incorrectly, it will take more time to eradicate the errors than it would have taken to guide them in a brief oral preview of the new vocabulary. Of course, you should give the students guided practice in using a dictionary and in utilizing contextual clues to help them select the most appropriate word from the numerous dictionary meanings. But how could they, without your guidance, decide which of the many meanings of words such as *time, give, run,* or *take* to select?

7. Language learning includes learning the culture, gestures, and spoken expressions which give added meaning to words or sentences. An intonation pattern may express anger in one language but delight in another.

• Dinner in the United States usually takes place about six or seven o'clock. In some regions of the United States, the noontime meal is called *lunch*; in others, it may be called *dinner*. In Spain, one has dinner after 9:30 P.M.

8. Another extremely important area of the English language we must help our students acquire is its vocabulary.

• Within vocabulary (the *lexicon* of the language), we distinguish between *content* words (*pen, school, go, pretty,* etc.) and *function* words (*with, for, may, will,* etc.). Function words need to be learned as quickly as feasible (in a logical order and sequence, however). Content words can be learned in small groups around "life" situations. At the beginning stages of language learning the same words are often used repeatedly to give practice in new structures (I need a pen; I'd like a pen; Will you buy me a pen? etc.).
• Although vocabulary is important, its overly rapid acquisition in the early stages should be subordinated to that of the sounds and the structure (grammar) of the language. Vocabulary can be accumulated quickly as the need arises later and as wider reading is begun *after* the basic sound and structure system of the language has been learned.

On the other hand, vocabulary items—although low on a word frequency list—should be taught as soon as feasible if such teaching stimulates students to talk about the immediate environment. For example, words like *skyscraper, cow, sheep* may have to be taught immediately if the classroom window looks out on them.

The watchword is *judiciously*. You should teach those items which will give the students the feeling that they are talking about real things in their environment which they would ordinarily talk about in their native tongue.

9. Especially at the elementary level, you should first go over in class all work assigned for the language laboratory. Moreover, at any level, the first part of the next class period should include activities that will permit the students to demonstrate the greater fluency and skill they have gained through work in the laboratory. Students will place more value on the laboratory session if you thus demonstrate that you consider it an integral and reinforcing part of their classroom work.

10. In order to develop reading comprehension, initially all reading should be of the intensive type. After an appropriate prereading period related to the students' experiences, you should clarify all difficulties in the reading passage: pronunciation, grammar, vocabulary, cultural allusions, situation. With the students' books open (since you are now emphasizing reading and not listening comprehension), you should read one or two sentences aloud and ask several types of questions about them (yes-no questions and questions beginning with one of the *wh* words). After you treat an entire portion in this way, you should ask for a summary—a sequential one—with each of several students contributing one idea and then one or two students giving the entire summary briefly. You should follow this with word study exercises, other types of questions, paraphrases, and related activities that will contribute to development of the total reading skill.

11. You should use dialogues for multiple purposes. In addition to using the utterances in them as models for grammatical or lexical study, you should also use dialogues extensively for question-and-answer practice. Some questions may be on the content of the dialogue itself; others may be of a personal nature but related to the theme of the dialogue. For example, if the dialogue is about movie-going, you might ask such personalized questions as "Do you like to go to the movies?" "What kind of movies do you like best?" "Do you ever see English films?"

The students should also practice entire alternative sentences that would be appropriate in the context of the dialogue. It goes without saying that you should encourage them to formulate their own questions on the dialogue, which they can then ask you or their fellow students.

12. Whenever possible, you should individualize instruction, fitting it to the abilities and interests of the students. This is desirable even at beginning levels. For example, you can ask timid students or "late starters" questions that require only a yes-no response, while you ask more advanced extroverts to make longer responses or encourage them to formulate their own questions.

13. You might wish to try the following sequence of student participation:

a. Question individual students or give cues to which individual students will respond. (It is a good idea to prepare a small card, to fit in your left hand, on which you have written cue words or questions. This makes for a brisk, rhythmic drill.)

b. In directed practice, have individual students question each other or make statements in chain fashion as they sit in pairs facing each other.

14. More essential than anything I have said to this point is that you give the students a constant feeling of success and of confidence in their ability to learn the language. Announcing all tests in advance; making sure that tests are based only on what has been taught *and learned*; individualizing instruction; providing many warm-up and summary periods; preparing all homework with the students except, perhaps, for those at advanced levels; planning for the inclusion of many audience situations in which more advanced students tell you and their peers about books they have read, things they have done, places they have visited, persons to whom they have talked—all these things will contribute to the feeling of security and accomplishment that students need to sustain motivation and enthusiasm.

15. Many other techniques could be noted, of course, but no article or book could ever hope to list them all. Only the teacher in the classroom can be fully cognizant of the problems and the joys, the frustrations and the satisfactions, and the intuitive procedures that ''work'' which are the very essence of teaching. Instructors with a sense of commitment to their profession, and with the conviction that people can learn, think primarily of the joys and satisfactions of teaching as they come into contact with human beings whose futures they may help to mold.

The important moment of reality comes when the enthusiastic and well-prepared teacher is aware of his or her students' unspoken ''well done'' and when he or she sees the glint of comprehension and the smile of confidence on their faces. For those of us who have made teaching our life's work, all myths are dispelled and we are left at the end of each day with a sense of fulfillment and enrichment gained from the interaction with our students.

Motivation: Its Crucial Role

Motivation is often extolled as the key to learning but is just as often misunderstood. While everyone would agree that motivation should be fostered and sustained, there has been little consensus on the what, when, why, and how that teachers must have to ensure that students will maintain the drive, the interest, and the desire to persevere in spite of the hurdles and plateaus which lie in the path of language learning.

Contrary to some popular misconceptions, motivation is not *either* extrinsic *or* intrinsic, or, if you prefer, instrumental or integrative; it is not something that is fostered only during the first half-hour of the academic year; it does not depend solely on the learner's aptitude, personality, or learning strategies. Motivation stems rather from positive learners and teacher attitudes which should permeate every stage of the learning process if it is to lead to pleasure and success in language acquisition. Motivation is the feeling nurtured primarily by the classroom teacher in the learning situation as he or she engages in carefully planned as well as empirical and intuitive practices which will satisfy one or more of the basic, universal, cognitive, and affective human needs identified by psychologists such as Maslow: the need for survival, belonging, identity, self-esteem and self-actualization.

I am not suggesting that teachers should be unaware of sound theoretical bases derived from linguistics, sociology, anthropology, and other sciences. What I am suggesting is that we devote more attention to the study of characteristics within the teacher, the learners, and the community in which they live and in which the learning institution is located—the real, human factors which may well have a greater impact on learning than the most rigorously constructed scientific theory.

How can the teacher develop the interest and attitudes needed to sustain motivation? Why is it that students' initial motivation very often wanes quickly? Let me try to answer these questions briefly by touching on techniques and strategies the teacher may find useful.

In order to do so, I will use the term *motivation* itself as a mnemonic device and indicate what each letter suggests to me with respect to language acquisition. Unfortunately, I can mention only a few of the concepts or procedures that each letter suggests. (I could, for example, have used the letter *A* as a reminder of such terms as *aptitude* and *aspiration*, in addition to *attitude*.) Keeping these reservations in mind, I now turn to our mnemonic.

The letter *M* reminds us of studies by Wallace Lambert and his colleagues on instrumental and integrative *motivation*. *Instrumental motivation* refers primarily to the learner's desire to acquire the language as an instrument of communication, which may lead to better grades in school, to better paid employment, and to upward social mobility. *Integrative motivation* relates to the learner's desire to be accepted by the speakers of the foreign or second language and to be identified with them. Where feasible, we should foster both types of motivation. In many places throughout the world where there are few native English speakers and no electric current for radio, tape player, or television, integrative motivation is difficult to achieve. In this regard, I was happy to read an article by G. Richard Tucker recently in which he cautions educators against replicating experimentation which has been carried out in totally different sociocultural circumstances.

A half-century or more ago, educators distinguished between *extrinsic* and *intrinsic* motivation. *Extrinsic motivation*, the desire to do well on an examination or in a class recitation, will often become *intrinsic* when the learner experiences a feeling of confidence and achievement as a result of successful performance. A primary responsibility of teachers—and I have seen thousands of them perform this miracle—is to transform initial extrinsic motivation into permanent intrinsic motivation.

The *M* in motivation, of course, also stands for *methodology*. Our methodology must be flexible and eclectic, *not* dogmatic or prescriptive. Language teaching has been set back fifty years and student motivation stifled by adherence to such statements as *Reading must be deferred for X number of years* or *Dialogues must be memorized* or *Translation must be banned*, or *We must never talk about the language*—with little consideration given to such important factors as the age and affective needs of the learners and the objectives of the program. Methodology, moreover, must be compatible with the time available, the aptitude and interests of the learners, and the personality and preparation of the teacher.

Nor, as some people seem to think, does *eclectic* mean haphazard. Quite the contrary. Eclecticism implies the careful selection of facets of various methods and their integration into a cohesive, coherent procedure. This must be in harmony with the teacher's personality, the students' needs and strategies for learning, and the aspirations of the community. An example of an eclectic approach to foreign language learning is a functional-notional curriculum. In this most recent addition to current approaches, the learners' communicative purpose is considered to be of central importance.

Subordinate, although still crucial, are the choice and presentation of grammatical, situational, and thematic aspects related to the speaker's or writer's purpose. To these are added basic tenets of semantic and humanistic theory which will certainly be motivating when learners feel that they can choose from among several alternatives to express their purpose (a principle of semantic theory) and, as important, when they feel valued and respected as human beings. It is interesting to note that the hierarchy of needs identified by Maslow and others is the basis for syllabus design in some functional-notional materials.

Allow me to continue with the letter *M*. The *meaning* of everything the learner hears and says must be made crystal clear to him or her through pictures or other aids and through use of the native language in situations where this is feasible. The native language should be used without hesitation in the classroom when comprehension fails and when the learners are frustrated or are merely repeating in rote fashion. Of course, there should be a gradual phasing out of the learners' native tongue as soon as their competence in English increases. On the other hand, students should always be encouraged to ask questions such as, "How do we say X in English?"

The teacher should lead the students very gradually in small incremental steps to *mastery* through varied activities and experiences, but never, except in rare instances, through memorization. Nor should we insist on mastery prematurely. We must learn to be satisfied with a gradual unfolding of the learner's potential to acquire English, through such techniques as the use of a spiral approach in lesson or unit planning, peer teaching, exposure to a variety of comprehensible materials, and opportunities to say or write increasingly longer sentences.

The letter *O* may represent *objectives*. I believe it would be appropriate to say that the primary goal of language teaching today is to help learners use language *fluently* through the multiple functions it serves in real life and to develop their communicative competence, that is, to enable them to understand and produce language that is not only correct but also appropriate and acceptable in the social situations in which it is generally used. In order to achieve such a goal, the curriculum should include not only provision for a discussion of the elements—people, places, time, topics—in the situation, but also the study of language varieties or registers and of nonlinguistic features such as distances between speakers, facial expressions, and unarticulated sounds normally used in spoken communication.

The curriculum should provide activities that stimulate learners to express themselves—to clarify and classify their thoughts, to agree, to disagree, and to express love, anger, and any other human emotion—as well as to interact with others. The curriculum should also give language practice needed to create sentences, stories, songs, poetry, or essays. It is no longer enough to teach the *forms* of linguistic items; we must also make students aware of the contexts and the situations—in other words, the dimensions of experience—in which the forms would be used by native speakers.

I cannot subscribe to the dogmatic emphasis on *performance objectives*, which holds that a specific body of knowledge must be acquired in a certain way within a prescribed time limit. Although some writers contend that performance objectives tell the student exactly what is expected of him or her, such objectives discount more important psychological factors, which causes unnecessary tension in the student. As we know, all human beings have different styles and different rhythms of learning. Only the perceptive teacher can pause, turn back when necessary, and realize merely by looking at the student when fatigue or anxiety may hamper learning and reduce motivation.

Another word about objectives: Teachers, schools, and education officials should ask continually, Are these objectives realistic for this age group, in this community, with these learners, and within the time available? Will they be valuable to the students not only in the future but also today? If not, how can we modify them?

The comments I might make under the letter *T* should be concerned primarily with the *teacher*—but it is obvious that the role of the teacher permeates this entire book. The enhancement of motivation occurs when the teacher closes the classroom door, greets the students with a warm, welcoming smile, and proceeds to interact with various individuals by making comments or asking questions which indicate personal concern. Allow me, therefore, to use the letter *T* for the term *technique*.

Let me enumerate a handful which I have found particularly stimulating because they satisfy one or more of our students' cognitive or affective needs.

Try engaging the learners' interest by doing some of the following:

1. Relate the presentation and practice of any communicative, grammatical, or lexical item or the reading and writing of any passage to *their* cultural and language knowledge and to *their* experiences, both past and present.

2. Make them consciously aware of redundancy clues in English as an aid in listening, speaking, reading, or writing, e.g., plurality—*Some* boy*s are* going to get *their* coat*s*.

3. Help them to guess word meanings from the relevant context or from the situation of the conversation or passage. If this is difficult or impossible, give or have someone else give the native language equivalent or encourage them to use a dictionary.

4. Enable them to understand the communicative message under a surface statement. For example, "Is that your new car?" may express admiration or anger depending upon the situation in which it is said and the intonation used.

5. Use the spiral approach in presentation and practice. For example, do not give fifteen ways to make a request in one lesson, even in your university classes. First give one or two and then return to them and give other alternatives in subsequent lessons.

6. In relation to item 5 above, proceed from simple to more complex utterances used to express a thought or function. Begin with nonverbal messages and move to simple verbal ones, starting, where possible, with the utterance *you* would use in expressing a function or concept.

7. Give the learners extensive practice in paraphrasing—in using alternatives for communicative expressions, structures, or lexical items. You and I know that they will seldom if ever encounter the same dialogue sequence again.

8. Help them to learn the reason for switching the language variety in a dialogue or passage. Help them also to produce different varieties by changing one or more elements in the situation under discussion.

9. Help them to play different roles in text or teacher-prepared dialogues and later in realistic scenes created by individuals, pairs, or groups. Do not, however, ask them to engage in spontaneous role playing without building up to that stage in carefully graded steps.

10. Enable them to recognize and use cognates in learning situations where such use is possible. Place these on the chalkboard under each other so that similarities of form will be immediately visible; for example,

difficult (English)
difficile (Italian)
difficile (French)
dificil (Spanish)

11. When using listening comprehension involving a connected text at beginning and intermediate levels you may need to adapt the passage or dialogue in three stages to produce a less complex text. (a) In the first stage, use simple, active, declarative sentences, omitting adjectives, adverbs, and complex sentences while still keeping the basic message authentic. Ask for yes-no or true-false responses. (b) In the second stage, reinsert the adjectives and adverbs. With this version, use *wh* questions, asking for utterances, not complete sentences. (c) In the third stage, introduce the original passage and use the questions above as well as inferential questions, for example, "Why do you think that?" and "How do you know that?"

12. With further reference to listening comprehension, two other suggestions may be in order. (a) Repeat or have the learners hear the same tape of a dialogue or role play at least three times. (b) Stop the tape or your reading at several points, asking questions which become increasingly more complex and require longer answers, for example, "Who is talking?" "What are X and Y talking about?" "What does X want Y to do?" and "Do they agree?" Later you may add "What did Y say? Use his exact words" or "What did you hear X say?" (Ask for indirect speech: "X said that. . . .".)

13. Try to get authentic materials, such as newspapers, magazines, journals, ads, and timetables. Duplicate relevant parts and use them for pair or group practice. Use the same piece of material over the semester for a variety of language-producing activities. In addition to saving your time, such multiple use is motivating because the students' expectation of familiar structure or vocabulary will help them to recall it easily and will result in increased fluency.

14. Help the students themselves (over the age of about eleven) discover the rule underlying the form and use of a structural item, a communicative expression, or a communicative formula by placing examples on the chalkboard, underlining the forms, and drawing arrows from key words to their referents. After presenting your oral model, ask questions eliciting the oral and written form, position, grammatical function, and meaning of the expression or structure.

15. Divide material such as dialogues or reading into two parallel streams: one for global comprehension only and the other for gradual mastery. As quickly as is feasible, learners should be helped to understand and read interesting, meaningful material although they may have only a global comprehension of it—even though some of the structures within it will not be presented for active production for several days or months. (I consider the first stream the most important one for motivation.) At the same time, of course, learners will be systematically but gradually introduced to the phonemes of the language, inflections and derivations, word order, sound-symbol relationships, words which may or must co-occur, and other significant elements of the English language.

16. Make use of an interdisciplinary, broadly based curricular approach not only in English for special-purpose classes but in all classes as well, for several reasons: (a) in countries such as Great Britain, the United States, and others where English is the language of the school and community, to enable learners to enter the mainstream; (b) to make them aware that English is an instrument of learning and communication, as is their native tongue; and (c) to give them interesting topics to talk and ask about, gleaned from several curricular areas.

17. Set realistic tasks and activities which can be accomplished within a reasonable time and which will indicate that you (a) have an awareness of the learners' communities and resources; (b) have an understanding of the fact that English may not be their only school subject; (c) (as is true in many situations) realize they may never hear English outside your classroom; and (d) understand that their cultural taboos may make certain tasks impossible to perform.

18. Make sure that, in presenting new materials, numerous receptive (recognition) activities precede your request for production or ''creativity.''

19. Learn to be content with compound bilingualism, particularly in older persons. We can no longer insist on coordinate bilingualism and especially on perfect pronunciation. Both for cognitive and affective reasons, we should recognize that—except for the highly gifted or fortunate learners who have wide access to native speakers and taped materials—our learners will generally speak a Chinese, an Indian, or an Italian English.

I shall use the letter *I* for the terms *involvement* and *integration*.

The need for *involving* students in all phases of the program is of central importance in sustaining motivation. We should rid ourselves of the outworn notion that listening and reading are passive communication abilities. On the contrary, both listening and reading require the most active involvement on the part of the student.

The strengths and weaknesses of individual students should be considered when we assign class tasks and homework, as we vary their roles in groups, and as we ensure that each one participates in every lesson to the best of his or her ability. We must, for example, realize that some students may never be capable of writing a ''free'' composition on an abstract topic. Neither would they be able to do so in their native language.

The term *integration* refers to several ideas:

1. The teacher will help students realize that all levels of language—phonological, morphological, syntactic, lexical, and cultural—are integrated, that is, interrelated, in every act of communication. Essential in bringing about this awareness is the deliberate reintroduction (spiraling) in lessons of the linguistic or cultural elements acquired at earlier learning levels or in previous lessons. Students gain a feeling of achievement as they meet, recognize, and produce known language—in wider contexts or in different, appropriate social situations—with increasing fluency.

2. The same text or passage should be used to engage learners in integrated listening, speaking, reading, and writing activities.

3. Communicative purposes, situational elements, grammatical structures, and specific notions, that is, vocabulary items, are integrated in a functional-notional or communicative approach to produce an utterance, in even the most simple message.

4. More important than the three ideas above noted are the following: The teacher's pivotal responsibility is to imbue students with confidence and self-esteem, ensuring that they will retain or develop emotional security and a well-integrated personality that will influence their entire lives.

The letter *V* is of paramount concern. The positive *values* that we help students acquire as they learn to use linguistic and cultural insights for real-world communication will remain with them long after they have forgotten an irregular past participle. Students should be helped to appreciate the universality of the human experience, their own culture and values, and those of other people.

Our goal should be not merely to make learners bicultural—increasing their awareness of their culture and that of English speakers—but rather to help them perceive, accept, and respect cultural pluralism. Concentrating on similarities among peoples rather than on differences will have a more far-reaching and positive psychological effect on learners than the invidious comparisons that often characterize the teaching of culture. Our hope for a pluralistic and harmonious world lies in helping our students realize that they are members of a world community which transcends individual and national boundaries.

In order to achieve this objective, we must start by recognizing and reinforcing the learners' sense of identity by giving them pride in their own language and culture, and then continue the process by teaching them the polite and tentative language which should be used to disagree or express uncertainty and by helping them—in carefully selected tasks—to make moral and ethical choices.

The letter *A* is also multifaceted. Let us start with *attitudes*. The attitudes of the students, teachers, community members, peers, and others with whom the student comes into contact all affect motivation to some extent, but it is the attitude of the teacher toward the student and toward his or her profession that is the essence and core of motivation. Is the teacher enthusiastic, empathetic, patient, and well-prepared? Does he or she respect each student's individuality? Does the teacher show a sensitive awareness of the language, the culture, and the educational system of the student's country of origin, as well as of any problems which may exist in the community?

On the other hand, returning to the correction of errors for a moment, let me say that, while I believe firmly in words of encouragement and praise whenever possible, the teacher should never praise a student for uttering a completely incorrect sentence, such as "He don't got no pencil." Such praise would do a grave disservice both to the student whose error might thus be reinforced and to other students in the class who are aware of the error and would thus become confused. The key word in correcting errors and, indeed, in any aspect of teaching is the adverb *judiciously*.

The letter *A* reminds us also that teachers should plan a wide gamut of *activities* for each lesson: I would say a minimum of five different ones for each class hour. Such activities should give students the feeling that they are achieving and making perhaps slow but nonetheless definite progress toward communicative competence.

A also stands for the educational term *articulation*. Articulation has two important dimensions: vertical and horizontal. *Vertical articulation* ensures that the student's progress from one learning level to the next is continuous and smooth. The teacher should provide for the review of material learned at lower levels and for the preparation of students for subsequent levels.

Horizontal articulation is particularly necessary when students in secondary schools and universities are taught pronunciation, reading, and grammar by different teachers, since this might preclude an appreciation of the interrelations among these different skills. As mentioned above, an interdisciplinary approach, as well as the integration of disparate linguistic or cultural items into meaningful acts of communication, would also come under the heading of horizontal articulation. Under this heading, too, would be placed the primary responsibility of the *special English* teacher in pull-out programs in the United States and Great Britain, who should relate the material he or she teaches to the subject areas the students follow during the remainder of the school day.

T may stand for *transfer* of learning, for *translation*, for *textbooks*, and for *testing*. Let us start with transfer of learning of one linguistic item—for example, verb endings transferred to other verbs at a beginning level. Transfer does not generally take place automatically. Unless the teacher specifically points out the common elements within the forms and, in addition, gives the students practice in using them in contexts or situations other than those in which they were presented, the majority of learners will not know how and when to transfer the knowledge they have acquired. The teacher must provide models and extensive practice with verbs such as *need, want, have*, and *like*, for example, in order to ensure transfer.

I should like to mention two facts about *translation* because both seem to cause misunderstanding. First, it is perfectly normal for learners above the age of about five to think of the equivalent of a term or a structure in their native language as they hear the term in English. The art and skill of the teacher will be called into play in eliminating this intermediate step of translation through a variety of briskly conducted activities. Second, although I do not advocate a return to the traditional grammar-translation method, I do think it is desirable at early levels to ask students—after they have carried out all other appropriate oral drills—to give native language equivalents of limited structural items from the target language, and vice versa. I realize that this is not possible in classes where learners have different language backgrounds. Where possible, however, at intermediate and advanced levels, equivalents of expressions, sentences, and even paragraphs may be extremely useful. Such practice could well lead to a saleable skill that we should help our students acquire. A total ban on translation—that is, giving equivalent expressions in the native language—is not realistic, particularly in countries where translation is feasible and is required on final examinations.

Moving to *textbooks*, we must accept the fact that the perfect textbook will never be written, especially for our learners in difficult situations. It is the teacher's responsibility to add dialogues and relevant lexical items, to change the order of exercises or of sentences within the exercises, and to modify or delete sections that might be particularly counterproductive.

Testing and evaluation of students' competence and performance, as well as of our teaching procedures, should be an integral part of the language-teaching program. I believe in frequent, brief, previously announced tests—both discrete point and integrative—designed to assess the quality and quantity of the learners' oral or written production. These formative tests will keep teachers and students informed of their progress toward the multiple goals they are expected to achieve. Parents and community leaders also have the right to know whether the schools are succeeding. I would not assign grades to all tests, however. Use some of them as learning devices instead.

Returning again to the letter *I*, I should like to mention two issues that appear with increasing frequency in language-teaching journals: (1) *linguistic interference* and (2) *individualization of instruction*.

A great deal of experimentation is being conducted at the present time to determine whether it is solely interference *between the first language and the target language* that causes students to make errors—in other words, whether the interference is *interlinguistic*. If the conflict *is* between L1 and L2, contrastive analyses of the native language and English would be effective in explaining and in determining priorities and emphases.

Other researchers contend that *intralinguistic* interference is equally important and that analyses of students' oral and written errors would demonstrate that they are not necessarily caused by a conflict between the first and second languages. They assert that incomplete knowledge of a linguistic class or category in the *target language* may produce false analogies and cause problems as students move toward more complete linguistic acquisition. Moreover, numerous studies on second and native language acquisition indicate that forms which are learned—either early or late—and errors which occur in the process are similar as one moves across age levels and across cultures.

All these research efforts are of crucial importance not only in order to plan for selection and gradation of material to be taught but also to reassure teachers—who often think "mea culpa" immediately when errors are made—that such errors are normal. The teacher's reassurance of the students as well as his or her conscious reintroduction in lesson materials of troublesome points—whatever their origin—will enhance motivation.

In theory, *individualization of instruction* is desirable and necessary. As a teacher, however, I would protest the exaggerations made by some journals. It would be an arduous and virtually impossible task for the teacher with 40 to 100 students in a class to prepare the many activities and tests that would be needed if all instruction were truly individualized. We should of course utilize the strengths and interests of individual students—in group work and individualized homework. And we should of course help them to overcome weaknesses through individual help and specialized materials, but we should also prepare classwide activities for a good part of each teaching lesson, especially for large classes, those below the advanced, professional level, and those held in small rooms.

I will be very brief here about the letter *O*. To me it symbolizes the need for guided teacher *observation* in elementary and secondary schools, not only of other master teachers but sometimes of less able teachers. Moreover, I have urged for years that college professors concerned with teacher training observe classes in lower-level schools. Only through direct observation can they become truly aware of the grim realities of some teaching situations. Videotape recordings are not always practical or satisfactory.

In a different sense, observation also serves as a reminder of the need for the teacher to be aware of the student's quality of involvement, participation, and attitude during the class hour. The teacher should evaluate the student's progress toward goals not only in formal or informal oral and written tests but also through sensitive observation.

In discussing the last letter in our mnemonic, *N*, I should like to start with a plea: that we help and indeed encourage our students to talk in English about their *native culture*. Such a procedure is psychologically sound and conducive to high motivation.

The letter *N* also stands for the entire range of the affective and cognitive *needs* of every human being. All pupils need to be exposed to a wide array of interesting, challenging experiences; they need to feel that they are moving forward continuously and that they are becoming increasingly able to perceive and to integrate the experiences to which they are exposed; they need to feel secure not only in their knowledge of the foreign language and culture but also in having the understanding and respect of teachers and peers. They need to feel that they belong to a group and that they can hope for many small successes. They need to enter their language classes not with fear but with a feeling of enthusiasm.

Finally, motivation for learning means not only understanding the learners, their feelings, their aspirations, and their spiritual and creative needs but also the world that they bring with them into the classroom. Most learners come to us with a perfectly adequate language and culture. One of our major responsibilities is to help them appreciate that we do not want to take away these precious possessions from them. We wish only to add another language to their abilities and help them to appreciate other cultures.

Teachers, too, have needs over and above the need for a knowledge of linguistics, sociology, and psychology. In order to sustain their student's motivation, they need the courage to scrutinize, challenge, and question nonproductive theories, panaceas, or slogans. They need to constantly live a commitment to teaching and to the idea that all normal human beings can learn. They need confidence in themselves to use their intuition and to develop their strong points. They need to have the conviction that their mission constitutes a most crucial task in any society. It is the teacher who will have the opportunity to meet and touch the minds and hearts of the majority of young people in a community.

Let me conclude by reaffirming my belief that the teacher is the crucial variable in a society. The language teacher, in particular, is aware that while teaching materials must be timely and relevant, it is infinitely more important that they be timeless and universal. A teacher is cognizant of the fact that material should be designed not only to teach language, literature, or culture but also to foster the moral, spiritual, and ethical values which can contribute to our goal of world citizenship.

Education in its broadest sense means helping our learners to grow, to change, to live—in sum, to be well-integrated, secure persons. Such an education can be provided in the school situation only by caring, sensitive, humane, knowledgeable teachers. And now, a truth which has been repeated often: While teaching is a science, it is primarily an art which only you, a teacher, can bring into your classroom. Your enthusiasm, your dedication, and your love for your profession and for your students cannot help but make every learning hour a stimulating, motivating experience—one which you and your students will look forward to with the keenest anticipation.

Theories and Principles of Language Learning

No one really knows how learning takes place. In fact, one of the major reasons for studying verbal behavior is to gain insight into the mental processes of human beings. There are two major theories currently in vogue and numerous research studies in linguistics and other sciences which make it possible for us to state some principles which can certainly guide us in our profession. The works of Lenneberg, Chomsky, and others (see Appendix V) underscore the existence in every human being of a language acquisition device. It is important to remember, however, that even in acquiring his native tongue, the child must be in an environment where *he hears* meaningful "noises" and where *other people react* to the sounds he makes. The stages of language development in all children appear to be biologically determined, but they must receive (hear) the primary data (meaningful speech) which they will then process.

TWO THEORIES OF LEARNING

The learner's active participation in the learning process is a fundamental premise of the two currently favored learning theories. Stated simply, one—the cognitive code theory—underscores the fact that the learner brings to the task of learning an innate mental capacity. S/he brings a perception of relationships and an unconscious formulation of the "rules" resulting from the discovery of the structure and organization of new material and from the perception of its relationship to known material. Closely tied to this theory of the importance of the individual's mental organization of learned material is research which seems to indicate that the nervous system stores images and memories which can then be evoked without a preceding stimulus.

The other theory—the association or operant conditioning theory—is based on experimentation indicating that bonds can be forged between a stimulus and a response and that responses are shaped and strengthened or extinguished by the reinforcements or rewards which should always follow the learner's response to a stimulus. Such a continuous association between stimulus and response, followed immediately by confirmation of the learner's correct response by a teacher, a tape, a record, and so on, leads to formation of the *habits* needed for placing sounds and words in appropriate arrangements.

Both of these theories have a place in language learning. After students have acquired *cognitive control* of the phonological, grammatical, and lexical patterns, they will develop the *habit* of using them with facility as they practice them in numerous activities.

A HANDFUL OF PRINCIPLES

1. Language items should be presented in *contexts* and *situations* which will clarify their meaning. Through the dramatization of a plausible, realistic situation, students should be enabled to grasp the essential features of sound, structure, words, communicative functions, and the arrangements of these in the utterances used in it.

- The separate elements of the utterances—presented and understood in a situation—may then be isolated and practiced, the presentation and amount of practice at any one time depending on whether an item is *of high frequency* and *useful in many other situations* (or needed by the students in order to use their textbook profitably.)
- The spiral approach should be used. Any new item of language should be continually *reentered in other larger language contexts* with which it can co-occur. (See the chart on p. 15.)
- We should distinguish between *active* and *passive* acquisition of structure and vocabulary. Active items will be learned by students for purposes of *production* (both oral and written); and passive items for *recognition* or *reception* only (listening and reading comprehension). Naturally, many passive items may be pre-

sented and practiced for active production in subsequent lessons or at more advanced levels.

2. The *sounds*—found in an utterance already understood—may be practiced one at a time in isolation and/or by contrasting them in what is called *minimal pairs*. For example, *pit* and *pet* is a minimal pair because *one* sound alone makes the difference in the meaning.

- It is important, however, that a sound which may have been practiced in isolation be inserted immediately in words, phrases, or sentences which have, in addition, the *stress, rhythm, pauses* (or *junctures*), and *intonation* which are characteristic of English.

- The grammatical interrelationships of phonemes should be pointed out; for example (with older learners especially), *serene, serenity; divine, divinity; meter, metric*.

3. In addition to the sound system, learners must be taught the *structure system* of the language. Through numerous examples, learners must be given insight into word order, inflection, and derivation and into the other meaningful features of the English language (e.g., The boy is going. The boys *are* going. I wash every morning. I'm wash*ing* now. I wash*ed* yesterday morning.).

- Insight into a pattern is not enough, however. Our students have to learn the basic rules which govern the arrangements of sounds, structures, and words in the English language.

- Through application of these rules in meaningful material, they should be enabled to create similar utterances in other communication situations in which they will find themselves.

- Learners must be taught which other words within word classes (nouns, verbs, etc.) can be used in the place (*the slot*) of each of the words in a pattern. In "Did he go to the store this morning?" for example, *she* can be used instead of *he, ride* instead of *go, office* instead of *store*, and so on.

- Such substitution of a word or expression is only the beginning, however. Pupils have to be given such thorough control of the sounds and structures of the new language that they can understand, speak, and perhaps read and write without having to worry about the position of each word in the sentence or the form of each word (e.g., when do they use *sing, sang, sung?*; *boy, boy's?*; *child, children?*).

- Second language learning, therefore, means acquiring new habits or ways of using the speech organs and learning the forms and the arrangements of forms required by the system. It means acquiring the habit of the language through the intensive and extensive practice of numerous examples.

- It means, with older learners, learning the rules, that is, putting to use the insight into the recurring patterns of the second language which has been gained through the study (listening, repeating, practicing) of many examples. (It is important to remember that any reference to the recurring pattern comes *after* the study of numerous examples. The reference is usually a description of what actually happens in speech and not a rule of grammar. We will have more to say about this later.)

- The sounds, forms, or word sequences must be taught and practiced *systematically* in a *progression* and *order* which will permit the learners to associate each little segment of newly acquired language with every other segment they have already acquired.
- Through listening to, repeating, and studying many examples, students should be helped to acquire a repertoire of items they may come to expect in an utterance. The ability to "anticipate" language appears to be an important factor in the development of communicative competence.
- They should be led to notice which features are *redundant* in the English language. In an utterance such as, The *three* boys *are* going to get *their* coats, there are several clues to plurality. (This awareness of redundant signals will be helpful to them in *listening*, but they will still have to be given extensive practice in using each one of the signals in their speaking and writing activities.)
- Through the study of various examples, pupils should be enabled to recognize those sentences which look alike on the surface but are not really alike, for example, "The man was drunk by noon" and "The man was struck by lightning"; and how to resolve ambiguity by expanding the context, for example, "Visiting relatives can be enjoyable," might be expanded to clarify its two possible meanings: "I always like to go to their homes" or "We always have fun when they come to see us."
- They should also be helped to recognize the relationships among the various possible transformations of a base sentence.
- Students need not only knowledge about features such as those mentioned above but also practice in them in varied, stimulating, meaningful situations which will lead to really stimulus-free (creative) communication.

4. Language learning means acquiring the ability to ask and answer questions; to make statements; and to produce the normal, authentic forms used by native English speakers. For example, when someone asks, "Where did you go last night?" a possible normal response is "To the library." It is *not* "I went to the library last night."

- The end result is "free" communication. This ideal can be reached, however, only if students are helped, through orderly presentation and extensive oral practice, to communicate from the very beginning of the course. More will be said about this later.

5. It is important to reaffirm that although the new language material may be *introduced* in situations (conversations or brief narratives in which people, events, and objects in the environment are clearly delineated), you will have to do the following: (a) *select* the material for intensive "active" presentation; (b) *grade* it according to its complexity; (c) *order* it according to criteria of frequency of use; for example, *teach I, you, we, they* first because they have the same verb form and because *I* and *you* permit immediate communication; (d) *arrange* the model utterances in a way which will permit students to perceive the recurring features and hence the underlying rule.

Some Features of the English Language

ITS SOUND SYSTEM

A parenthetical statement may be in order before we proceed. Linguistics is a comparatively young science. Many experiments in the field are still in progress, and their results may not be known for years to come. It is natural, therefore, that some controversies exist among linguists about some symbols, some terms, and even some concepts. The facts given below are those *generally* accepted by a majority of linguists.

Since we will have occasion to refer to them several times in this book, the organs of speech, or *vocal organs*, are indicated on the accompanying diagram.

The accompanying table shows two sets of symbols representing the significant sounds of the English language. These sounds, the *phonemes*, are those which produce a difference in meaning.

The Vocal Organs

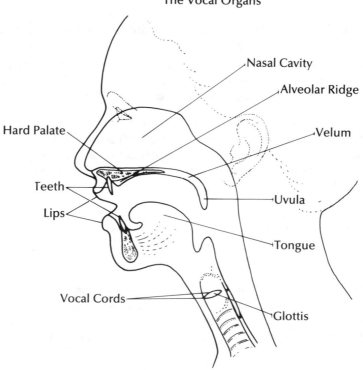

IPA	T and S	English Word	IPA	T and S	English Word
Consonants					
b	b	boy	s	s	soap
d	d	do	ʃ	š	ship
f	f	first	t	t	tie
g	g	go	θ	θ	thin
h	h	hit	ð	ð	then
k	k	cook	v	v	very
l	l	let	w	w	water
m	m	man	y	y	yes
n	n	no	z	z	rose
ŋ	ŋ	sing	ʒ	ž	pleasure
p	p	put	tʃ	č	cheese
r	r	robe	dʒ	j	judge
Vowels					
a	ɑ	hot	ɔ	ɔ	law
æ	æ	map	o	ow	hope
e	ey	made	u	uw	spoon
ɛ	e	let	ʊ	u	foot
i	iy	eat	ə	ʌ	but
ɪ	ɪ	sit	ə	ə	above
Diphthongs					
aɪ	ay	tie			
aʊ	ɑw	how			
ɔɪ	oy	boy			

The first column (headed "IPA") gives symbols of the international phonetic alphabet with slight modifications (e.g., a for ɑ; y for j), since these are widely accepted. The second column (headed "T and S") gives the symbols used by Trager and Smith in their text *An Outline of English Structure* and adopted by many American linguists with various modifications (e.g., ɑw for aw, ɔy for oy).

In addition to the symbols shown here, many texts contain other variations of these two major systems. It is important, therefore, that you study carefully the pronunciation symbols in any text that you use.

Since the IPA has been the basis of many of the variations and since it is widely known throughout the world, I shall use its symbols in future examples throughout this book. The symbols will be within slant lines (/ /) to indicate that they are the *phonemes* of the language. Phonetic symbols, covering a much broader range of sounds, are generally enclosed within brackets ([ ]).

In working with phonetic and phonemic symbols, it is important to remember that *no* symbol can help a student to *make* a sound. What is significant is that we know (1) the *sound* associated with the symbol and (2) the techniques to help our students *hear* and *produce* the sound. It is also important that we and our students attach the *same* sound to a symbol or to a gesture. The symbols serve only as memory clues when the students do their assignments or as a help to them when they look up a word in the dictionary.

One of the important things we should know about the English sound system is how the sounds are made—particularly those which could cause a *difference* in meaning in the language. As noted above, we call such sounds the *phonemes* of the language. The sounds /I/ and /ɛ/ between /p/ and /t/ in *pit* and *pet*, for example, are phonemes because they alone make the *meaning* difference in the two words. We know that /p/ and /b/ are phonemes because in the words *pit* and *bit* only the sounds /p/ and /b/ make the meaning different. Each language has its own phonemes. In some cases, however, the same phoneme may exist in the native language of your learners and in English, but it may exist in a different position within a word. For example, we can put together (cluster) /sk/ at the *beginning* of a word (e.g., school). Spanish speakers never have this cluster at the beginning of a word and therefore will find it difficult to produce.

What other features are phonemic in the sound system of English? Three: *stress, intonation*, and *pause (juncture)*.

Let us examine each of the features of the English phonemic system in turn. We will start with the vowels and consonants.

First, what makes a difference in sounds? Several things:

1. The vibration of the vocal cords. Pronounce /b/ several times putting your hands on your throat. Now pronounce /p/ several times. The vocal cords were vibrating for /b/. They were not vibrating for /p/. We call sounds which are made with the vocal cords *vibrating* or *voiced* sounds. When the vocal cords do not vibrate, we say the sounds are *voiceless* or *unvoiced*. All vowels are voiced.

   The voiced consonant phonemes in IPA symbols are /b/, /d/, /g/, /l/, /m/, /n/, /ŋ/, /r/, /ð/, /v/, /w/, /y/, /z/, /ʒ/, /ʤ/.
   The voiceless consonants are /f/, /h/, /k/, /p/, /s/, /ʃ/, /t/, /θ/, /tʃ/.
   Notice the pairs of voiced and unvoiced consonants (the voiced consonant is first): b/p, d/t, g/k, ð/θ, v/f, z/s, ʒ/ʃ, ʤ /tʃ.

2. Does the breath come out of the mouth or the nose? In the nasal sounds /m/, /n/, and /ŋ/, the breath comes out of the nose.

3. Is the air stopped in our mouths as we make a sound? Could it continue? Where is it stopped? (If it is stopped, for example, we may call the sound a *stop*.) *T* is a stop. (Try it!) *M* is a *continuant*.

4. What happens to the position of the vocal organs as we make a sound? Where do the vocal organs come together? To what other position do they move? What is the position of the tongue, of the lips, of the teeth? In other words, what about the articulation?

The Vowels.   I studied French with the accompanying vowel triangle. It is just as useful in studying English. Notice how your tongue moves from front to back; notice how your lips become more rounded or less rounded as your jaw opens and closes.

The accompanying vowel chart, although in another form, gives you the same information about the tongue position of the phonemes shown and will help you to help your students make the sounds.

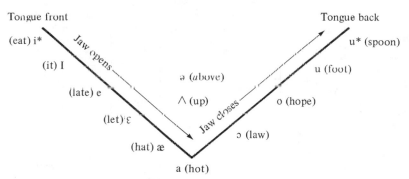

Victor Triangle

*Some linguists do not consider these simple vowels *phonemic*.

The highest part of the tongue is		front	central part	back	
high	in the	i† I		u† U	of the mouth.
mid		e ɛ	ə ∧	o	
low		æ	a	ɔ	

†Simple /i/ and /u/ are not considered phonemic because some English speakers do not use them in their dialects.

As you make each vowel sound, study carefully the position of your lips. Are they rounded or stretched back? Are they tense?

All the simple vowels (above) can occur alone or with /y/, /w/, or /h/* so that the tongue glides (goes) from the vowel position to the /y/, /w/, or /h/ or from the /y/, /w/, or /h/ to the vowel position. Pronounce: *toy* /tɔi/, *ice* /ais/, *how* /haU/, and *hoop* /hup/.

We know, then, that in English (1) there are nine *simple vowels* which can be used alone or in combination with /y/, /w/, or /h/. (2) The vowels are voiced. (3) The differences in sounds are produced by the position of the tongue in the mouth. It may be relatively high, mid, or low, *and*, at the same time, it may be relatively in the front, center, or back of the mouth. (4) The difference is produced also by the shape of the lips (rounded or stretched).

The Consonants.   Let us turn our attention to the consonants. We will examine, as we have pointed out, whether these are voiced or unvoiced; what happens to the air in the mouth; and the positions of the tongue, lips, and teeth.

Study the accompanying chart carefully. I have purposely used simple terminology that you could use in teaching your students.

*/y/, /w/, /h/ are sometimes called *semivowels*. These combinations with /y/, /w/, and /h/ are sometimes called *complex vowel nuclei*.

Passage of Air	Vibration of Vocal Cords	Two Lips	Lower Lip, Upper Teeth	Tip of Tongue, Upper Teeth	Tip of Tongue, Back of Upper Teeth	Front of Tongue, Front of Palate	Back of Tongue, Soft Palate	The Vocal Cords
Completely stopped	No voiceless	p			t		k	
	Yes voiced	b			d		g	
Two sounds: A stop followed by a continuant	No voiceless					tʃ		
	Yes voiced					dʒ		
Through a narrow opening	No voiceless		f	θ	s	ʃ		
	Yes voiced		v	ð	z	ʒ		
Through the side of the tongue	No voiceless							
	Yes voiced				l			
Through the nose	No voiceless							
	Yes voiced	m			n	ŋ		
No stoppage	No voiceless							
	Yes voiced	w			r*	y		h

*Tongue curls toward back.

You see that there are twenty-four consonants in English. (Some linguists consider that there are twenty-one consonants and call /w/, /y/, and /h/ *semivowels*.) Three factors enter into the formation of a consonant: (1) the vibration or lack of vibration of the vocal cords; (2) the point of obstruction of air in the mouth, if at all; and (3) the points of meeting (the articulation) of the lips and the relation of the tongue to the teeth and the palate.

Stress

Stress is the name given to the relative degree of loudness of a part (syllable) of a word, of a whole word, or of a syllable within an utterance.

For our purpose, we may distinguish two kinds of stress. There is *word stress* and *sentence stress*. Each word or word phrase has one primary stress. We say agaín, néver, ápple tree, bús route, good býe, go ín, try ón, come báck. Word stress can be phonemic. Study, for example, "cóntract" and "contráct." Word stress is often called *accent*.

There are four possible phrase* stresses in English:

1. The loudest—called *primary*—usually marked /
2. The next to the loudest—called *secondary*—usually marked ˆ
3. The third loudest or medium soft—called *tertiary*—usually marked \
4. The least loud—called *weak*—usually marked ˘. (Many books, however, do not mark weak stress.)

Let us examine sentence stress. In a sentence like "I'm studying English," the stress is on the *E* of English. Every sentence has at least one stress, but it may have two or more depending on the length of the sentence or the meaning you want to convey. A sentence like "What are you doing?" for example, may have stress on *What* and stress on *do*. A short answer such as "Yes, I did" may have stress on *Yes* and on *did*. Almost any word in a sentence can be stressed depending upon the situation or on the meaning one wishes to convey; for example, "It's *my* business" or "It's my *business*." A question such as, "Do you see that *man*?" has a difference in stress in the answer, "Yes, I *see* him."

Stressed syllables are usually longer and louder, giving English the *rhythm* which we say is characteristic of English.

Rhythm

Rhythm, which depends on the accented syllables in each utterance, is rather regularly spaced in English. In speaking we try to maintain the same *time* between one stressed syllable and the next stressed syllable in the utterance. In order to maintain the rhythm, we say the unstressed (unaccepted) syllables *faster*. We do that by crowding them together and by pronouncing all or most of the unstressed vowels as /ə/ or not pronouncing them at all. Notice how people normally say a sentence like

What are you going to do?   /wat ə yə goiŋ tə du?/

Intonation

Intonation is the name given to the levels of pitch (the relative height of the voice) in a sentence. When we talk about intonation, we include, too, the rising of the voice or the fading of the voice into silence at the end of an utterance as well as the sustained pitch of the voice near the end of certain sentences we will examine later.†

There are four relative levels of pitch. (We use the term *relative* because the height to which the voice rises varies from speaker to speaker.) These are marked in different ways by various linguists. Some use 1 for the lowest pitch, and some use 1 for the highest pitch. Some use lines, and some use arrows. I will use lines and numbers (to reinforce the lines). Most people start to speak at pitch level 2. Pitch level 2 is *normal* level. The voice then usually rises to 3 and then remains at 3 or

---

*No single word has four accents, but word combinations or phrases do, for example, élěvâtŏr òpěrâtŏr.

†Some linguists prefer to call these intonations *terminal contours* since they mark the end or termination of an utterance.

falls to 1. Level 3 is *above normal*; level 1 is *below normal*. Level 3 is usually (but not necessarily) the level of the stressed part of the sentence. Level 4 is *way above normal*. It is usually used to express emotion, anger, surprise, delight, and so on.

This is how I will mark the examples:

$$_2 \underline{\hspace{1cm}} \text{What are you} \begin{array}{c} 3 \\ \boxed{\text{do}} \end{array} \text{ing?} \underline{\hspace{0.5cm}} _1$$

When the word on which there is stress is the last word in the sentence and is a one-syllable word, we use a *diagonal* line to show that the voice glides from one position to another. Notice:

$$_2 \underline{\hspace{1cm}} \text{When did he } \begin{array}{c} 3 \\ \end{array} \text{leave?} \searrow _1$$

There are two important intonation patterns in English. It is desirable to concentrate *only* on these two in teaching English at the beginning and intermediate levels of elementary and secondary schools and at the beginning college level.

1. We use *rising-falling* intonation in
   a. Simple statements:

$$_2 \underline{\hspace{1cm}} \text{He came to} \begin{array}{c} 3 \\ \boxed{\text{see}} \end{array} \boxed{\text{me.}} _1$$

   b. Commands:

$$_2 \underline{\hspace{1cm}} \text{Go to the} \begin{array}{c} 3 \\ \end{array} \text{door.} \searrow _1$$

   c. Question-word questions:

$$_2 \underline{\hspace{1cm}} \text{Why did he} \begin{array}{c} 3 \\ \end{array} \text{leave?} \searrow _1$$

   d. Attached questions* sometimes (when we're *not* asking for information.)

$$_2 \underline{\hspace{1cm}} \text{He didn't} \boxed{\text{go,}} \begin{array}{c} 3 \\ \end{array} \boxed{\text{did}} \text{he?} _1$$

The fall and fade out of the voice is often designated by a # (double cross). For example,

$$_2 \underline{\hspace{1cm}} \text{Why did he} \begin{array}{c} \\ \end{array} \text{leave? } \searrow _1 \text{ \#}$$

*In attached questions, when we're asking for information, we use *rising* intonation:

$$_2 \underline{\hspace{1cm}} \text{He didn't} \begin{array}{c} 3 \\ \boxed{\text{go,}} \end{array} _2 \underline{\hspace{1cm}} \begin{array}{c} 3 \\ \text{did} \end{array} \text{he?}$$

2. We use *rising* intonation at the end of questions which do *not* begin with a question word. For example,

$$\text{Is he}\overline{\text{ there?}}$$

$$\text{Can you}\overline{\text{ get it for me?}}$$

Notice that in sentences with *rising* intonation, everything that follows the *rise* (the stressed syllable) is also pronounced on the high pitch or level.

The rising and fade out of the voice is often designated by a || (double bar). For example,

$$\text{Can you}\overline{\text{ get it for me?}}\ ||$$

We also use *rising* intonation in direct address and in introductions. Notice:

$$\text{Mr.}\overline{\text{Brown,}}\quad\text{this is Ms.}\overline{\text{ Jones.}}$$

$$\text{How are}\overline{\text{ you,}}\quad\text{Ms.}\overline{\text{ Jones?}}$$

In a *series*, we are *rising* intonation until the last item where we use *rising-falling* intonation.

$$\text{I need}\overline{\text{ books,}}\ \text{pen}\overline{\text{cils,}}\ \text{and}\overline{\text{cray}}\text{ons.}$$

Sustained pitch in utterances is designated by a | (single bar). It is used where in writing we would ordinarily place a comma or a dash. Notice:

$$\text{Are you}\overline{\text{there}}\ |\ \overline{\text{John?}}$$

The pitch of *there* and the pitch of *John* are the same, but if you say the sentence aloud, you will note that you have prolonged the sound of *there* more than if the sentence had been "Are you there?"

One last brief word before we leave the important subject of intonation. A contrast, such as

$$\text{Was he}\overline{\text{angry?}}\qquad\text{and}\qquad\text{Was}\overline{\text{he ang}}\text{ry!}$$

will show immediately that intonation is phonemic.

Internal Juncture or Pause

Another important feature of the English sound system which makes a difference in meaning is *internal juncture*. The word *pause* is often used to indicate juncture. This type of pause is unmarked in writing:

> The night rate /nait + ret/ is cheap.
>
> The nitrate /naitret/ is cheap.
>
> Ice cream /ais + krim/.
>
> I scream /ai + skrim/.

We would say that, in the first sentence, there is *plus juncture* between *night* and *rate*. In the second pair of utterances, the plus juncture comes between *ice* and *cream* in Example 1; it comes between *I* and *scream* in Example 2. There is no difference in the pronunciation of the other sounds. The difference in meaning is caused *only* by the slight pause.

One other remark needs to be made about the sound system. As far as speech is concerned, what is considered a sentence? Look at this example—Question: "Where did you go yesterday?" Possible answer: "To the movies." For the purposes of *speech*,

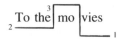

where there is a complete fading out of the voice after ₁, may be considered a sentence.

Some linguists distinguish between *sentences* (a group of words with a subject and predicate) and *nonsentences*. In order to avoid discussion, the term *utterance* is used more and more frequently. An utterance is the name given to any meaningful act of speech which includes the features of the sound system we have been discussing (i.e., pitch, rising or fading of the voice, stress, or pause). For example, in an exchange such as "Who came in?" "John" *John* is an utterance.

We have seen that *sounds, stress, juncture*, and *intonation* are at the very core of spoken language. All are important in understanding and speaking English, and all of them must be taught. Since the teacher must be concerned with helping students learn these features, more will be said about the method of teaching them in Chapter 4.

SOME NOTES ON STRUCTURE

In this section, I will confine myself to pointing out only some of the basic features of the English system. I will do so by presenting some examples of speech and posing some questions. Suggestions for further study will be found in Appendix V.

- We noted earlier that an important aspect of the system is the use of *word order*.

  Compare "Mary is home" and "Is Mary home?"

  Can you say "Spoke to I him" and be understood?

Where is the word *not*—before or after *is*?

He is not (or he isn't) an American.

Wouldn't "I go every morning to the park" sound "foreign" to your ears?

Is a *station bus* the same as a *bus station*?

- English uses *inflection*, that is, it may add or take away something from a word or change the form of the word to show number (singular or plural), tense (present or past),* and so on. Notice:

   The *boy* is here. The *boys* are here.

   The *boy* is in the classroom. The *boy's* book is in the classroom.

   This is *my* book. This is *mine*.

   I gave *him* a book. *He* gave *me* a book.

   I *talk* to John every day. I talk*ed* to John yesterday.

   I *sing* every day. I *sang* yesterday.

   Sally is *pretty*. Joan is prett*ier*.

- English uses *function* (structure) *words* to express relationships or meanings. There are over 150 such words in English, the number depending upon the linguist's preferences, for example, the inclusion of pronouns. Some of those we use most frequently are

   1. *Articles* (or determiners): *a, the, an, this, some*
   Give me *a* book (any). Give me *the* book (already mentioned).

   2. *Auxiliaries: do, have, be*
   I want to go. I *do*n't want to go.

   I saw him. I've *seen* him many times.

   John wrote the letter. The letter *was* written by John.

   3. *Prepositions: at, by, for, from, of, on, in, with, to*
   The book is *on* the desk. The book is *in* the desk.

   4. *Conjunctions* (coordinate and subordinate): *and, but, until, although,* etc.
   I want the book *and* the pencil.

   I want the book, *but* I don't want the pencil.

   5. *Interrogatives: when, where,* etc. (often called *wh* words)
   When did you go? *Where* did you go?

   6. *Degree words: more, most, very, too*
   May I have *more* bread?

   It's *very* hot today. It's *too* hot to go out today.

   7. *Modals:* English uses modals—*may,* and so on—with verbs to indicate different degrees of reality or possibility. Consider:

   I *may* go to the movies.

   I *might* go (a little less probable).

---

*Linguists today prefer to talk about two *tenses* only. They consider expressions like "I've *talked* to John" and "I had *talked* to John" *verb phrases*.

I *can* go.

I *should* go. I *ought to* go.

I *must* go. I *have to* go.

Notice these additional examples of features of English structure.

1. I like *cheese.*   Give me a *cheese sandwich.*
2. Give me the *lamp oil.*   Give me the *oil lamp.*
3. It's a *long foot.*   It's a *foot long.*
4. He walked *along the street.*   He *walked along.*
5. He *took* his coat.   He *took off* his coat.
6. *Look! There's* an airplane.   *There's* an airplane in the sky.
7. *It's* cold out today.   Poor dog. *It's* cold.
8. *Go* to the shop every day.   *I go* to the shop every day.
9. *Sing.*   *Let's sing.*
10. The *man's legs* are long.   The *legs of the table* are high.
11. The boy is *tall.*   The *boys* are *tall.*
12. He's *a tall* boy.   He's *a very tall* boy.
13. *You're* going, *aren't you?*   You're *not* going, *are you?*
14. *One* never knows.   Let me have the *one* in the window.
15. He's *un*able to speak.   His *in*ability to speak is sad.
16. You understand me.   You *mis*understand me.
17. He usually eat*s* at one.   He *can* eat at one.
18. He's walk*ing* there.   He *might walk* there.

Notice these responses:

1. Are you going to be a doctor?   Yes, I *am.*
2. What did you *do* yesterday?   I *studied.*
3. Do you think it's going to rain?   I think *so.*
4. Do you have *any pencils?*   Yes. Here's *one.*
5. Who'*s* at the door?   Mary *and* John.
6. You like rice, *don't you?*   No, I *don't.*
   Yes, I *do.*

Basic sentence patterns in English include the following:

Two parts: Boys / eat.

The little boys at school / like to eat all the time.

Three parts: John / wrote / a letter. (This is a favorite sentence type).

The men in the office / have had to write / long letters to their clients.

Four parts: John / wrote / me / a letter.

The women of the Colonial Association / are going to write / all the people they know / several letters.

Basic types of English sentences include:

1.	*Subject*	*Verb*	*Object*	*(Adverb)*
	He	saw	John	(yesterday).
2.	*Subject*	*Verb* (be)	*Predicate*	*(Adverb)*
	He	is	well	(now).
3.	*Subject*	*Verb* (look)	*Complement*	*(Adverb)*
	Rose	looks	fine	(again).
4.	*Subject*	*Intr. verb*	—	*(Adverb)*
	Birds	fly	—	(gracefully).
5.	*Subject*	*Verb*	*Ind. object Dir. object*	*(Adverb)*
	She	gave	John a book	(last week).

Transformations include:

1. Sentences with an unstressed *there*

There's a man at the door.

There are four books on the table.

2. Inverted questions

Will he study later?

3. Question-word questions

What do you want?

Whose son is that?

4. Commands and requests

Speak to him.

Let's speak to him.

5. Emphatic expressions.

He saw it *himself*.

This brief listing was obviously not intended to cover all the features of English. It will serve, however, to point up, particularly to native English speakers who have never had to think about form, order, inflection, or function, some of the more important characteristics of English which signal meaning.

ITS VOCABULARY (LEXICON, SPECIFIC NOTIONS)

Following are several comments with respect to the *lexicon* or the *vocabulary* of the language.

Words become meaningful only when studied and considered in *context*, that is, with all the other words which surround them and which help give them their meaning. Note, for example:

> Show me your hand.
>
> Hand in your papers.
>
> Language is handed down from mother to child.

Linguistic science has pointed up the fact that our old definitions such as "A noun is the name of a person, place, or thing" are not accurate. Is *hand* a *noun* in the sentences above?

It is not even a question of the *idioms* of the language. The word *get*, for example, has over 200 meanings. Notice:

> Here's fifty cents. Get the paper.
>
> Get the paper. It's on the table.
>
> He got a good mark on the test.

One of your students' learning problems will be caused by the fact that the semantic areas in their native languages do not necessarily overlap with those of English. For example, we use *thin* when talking either about a human being or about a piece of paper, while other languages have two different words to express the concept. To illustrate further, "a cake of soap" in English may be (literally) a "bread of soap" in French or a "piece of soap" in Italian.

A vocabulary item may use a different prefix to mean *not*, for example, even when the root is the same, for example, *unable* but *inability*. Words may add formal suffixes, for example, *man, manly, manlike, mannish*, or they may change their base form completely, depending on the "register." Note, for example, *man, fellow, chap, guy, bloke*.

In *Teaching and Learning English as a Foreign Language*, Charles C. Fries divided the content* words of our language into *things*, *actions*, and *qualities*. He further subdivided words into *simple, compound*, and *derived*. Let us examine several examples:

Content Words

> *Things*:
>
>   Simple — *door*
>
>   Compound — *doorknob*
>
>   Derived — *arrival, goodness, ability* (These come from nouns, verbs, adjectives, or adverbs)

*In addition to content words, there are the function (structure) words studied above.

Actions:

      Simple — *run, walk*

      Compound — *call up, take off, put on*

      Derived — *enjoy, soften, harden*

Qualities:

      Simple — *true, false*

      Derived — *misty, childish, broken.*

Specific Notions

As you will recall, in the functional-notional (communicative) approach, the vocabulary (lexical) items are subsumed under larger categories—the general notions, which include space, matter, quantity, time, case, and deixis. *Deixis* refers to the grammatical (functional) relationships between parts of sentences. For example, in "John arrived yesterday. I'd like to see him as soon as possible," *him* refers to *John*.

Specific notions are the nouns, verbs, pronouns, adjectives, adverbs, prepositions, numbers, days of the week—all the vocabulary needed to complete the communicative function. (See Figure 2.)

For Review and Discussion

1. What are some premises about the staying power of methodology?
2. Have we completely discarded the audio-lingual method?
3. What are some characteristics of the Gouin method and the direct method?
4. Why was the basic English method not popular?
5. What did the Coleman report advocate about reading?
6. What are some tenets of Chomsky's theories?
7. Can you make a list of ambiguous utterances such as "Flying planes can be dangerous" and tell us how you would clarify them?
8. Who played prominent roles in the development of sociolinguistics? What were their beliefs?
9. Have you used any of the new methods or techniques such as the silent way, community language learning, or total physical response? How did you use them?
10. What are the major elements of the functional-notional approach?
11. In groups, prepare several situations where you have to refuse, accept, or negotiate an invitation.
12. Prepare outlines of five sample units containing functions, situations, notions, and activities.
13. Give an example of levels of a grammatical structure using the spiral approach.
14. Give examples of exponents for each communication category.
15. What are phonemes in a language?

16. Give minimal pairs, for example, *bear/bare, hair/hare*.
17. What makes a difference in producing consonant sounds? With partners, prepare lists of words for each vowel sound using the vowel triangle.
18. Prepare lists of common words with the three diphthongs.
19. With partners, prepare lists of commonly used words which are stressed in different syllables but which are spelled the same.
20. Use the words in short utterances which will signal the difference in meaning.
21. How many pitch levels are there in English? Which does each signify?
22. When do we use rising-falling intonation? Give examples.
23. Make a list of tag (attached) questions (a) when you are asking for information; (b) when you are not asking for information. Supply answers to the questions which will clarify the communication, that is, the message.
24. What is the usual intonation in a series?
25. Give examples of one-word (or phrase) utterances in reply to a question.
26. Give ten words using prefixes and suffixes.
27. List several specific notions under each general notion.
28. School and community
    a. What resources do you have in your school?
    b. How do you utilize them?
    c. How can the community help you? What facilities are there? Are there parent and/or community volunteers?
    d. Are there printing facilities you or your students can use to print a newspaper (bilingual if possible)?
    e. How many persons in your community use English? Can they be called upon to speak to the students?
29. You, the teacher
    a. What are your multiple roles?
    b. Do you belong to a teacher's association?
    c. Are you aware of your learners' problems? What are some of them?
    d. Do you read teachers' journals? Do you ever use innovative ideas which you find in journals?
30. The learning environment
    a. Is your classroom cheerful? Is it full of books, magazines, charts, bulletin boards?
    b. How do you distribute materials?
    c. How do you handle homework correction?
    d. Do you give a daily, preannounced test?
31. Innovations
    a. Think of the mnemonic MOTIVATION and give two ideas for each letter.
    b. Is integrative motivation possible in your community?

2

The Curriculum

If you are asked to teach English in a school where no curriculum exists, if there is a need to revise the curriculum which does exist, or if you cannot obtain graded textbooks, the material in this chapter should be of particular interest to you. Even where a curriculum and textbooks exist, however, you may wish to round out the content of your English program by considering the items and suggestions in this and the following chapters.

Some Basic Premises in Curriculum Development

- A curriculum guide for an English program usually includes the following for each learning level:

  1. An analysis of its aims and goals (the behavior and skills the students will be expected to acquire)
  2. A list of the language items to be taught (phonology, structure, vocabulary, and communicative expressions)
  3. A list of the cultural concepts to be discussed
  4. An analysis of the language abilities and enabling subskills to be developed (listening with understanding, speaking, reading, and writing)
  5. A description of the activities and realistic situations through which the language items will be introduced and practiced
  6. Suggestions for evaluation (testing) of the learners' language growth in linguistic competence and performance
  7. Sources for teacher reference and pupils' texts

- The content of the curriculum at any level will depend on several factors: the *age* of the pupils, the *number of years* the English course will last, the *aims and scope* of each program. For example, will there be emphasis on listening and speaking only, emphasis on reading (for those in need of reading scientific journals), and so on?

- With these considerations in mind, curriculum writers select and grade the material for each level, determine the number of items to be learned, and weigh the relative emphases of the skills at each level. (How much listening and speaking will be done at Level I? How much reading? How much writing? Will the same proportions in skill development be maintained after the first level?)

- Since language learning is *cumulative,* provision is made to relate all new language knowledge and skills to those which the students acquired at previous levels or in previous units.

- No skill which has been developed (listening or speaking, for example) is (nor should it be) entirely neglected *even when* another skill is being emphasized in teaching.

- Although each facet of a skill or feature of English may be practiced separately, these are brought together in real situations constantly so that pupils become aware of their interdependence or relationship in actual use.

- The curriculum of the English program is so designed that it enables the pupils upon completion to continue to study and read by themselves, to develop their skills, and to specialize in any aspect of English of their choice.

- Unless there is some urgent reason to change the order, priority in the curriculum is given to (1) all the sounds and entire phonemic system; (2) the basic word-order arrangements; (3) the function words; (4) the communicative expressions; (5) the inflections and derivations which are the most frequent; (6) the vocabulary which (7) will help the students practice the structures; (8) is useful in the pupils' immediate lives; and (9) will strengthen their conviction that English can be used to express the same ideas they express in their native tongue.

   These language features are not *presented* separately. Sounds and intonation patterns are learned as they are found in a dialogue or in a reading passage; communicative expressions, structures, function words, and arrangements of words are learned and practiced as they are found in meaningful material which duplicates the communication situations of real life. It cannot be underscored frequently enough that each item of language in a text, depends upon and is related to every other item.

- The oral language activities which are written into the curriculum afford the students practice in understanding and in answering questions; in making statements in the affirmative and in the negative with long or with short answers; in responding by carrying out directions; in communicating and interacting; in making comments (of agreement, of disagreement, of surprise, etc.); or in asking questions. The oral practice activities should enable them gradually but with perceptible progress to carry on a conversation about things they would ordinarily talk about in their own language with people of their own age group.

- The content of the curriculum starts with the students themselves and with their environment. It is only by relating it to their own experience that a new item becomes meaningful to them. If, for example, the reading material in your text refers to transportation in a large city in the United States or in Great Britain, it is desirable to discuss transportation as your students see it and live it before proceeding to the unfamiliar concept.
- The primary aim of language teaching is to develop communication competence, that is, to help students recognize and produce fluent language which is not only correct but also appropriate in the social situation in which it is being used.
- Whatever the aspirations or needs of the learners, they should first be enabled to acquire a *basic common core* of English. Later, or concurrently—in situations where immediate communication is a necessity—they should be made aware of the varieties (formal, informal, etc.) and registers which would be most appropriate in a given situation.
- One further comment is made here and noted throughout this book. The selection and presentation of linguistic material should permit the learners to make functional, that is, *communicative* use of the language at *all* points of the English program from the very first day. The communicative and the linguistic aspects should be presented and practiced simultaneously.

AIMS AND LEVELS

Two words I have used—aims and levels—need further explanation. What should be the *aims* of the program? What do we mean by *levels*?

In a regular English program, whether it starts in the elementary or secondary school or the university, we usually talk about five principal aims. We aim to give students:

- The *progressive* ability to understand the English used at their age by a native English speaker. (By native speaker, we mean a person who either was born in and learned English in an English-speaking country or a person who has learned English well enough to sound like a native English speaker.)
- The *progressive* ability to carry on a conversation with a native English speaker on topics of interest to persons of their age group.
- The *progressive* ability to read material in English with comprehension, ease, and enjoyment.
- The *progressive* ability to write correctly and perhaps creatively in English.
- The information, knowledge, attitude, and insight to appreciate the cultural similarities and differences (if such exist) between English-speaking peoples.

A brief comment should be made here. The culture need not and should not be taught systematically. When a word or a concept arises which needs special explanation, and you know the explanation, give it by all means. But, particularly at the beginning level, we should try to remember that language *is* culture and that culture is learned automatically as language competence is developed.

Since an English learning program may start in elementary school, secondary school, or the university, it is desirable to talk about levels of English learning. The first level is the *beginning* level of English language learning; the second is the *intermediate* level; and the third may be considered the *advanced* level. In a regular secondary school (high school) program, the first level is the first year of high school. If the language is begun in junior high school,* the first level may be the first two years of junior high school. In that case, a student who has begun English in junior high school may enter the second level or intermediate level in high school. When language is started in elementary school, the first level may be spread over three or four years. At the university, the first level may be of only one semester's duration. All the factors we have already discussed (age, length and type of course, etc.) must be considered in talking about levels.

CURRICULUM PLANNING

Some factors in curriculum planning are important: (1) The material from one level should lead naturally and sequentially to the next level. (2) The material should be graded. For example, we would start with one modifier of a noun before giving three modifiers together; we would teach the regular *s* plural (/z/, /s/, /IZ/) before we teach the exceptions. (3) There should be provision for constant reintroduction of all the material we have taught with the new material we are teaching. (4) We should not try to teach *all* the vocabulary around a topic or all the forms, meanings, or uses of an item of structure. Instead, we should use a spiral approach.

Let us study an example of the spiral approach within a cultural topic: The first time (at the first level) we speak of *family*, we may present the names of immediate family members—*father, mother, brother, sister*. At the second level, we may add to the family members list the words *grandmother, grandfather, uncle, aunt, cousins*. At the third level, perhaps, we may want to teach *mother-in-law, son-in-law, great-aunt, relatives*, and so on.

Where English must be learned quickly because it is the language of school instruction or the language of the surrounding community, attention (and priority) will have to be given to the structure and vocabulary items needed not only for participating in the other areas of the curriculum but also for making an effective personal and social adjustment to the life of the community.

NOTES ON CURRICULUM DESIGN

A well-designed curriculum for EFL or ESL situations—one that would facilitate learning and teaching—should have the following characteristics:

1. It uses the students and their background as the point of departure for the teaching of any aspect of the communication skills and of the culture of English-speaking peoples.

*A school which pupils enter after about six years of instruction.

2. It reflects realistic objectives. It asks what knowledge and skills the students for whom the curriculum is intended need in their immediate future and how much one can reasonably hope to accomplish in the time available and in the community in which the school is located. Is it, for example, an English-speaking community? Is it a foreign language enclave within an English-speaking community? Is it in a country or city where English is seldom seen or heard?

3. It assigns priority to the communicative structures and cultural insights students need in order to (a) speak about matters relevant to them; (b) use the language as a medium of instruction, where necessary; or (c) enter academic or vocational programs they aspire to.

4. It presents the students with the knowledge they need about the meaning and appropriateness of linguistic items in particular contexts and situations, and about the presuppositions and sociocultural assumptions which underlie their use.

5. It generally recommends starting with listening and speaking skills but moves ahead as quickly as possible to reading and writing. The age level of the students, as well as their ability to understand and say—with reasonable facility—the material they will be asked to read, helps determine when reading and writing in English can be introduced. With older university students from abroad, who feel they need only translation or reading comprehension skills to enter the upper levels of specialized programs, even the brief period of listening-speaking is often omitted—generally, however, to the later regret of persons involved in crash programs of this type.

6. It does not neglect the listening and speaking skills even after reading and writing are introduced. On the contrary, reading and writing experiences are used as a basis for stimulating the kinds of activities which enable students to agree, disagree, discuss, and debate, or to express surprise, disappointment, anger, sympathy, and compassion. Learners are made to realize from the first day that the new language will permit them to say anything they would say in their native tongue. As we know, a primary objective in today's programs is to develop communicative competence in learners, that is, to help them understand and produce language which is not only correct but also appropriate for the varied functions which language serves in real-life situations.

7. It suggests experiences and procedures which require the learners and *not* the teacher to do most of the talking in English.

8. It makes provision for relating all new linguistic and cultural items to those which students have learned in previous units of work or at lower learning levels. It usually recommends that lessons start with a wide-ranging, creative "warm-up" period in which material acquired previously is reinserted frequently into a variety of communication activities, thus facilitating its retrieval from the students' memory stores. Moreover, materials such as dialogues, reading passages, and grammatical structures are recombined often so that students develop awareness of the facts that language learning is cumulative, that the same material may be used in situations other than the one in which it was first presented, and that language makes infinite use of finite means.

9. It integrates language material which may have been taught in isolation—

features of pronunciation, vocabulary, structure—in authentic communication situations. Students are asked to dramatize dialogues, to formulate and answer questions about them, and especially to suggest alternative utterances in them; to listen to broadcasts; to play communication games; to write letters; to take notes; to engage in directed and free question-and-answer activities, in guided or spontaneous role playing, and in broader simulation activities; in sum, to participate in activities appropriate to their age and to their learning levels, which will reaffirm their conviction that English is another vehicle for normal communication.

10. It provides for continuity of instruction—both horizontal and vertical. Integration of the abilities of listening, speaking, reading, writing—one of the facets of horizontal articulation—is vitally important in curriculum design. Continuity of instruction in vertical articulation is also essential. A curriculum for each learning level is generally explicitly spelled out so that teachers are made aware not only of the probable linguistic and cultural content, activities, and experiences of students who come to them from less advanced levels, but also of the expectations of instructors who will teach these students at the next higher level.

11. It recommends integrative language and cultural experiences in which all students learn a basic body of material. A good curriculum, however, also provides for the inclusion of differentiating experiences which recognize the uniqueness of each individual and, where essential, his or her vocational and professional needs. Today, there is a greater realization, for example, that not all students can be expected to create plays or write essays on abstract topics; not all students need produce a variety of intonation patterns unless they are going to be broadcasters or teachers. Enrichment activities are generally suggested, however, which can be offered to individuals who have the potential and will later be engaged in teaching, broadcasting, or playwriting. The help of other teachers in the school or of competent community members should be sought when necessary.

12. It encourages learners to speak about their native culture in English. Please permit a personal comment here. If the English language is indeed another instrument of communication, what better way to demonstrate that we believe in the truth of that statement than by having students talk about their foods, their holidays, their folktales, or any other cultural aspects of interest to them? The unrealistic notion of complete immersion in English culture has been reevaluated in recent years in schools in which there exists a genuine concern for integrating the affective and cognitive domains in language programs.*

I will now make some suggestions with respect to the content at each level. Remember that this same content may be spread over a longer period or condensed into a shorter period. If your school system uses a syllabus or books and if the year-end examinations are based on the books, *use the content of the texts*, adapting or enriching it judiciously in harmony with your students' interests.

After listing some structural items, some cultural topics (which will suggest

---

*At beginning levels in EFL or ESL situations, students should be encouraged to talk about their cultural heritage, values, and customs in their native tongue.

the vocabulary content), and some features of the sound system, I will indicate generally desirable proportions for emphasis within the skills of listening, speaking, reading, and writing. For the sake of convenience, I have separated word order, inflections, and so on. It is immediately obvious, however, that inflected nouns or verbs are placed in a certain order in an utterance and that there is overlapping.

Some Suggestions for Content

LEVEL I

The Sound System

Present *all* the vowel and consonant sounds in English, the two basic intonation patterns (with emphasis on statements, inverted questions, and short answers), and the characteristic stress and rhythm of English (reduced and contrasted forms) in the grammatical patterns you teach.

Communicative Functions

Greetings, leave takings

Making introductions, identifying oneself and others

Apologizing

Asking for or giving instructions

Asking for or giving information

Asking permission to do something

Asking for or giving directions

Asking someone to do something

Expressing likes and dislikes

Expressing agreement, disagreement, or indifference

Indicating lack of comprehension

Purchasing things in shops or markets.

Structure

1. The simple and continuous present of *be, have,* and regular verbs (*eat, sing,* etc.) in statements.
2. Questions with *be.*
3. The place of *not.* (Teach both forms: He's *not* a student. He *isn't* a student.)
4. The place of the auxiliary *do* in questions and negative statements with *have* and regular verbs. (Teach *Have you?* etc., i.e., the interrogative of *have* without *do.*)
5. The place of the noun complement. (I'm a student. This is my book.)
6. The place of the adjective after *be.* (He's tall. It's green.)
7. The place of the descriptive adjective before a noun, singular and plural. (I have a red pencil. She's a good student. They're good students.)

8. Question-word (Wh) questions with *who, where, when, how, what,* and so on.
9. Adverbs of frequency, place, time.

Function Words (Structural Words)

>Prepositions: *in, on, at, for, from, of, with, by, near*
>Determiners: *a, an, the, this, that, these, those*
>Conjunctions (coordinating): *and, but.*

Inflections

>Plurals of nouns: *boys, girls,* (some irregulars—children, men)
>Regular comparisons and superlatives
>Count and mass nouns
>Possessive with singular nouns.

Pronouns

>Personal: *I, you, he, they,* etc. (The major emphasis should be on the *I-you* alternates.)*
>Impersonal: *it.*
>Possessives: *my, your, his,* and so on.

Verbs and Verb Phrases

>Simple present: I eat every day.
>Present with *now*: I'm eating now.
>The *going to* future: I'm going to eat soon.
>Commands (simple and polite): Go to the door. Please go to the door.
>Requests: Let's and Let's not. (Speaker is included.)

Responses

>Short answers (affirmative and negative with verbs taught): Yes, I am; No, I'm not; No, it's not; Yes, I do; and so on.

There

>There's a book on the table. There are two books on the table.

Miscellaneous Items (Only a sampling)

>Numbers one to twenty.
>Days of the week.
>Months of the year.
>Courtesy formulas, for example,
>>How are you? I'm fine.
>>Thank you. You're welcome.

*Some linguists consider pronouns function words.

Greetings and leave takings.

Classroom formulas, for example,

> Show us ———.
>
> May I have (leave) ———.

Time— hours and half-hours.

Vocabulary (Cultural) Content

Introductions and Self-identification

Names of students in the room. (You may wish to assign an English name to each student.)

The Immediate Classroom

Instructional materials

Parts of the room

Activities such as listening, reading, writing

Subjects such as English, mathematics, social studies.

The School

Location of rooms.

People in the building [names, titles (*Mr., Mrs., Ms.*)].

Procedures and schedules (We come to school at eight o'clock. We come to school on Mondays.)

The Family

Names of immediate family members.

Relationships.

Ages (He's . . . years old.)

Occupations (My father is a carpenter.)

The house (its rooms).

Activities (e.g., I get up at seven; I eat breakfast.)

Curriculum and Other Areas

The Skills

Suggested proportions of time. (We will discuss the place of reading and writing in the next chapter.)

Listening, 40%

Speaking, 40%

Reading, 15% ⎫ Reduce or *omit* entirely in the elementary school course un-
Writing, 5% ⎭ der the second grade or year.

LEVEL II

The Sound System

Review all the sounds and the two basic intonation patterns. Teach the change in stress when noun complements are replaced by pronouns:

$$_2\underline{\text{He bought the}}\overset{3}{|\text{gro}|}\underline{\text{ceries.}}_{|} \qquad _2\underline{\text{He}}\overset{3}{|\text{bought}|}\underline{\text{them.}}_{|}$$

Teach the intonation of attached (tag) questions with the stress on the second part of two-word verbs in sentences such as

$$_2\underline{\text{Take it}}\overset{3}{\backslash}\text{ff.}_{|} \qquad _2\underline{\text{Turn them}}\overset{3}{\backslash}\text{n.}_{|}$$

Teach word stress (accent) and word pause if the materials of instruction you are using contain examples. Work on increased fluency in increasingly longer sentences and on stress and rhythm.

Communicative Functions

Review the functions taught at Level I and teach the following:

> Asking for things
> Offering things
> Congratulating someone
> Making requests and suggestions
> Getting things done
> Making phone calls
> Writing letters
> Issuing invitations
> Accepting or declining invitations.

Structure

Review the structures taught at Level I. In the review, strive for more accuracy, more habitual control, more immediate and fluent response.

Word Order

> Expressions of time, such as *in the morning; at noon.*
> Expressions of place, such as *at the office.*
> Expressions of place and time, such as *to school in the afternoon.*
> Frequency words, such as *usually, always.*
> *Some, any, a lot of,* and so on before countable and noncountable nouns.
> Comparisons with *more* and *most.*
> Verb followed by two complements (objects): He gave *her a book*; He gave *it to them.*
> Noun-noun combinations: Give me a *ham sandwich*; Show me a *pocket comb.*

Inflections

Pronouns:

Direct and indirect object (*me, him*, etc.): Give *me* the book. I saw *you* take it.

Possessive: *mine, yours*, and so on.

Whose.

Nouns:

Possessive: the *man's* hat.

Countable and noncountable nouns: Give me the *books*. Give me the *ink*. I need *water*.

Comparisons with *er* and *est* (irregular forms).

Adverbs: *slowly, quietly.*

Verbs and Verb Phrases

Past tense: affirmative, negative, and interrogative of *be, have*, and other verbs.

Two-word verbs: *take off; put on.*

Commands in the negative: *Don't go.* (This may have been taught at Level I.)

The verb *do* as a substitute word (What did you do yesterday?)

Function Words

Modals: *can, may, must, should*

Will future: negative and interrogative.

Responses and Attached Questions

Short answers (affirmative and negative): *Yes, I did; No, I didn't.*

"Tag" (attached) questions with all the verbs already studied: He's tall, *isn't he*? She isn't pretty, *is she*? I can go, *can't I*, and so on.

Miscellaneous Items

The clock: quarter-hour, time *past* (after) and *to* the hour.

Intensifiers: *too, very.*

Too and *either* in: I like it *too*; I don't like it *either*.

Exclamations: *What* a pretty dress! *How* pretty!

The months of the year; the seasons (Many of the months will have been learned "passively" as you placed the date on the chalkboard each day and had the students repeat it.)

Vocabulary (Cultural) Content

Remember that as you review known classroom objects, places, and people in the school, you should *add* new vocabulary items within those same topics.

The Home

Meals (items, hours)

Health and health practices (dressing, illness, bathing, etc.)

Clothing (include reference to seasonal changes); fabrics (wool, silk, cotton, etc.), sizes, colors; making, buying.

The Family

Names of more distant relatives (aunt, uncle, cousin, etc.)

Activities and likes or dislikes of family members.

The Surrounding Community*

Transportation facilities

Communication facilities

Stores (kinds)

Shopping (money, courtesy expressions, expressions of quantity, etc.)

Government agencies (police station, post office)

Places of recreational interest (park, movie, library, theater)

Addresses, names, numbers to 1000, and the use of numbers in an address (1822 = eighteen twenty-two).

Holidays

As they occur (if possible). You should also teach the vocabulary of holidays which are *not* typically American or British but which are within *your* students' experience.

Gifts; visiting; greeting cards.

The World of Work

Occupations and some responsibilities within each.

The Skills
Suggested proportion of time:

Listening-speaking, 40%

Reading, 40%

Writing, 20%.

LEVEL III

The Sound System
Review the phonemes; give extensive practice in contrasting words and phrases; teach the intonation patterns in emphatic speech, particularly those found in your

*In an English-speaking community the vocabulary items in this topic would have been taught at Level I.

texts; give drills in sentences of increasing length; emphasize rhythm; teach reduced forms (the use of ə) in spoken language.

Communicative Functions

Review the functions taught at Levels I and II and teach the following:

Solving a problem

Getting information and reporting on it

Going for a job interview

Getting along with others (at home, at work, etc.)

Expressing emotions (concern, frustration, disappointment, surprise, joy, etc.)

Evaluating the results of an action or an event

Discussing music, art, literature, and scientific discoveries

Making value judgments.

Structure

Review the structures taught at Levels I and II, striving always for greater ease and fluency and for a more sustained response, that is, for more than one statement or question as a response to your question or statement. For example,

Statement 1: That's a pretty dress.

Response 1: Thank you.

Statement 2: That's a pretty dress.

Response 2: Thank you. It's new. I bought it last week.

Word Order

Multiple modifiers before a noun: I bought *several very pretty white* dresses.

Prepositional phrases: The girl *with the green eyes*, the book *with the long title*, the legs *of the table*.

Included sentences or clauses: I'm sure *he's in the house*. The girl *who is near the table* is my friend Alice. I was eating *when he came in*. I'll study *while you eat*. And so on.

Questions with *how long*, referring to both time *and* measurement; *how much*; and so on.

Indirect questions and statements: Does he know where he wants to go? I know what he wants. The man asked me where I lived.

Verbs and Verb Phrases

Aspects and time in verb phrases: I've known him for a year. I've known him since Monday. I've been waiting for an hour. He shouldn't have taken the car.

Sequence of tenses after *if*:

If it rains, I'll go. If it rains, I can't go.

If it rained, I wouldn't go.

If it had rained, I wouldn't have gone.

The *ing* form after verbs like *enjoy, prefer*, for example, She enjoys *swimming*; he prefers *fishing*; and expressions such as Thank you for *helping* me.

The *ing* form after adjectives, for example, I'm interested in *learning*.

The "marked" infinitive: I'd like *to eat*. I want *to see* him. I want *you to see* him. I'm happy *to be* here. Tell her *to study*.

Short answers with the marked infinitive: Yes, I'd like to. Yes, I want to.

Special verbs taking two objects: *tell, read, write, ask*.

The passive with *be*: Teach only the forms commonly used in "real" speech. English speakers do *not* say, for example, "It was sewn by the tailor."

Modals: *might, could, have to, ought to*.

Adverbial Expressions

He went *by bus*. He did it *through hard work*.

Too, very, more, before adverbs: He drives too quickly. Speak more slowly.

Miscellaneous Items

Substitute expressions such as I think so, I'm sure of it, and I know so, as responses to questions like: Do you think it's going to rain this afternoon? (Yes, I think so.), etc.

*Some*one, *every*one, *no*body, *one*, and so on.

Linking words: however, moreover, and so on.

Vocabulary (Cultural) Content*

Educational opportunities (for more advanced study)

Government, religion, social agencies

Travel to the wider community (by ship, by plane)

Family—more distant relationships

Holidays (customs)

Vacations (mountains, beach, at home)

Music, literature, the arts

Leisure-time activities—hobbies, community centers

The world of work (including labor laws)

Cross-cultural concepts.

The Skills

Suggested proportion of time:

Listening-speaking, 40%

Reading, 40%

Writing, 20%.

*Other topics can be added, depending upon your students' needs and interests.

The methods and devices you may wish to use to present the contents of the curriculum, the activities which will help in the development of each of the skills, and some suggestions for integrating the skills into real communication will be the subject of the next chapter.

Additional Comments on Curriculum Design

You should examine as many textbooks as possible in the field of teaching English as a second language. The sequence, organization, and content of the materials in the textbooks and a realistic appraisal of your students and community will help you in planning the curriculum for your course.

You will find that there are available many excellent textbooks in the field. It is not usually necessary to write completely new material. You can adapt existing materials to your classroom needs and add readings, dialogues, and other activities to supplement traditional or "dry" basic content. The ideal textbook for every situation will never be published, but the conscientious teacher can usually breathe life into *any* textbook. In examining a book, it is good to remember, however, that the author may not necessarily intend the book to be used at a specific level or for a specific period of time.

USING EXISTING TEXTBOOKS

The author's introductory remarks should always be studied carefully. An author does not usually expect a teacher to follow the items within each unit or lesson exactly as they are written. For example, a textbook may start with a conversation or reading passage containing new vocabulary, then give five grammar points, then give ten exercises, and then list the vocabulary. It is not intended that in presenting the units the teacher will do *all* the conversation or reading first, then *all* the grammar, then *all* the exercises. For example, the new vocabulary should be clarified and practiced when it is needed, that is, *before* the conversations are learned or before the exercises are done.

Beginning teachers will find it desirable to study the entire text if possible, but certainly each unit of work (or lesson)* to be learned. *All* the new material in the lesson should be listed and then divided into three or four categories: (1) pronunciation problems; (2) functions and structures; (3) vocabulary and culture; (4) practice activities (including reading, writing, and homework).

You should then study the items in the *new* material in order to decide (1) the number of teaching lessons necessary to treat all of the material, (2) the review needed to relate the new material to familiar, known material, (3) the gradation of the material in a logical sequence. You should ask yourself: Which communicative functions and structures will be taught first? Which practice activities will be used with which new functions and structures? When will the new vocabulary items be taught? How will the material be approached—through a conversation, through a story, through a related structure? What homework can be assigned? What materials will be needed for presentation and practice?

*By *lesson* here I mean the unit of work which must be divided into several teaching lessons.

DIVIDING A UNIT OF WORK

Let us study a possible example. We will assume that your unit* is on the past tense (negative, interrogative, etc.) and contains a dialogue and a reading passage with about thirty new vocabulary words.

Lesson I†

1. Motivate the need for the new material.
2. Review the simple present, the days of the week, the clock, words like *today* and *yesterday*. (Have a clock and a calendar available.)
3. Teach (in mini situations) and give practice in the *function, meaning*, and *one* sound form of the past (with nouns and with *I, you*, etc.). You might start with the known verbs whose *past* ends in the sound /t/ (washed, walked).

Lesson II

1. Before starting to present the new material, review the material in the previous lesson.
2. Teach and practice the /d/ past of verbs (I opened, closed, etc.).
3. Teach the interrogative of /t/ and /d/ pasts: Did you . . .? after reviewing the Do you . . .? form.

Lesson III

1. Teach the /təd/ form (wanted, needed). Use questions with *why*, for example, Why did you go to the (post office)?
2. Teach about five new vocabulary items needed to practice the structures.
3. Teach the negative after reviewing *I don't*, etc.

Lesson IV

1. Teach about five irregular verbs (*saw, went*, etc.) in the affirmative, negative, and interrogative. Use these in dialogues and other situational contexts. Teach the communicative expressions necessary, for example, What did you do last night? I went to the movies.

Lesson V

1. Teach the past of *be* and *have*—including the affirmative, negative, and interrogative.
2. Create brief dialogues in which the new items are inserted. Ask learners to create brief dialogues and to use them in role plays.

Lesson VI

1. Teach some other irregular verbs (if they appear in the exercises, in the reading, or in the conversation of the textbook).

*This example is based on an actual text in wide use in many school systems.

†It is expected that university students will need about three or four hours to cover the material and that younger or less able students will need more than eight hours to cover the same material.

2. Teach the short answers: Yes, I did; No, I didn't; No, I wasn't.

3. Begin the reading passage. (A technique for teaching reading will be found in Chapter 3.)

4. Have other pairs or triads perform role plays.

Lesson VII

1. Complete the reading lesson.

2. Dramatize the dialogues again and get feedback from other students.

Lesson VIII

1. Engage in oral activities which add the past tense verbs to other structures you may have taught, for example, I found the man's hat.

2. Give a short test, a dictation, cloze test, or an aural comprehension exercise. (The procedure will be explained.)

THE LANGUAGE LEARNING CLASSROOM.*

Universal Needs ⟶	A Lesson	⟵ The Needs and Goals of Education in Society
The individual's affective and cognitive desires for	Preliminary activities	Civic responsibility
	Greetings and interaction with and among individual students ⎱ 3–5 minutes	Social relationships
Survival and security		Economic efficiency and sufficiency
Identity	Immersion in known material	
Belonging	Warm-up activities	Self-realization
Self-esteem	Homework correction ⎱ 10 minutes	Global understanding
Self-realization	Thirty-second quiz	
	Intensive pronunciation practice	
	Presentation and practice of new material	
	Motivation	
	Statement of aim ⎱ 8 minutes	
	Review of related material (spiral technique)	
	Awareness of situational elements	
	Perception of language in dialogue, reading, structural examples, etc ⎱ 5–10 minutes	
	Student discovery of generalization (underlying structure and function), global comprehension of reading	
	Practice: controlled, guided, free (class, groups, pairs, individuals) ⎱ 15 minutes	
	Feedback and evaluation ⎱ 3–5 minutes	
	Looking ahead	

Constraints:

Level of educational development   Political climate
Paucity of financial and other resources   Resistance to change
Philosophy of education   Teacher's knowledge and skills
Ministerial policies (e.g., preservice training and in-   Community interest and support
service training, criteria for teacher selection and
advancement)

*Reprinted from Finocchiaro, M., "Teacher Education: Problems, Practices, Expectations," Georgetown University Round Table Conference, 1983, pp. 171–186.

A POSSIBLE LESSON PLAN

Let me summarize this section on curriculum design by diagramming the three pillars which hold up and should serve as the underpinnings of a language class. (See the accompanying table.) The central pillar—the lesson—reflects activities in the classroom and the interaction between the teacher and the learners and among the learners working in pairs or groups. Activities in any class hour are based on the teacher's awareness of the contribution he or she can make to the cognitive and affective needs of the individuals and to the needs of society. The individual's needs, goals, and hopes, as well as those of society, are nurtured and enriched by the varied experiences suggested and often initiated by an aware, knowledgeable, skilled teacher.

The stages noted in Column 2 should not limit the creativity and uniqueness of the individual teacher. (Nor should we fear the constraints which can impinge upon the language classroom. The secure teacher can overcome most problems with ingenuity, common sense, and skill.) Note that the time indicated on the chart is flexible.

For Review and Discussion

1. With partners or in groups, discuss the major contents of a curriculum.
2. What should be given priority in a curriculum?
3. What skills should we develop in our learners?
4. What would you add or delete in Level I?
5. What would you add or delete in Level II?
6. What would you add or delete in Level III?
7. Which situational topics would you use in Levels I, II, and III? Why? (See Appendix III.)
8. Discuss some principles of curriculum development.
9. How would you ensure reentry of known material in your lessons?
10. What do we mean by continuity of instruction?
11. How do you provide for differentiating experiences in your lessons?
12. What should be evaluated in teaching?
13. How can you set down a basic curricular plan if you have no textbook?
14. What are the basic needs of human beings in society?
15. How can your lessons contribute to the satisfaction of these needs?

3

Developing Language Abilities and Cultural Insights

Approaches

There are many generally accepted ways of approaching (leading into or introducing) the teaching of the sounds, communicative functions, structure, and vocabulary of the language and of the normal forms of conversation. Some teachers prefer to start by having students listen to and dramatize a conversation or a dialogue; some prefer to start by helping students read a narrative paragraph; some start directly by presenting the new communicative expression or structure in authentic utterances* which are later used in a conversation; some start by telling well-known stories (fairy-tales or folktales); some even start by dramatizing an action series such as "I'm getting up. I'm going to the door. I'm opening the door. And so on."

The approach you use should depend on the age of your students, on their interests, and on the length and major aims of your course. Each approach has merit. Many teachers today prefer the situational or communicative approach in which students hear, dramatize, and internalize a short dialogue. They consider that the dialogue duplicates most closely the normal speech of native speakers. Whichever other approach you use to teach any feature of the language and whatever the needs of your students, provision should be made for giving them practice in the normal forms of conversation; that is, in listening to questions and answers, in making responses, and in participating in conversational exchanges of varying lengths.

You may prefer to vary your approach depending on the structure you are going to teach. With one, you may find it most desirable to start with a dialogue; with another, you may wish to start with the structure and then (after you have practiced several examples) to incorporate it into a real conversation. Certainly, within every unit of work there should be provision for the study and dramatization of two

---

*Let us remember that an *utterance* unit is a stretch of speech by one person before which there was silence on his part and after which there was also silence on his part. (Fries, *The Structure of English*, p. 23.)

or more dialogues of four to eight utterances each. These dialogues may be in addition to or they may include questions and answers related to the communicative expression or structure you have been practicing. The dialogues should not be confined to questions and answers alone but should include all forms of normal speech such as statements, questions, responses, commands, formulas, complete sentences, and one-word utterances.

One dialogue could serve to *introduce* new communicative functions and structures (in combination, of course, with structures and vocabulary which are familiar to the students). One could serve to *reinforce* the new structures after they have been practiced. The cultural setting may be similar to the one in which the structures were introduced. Another dialogue may give practice in the same language items, but in different sociocultural situations.

Stages In Language Growth

Whatever the approach (conversation, story, etc.), your teaching of any language item should follow six sequential steps:

1. The pupils should be led to *understand* the material. This may be done through pictures, blackboard drawings, diagrams, or charts; through paraphrases (sentences using familiar words which explain the new word, for example, "A butcher is a person who cuts meat"); through dramatization of a situation in which the item is embedded; through a brief explanation in English; through an equivalent expression or a summary in the pupils' native language.

The use of the pupils' native tongue is a controversial issue. If all pupils speak the same native language, if you know the language, and if it will save time and lift morale, no harm will come to the students if the native language is used occasionally and *judiciously*. If you do use the native language, do it in the following way: Say the English in a normal voice, give the native language equivalent *once* in a low voice, and then give the English again. In general, unless there is misunderstanding, do *not* repeat the same expression in the native language in a subsequent lesson. The use of the native language should not be allowed to become a permanent crutch.

Pupils should never be asked to repeat or otherwise practice material whose meaning is not clear.

2. They should be led to repeat the material after you say it as often as is necessary. Do not strive for mastery at this stage.

3. They should be led to give a description of the *sounds, form, grammatical function, position,* and *meaning* of a grammatical item. This is often called a descriptive rule or a generalization. This step would be omitted in the lower levels of elementary school.

4. They should be led to practice the material in as many ways as possible.

5. They should be led to choose the correct word, expression, or structure (in statements, responses, or questions) from several choices.

6. They should be helped to use the new material in *every* communication situation where they can express ideas without worrying about inflection, word order, stress, or any other feature of the English language system.

As noted earlier, an English program usually aims to develop the skills of understanding, speaking, reading, and writing while giving insight into the culture of which the language is a part. Within each of the skills, attention must be given to phonology (the *phonetic and phonemic system*), to grammar (the *structure system*), and to vocabulary (the *lexicon*). Each of the language skills makes use of sounds (even reading, as we will indicate later), structure, and vocabulary. I will therefore take these three major areas of language in turn and give some brief suggestions for teaching them. As I do so, I will make continuous reference to the six stages listed above. I will start with phonology since what we say and hear in any speech act is a string of sounds, the *output* of the prior mental combination of the semantic and syntactic components.

The Listening-Speaking Skills

(The Audio-Oral or Audio-Lingual Skills)

THE SOUND SYSTEM

The sound system is learned best through imitation of the teacher or of a tape or record. It goes without saying that the teacher is preferred to any electronic or mechanical device for the first presentation of the new material. The only situation in which we can justify the use of a tape or record *before* the teacher's live presentation is one in which the teacher feels that his or her command of the language is not at all adequate. Many teachers also prefer to introduce songs through recordings.

Tapes and records are very effective, however, in making possible the additional sustained practice which language learning requires. Where possible, these should be used *after* the live presentation.

With older students whose ingrained native language habits may seriously conflict with the production of new language sounds, guided imitation of the teacher is usually not enough.

After identifying the sounds which cause the most difficulty to your students, you might use several techniques or a combination of techniques to teach them: (1) a *description* of the speech organs as the sound is being produced, (2) a *diagram* of the speech organs, (3) a *comparison* with the nearest sound in the students' native language (if you know the language)*; (4) a *modification* of a known English sound. (This may be particularly good in teaching the voiced and voiceless pairs—b/p, f/v, s/z.)

---

*If a similar sound exists in the pupil's native tongue but in a position which is not similar to its position in English, you may make the students aware of the fact that they *do* know and use the sound. You will help them isolate, extract, and use it in its new English position.

All descriptions should be simple, for example, for /u/, "The lips are rounded (show yours and/or draw a sketch on the board); the tongue is back."

A diagram should be uncluttered and clear. You should learn to sketch the lips, teeth, palate, and tongue on the board. Using dotted lines, indicate the position of the tongue or the movement of the tongue from one sound to the next.

A very effective device is to sketch a large profile on cardboard, indicating the lips, teeth, palate, and bottom of the mouth. Omit the tongue. Cut out the cardboard to show the mouth cavity. Make a red mitten for your right hand. As you teach a sound, use your gloved hand in the open mouth cavity to simulate the tongue. Move it against or between the teeth, bunch it up in the back, curl it up to the palate for /r/, or indicate movement from one sound to another.

After you teach one sound (the sound of *th* in *thin*, for example), teach a contrasting sound (/d/ or /t/ or /ð/) in familiar words, in those needed in the new lesson, and even in unfamiliar words.** Teach them in minimal pairs, if possible, that is, in words in which there is no difference except for the sound you are contrasting—for example, thin/tin, tin/din, beat/bit, Pete/pet, wine/vine, yellow/Jello, zoo/sue.

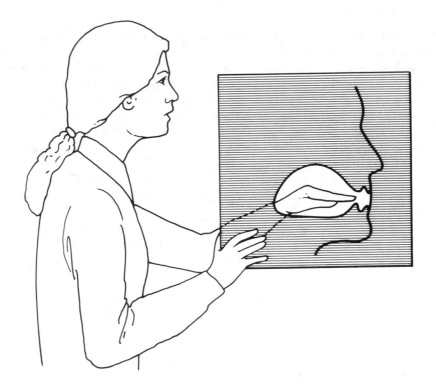

With older students, you may find it desirable to give the meanings of the pairs in the native language to convince them that the phonemes *do* make a meaning difference. You may find it necessary, too, to give pronunciation practice which does not exist in the textbook if your students have difficulty with certain sounds. You may even have to change the textbook order of teaching the sounds.

There are three essential steps in teaching your students to make sounds. They must be able to (1) hear the sound, (2) identify the sound, and (3) produce the sound.

Following is a brief illustration of a procedure you may wish to use to ensure recognition and production. Let us assume the problem is the /g/ and /k/ in a final position. Use simple pictures illustrating the words or the words themselves (which can be placed on the board in print or in cursive writing).

I	II
bag	back
hag	hack
rag	rack
sag	sack
tag	tack

1. Say all the words in Column I (or Set 1 of the pictures) two or three times.
2. Say all the words in Column II two or three times.
3. Say the words across several times.

***

4. Give two words from either list and ask the students to indicate whether they are the same or different, for example, *bag/bag*—same.
5. Give three words from either list and ask the students to indicate which two are the same. For example, you say, "tag, tag, tack." Individual students say "one, one, two."
6. Give a word from either list and have the students indicate on which list or set of pictures it appears by holding up one or two fingers.

***

7. Say each word in Column I or in the first set of pictures. Have the students repeat each word.

⁺Most teachers prefer to give practice with words which students can use immediately in communication situations. When incomplete words are used, indicate the missing segment by a line, for example, prob— (problem), —ferent (different).

8. Say each word in Column II. Have the students repeat.

9. Say the words across, followed by student repetition (whole class, groups, or individuals).

10. Say a word in one column. Have individuals give you the contrasting word.

11. Have a student give one word and a fellow student give the contrasting word.

12. Use words from both columns in short utterances. Have the students listen to and repeat each one in the ways suggested above.

A few other points about the teaching of sounds are necessary: (1) Remember to teach minimal pairs in positions other than initial or final (e.g., miller, mirror). (2) Present minimal pairs in situations whenever feasible; for example, Student 1: This mitt is no good. Student 2: Then don't play with it. Student 3: This meat is no good. Student 4: Then don't eat it. (3) Remember to point out the correlation between pairs like *meter* and *metric*, *insane* and *insanity*. (4) Teach consonant clusters in a gradual buildup of words, for example, *were, word, world, worlds*. (5) A technique you may use to correct particularly troublesome sounds is to have some pictures available showing minimal pairs of phonemes. When a student or the class mistakes one sound for the other, point to the correct one and say, "It's this sound." (e.g., *bag, back*) or whatever picture is more appropriate in the cultural setting in which you are teaching.

The "test," of course, is Stage 6 in our language learning process: Can students distinguish between sentences like "The sentence is long" and "The sentence is wrong" or "I see the ship" and "I see the sheep," and can they produce the correct sound in free communication situations?

A word of caution is in order before we proceed to the other elements in the sound system: You may have to reteach the same sound or remind the students of the pronunciation of the same sound 100 times or more. With older students particularly, habits of using the speech organs in one's native tongue are strong. Of the three major components of language, the sound system is the most difficult to acquire.

Intonation is taught by imitation of many similar sentences. I would recommend that you teach only the two basic intonation patterns first: the rise-fall intonation, and the rising intonation used in inverted questions (those usually requiring a yes-no answer).

It may be desirable to indicate intonation lines on the board or the numbers one to four, or to use an upward arm gesture to show rising intonation and a downward arm movement to show falling intonation, or to place up or down arrows (↑ ↓) at the end of the sentence, or to place curved arrows (↗ ↘) over the words having the highest or lowest pitch, or whatever helps *your* students.

Any of the techniques for indicating intonation will help. Combinations of the techniques are even more helpful.

Phonemic stress (word accent) is taught by contrast. Hearing, identifying the difference, producing the difference, using the words in sentences which show meaning differences, and finally using the contrasting words in real speech situations are the steps needed to ensure a knowledge of words in which stress is phonemic.

I would reserve for the intermediate or the advanced level the placement of stress on different parts of a sentence to show varying emphases. For example,

$_2$Did^3 ⌐ you go to the movies yesterday? (or your brother?)

$_2$Did you go to the movies ^{3} ⌐ yesterday? (or last week?)

$_2$Did you go to the ^{3} ⌐ movies yesterday? (or to the library?)

The typical rhythm of English is learned by imitation and by practice in saying increasingly longer sentences using the words in the first sentence in the longer sentences: May I have that book? May I have that big book? May I have that big history book? May I have those two big history books?

With older students, you may also wish to teach the symbol /ə/ and to write it over words which are "weakened" or reduced in speech, for example, Can (/kən/) you go to the movies? Yes, I can (/kaen/). (Notice the full value of the vowel in the short answer.) You may also wish to teach older students the phonemic symbols as reminders of the sounds. Whether you do or not will depend on your experience in using them, the students' writing system, their age, their needs, and other factors.

The emphasis in language learning today is on achieving understanding. It is recognized by most authorities that the complete elimination of a foreign accent in the majority of adults is impossible without a tremendous expenditure of time and effort. This effort might better be given to acquiring greater fluency and control of structure. The practice of structure patterns will automatically contribute to more accurate sound production. You should strive for comprehensibility at all times, however, even during those periods in the lesson when you are not giving concentrated practice on elements of the sound system.

With youngsters, the situation is different. It is always amazing to hear the accuracy with which many will mimic your speech.

LISTENING COMPREHENSION

Up to now, we have been concerned with learners' speech *production*. Let us turn our attention to their *comprehension* of the speech that they hear, that is, the decoding of the stream of speech, which involves continual mental processing, concentrated attention, and memory.

Comprehension of an utterance requires (1) *perception* of the sounds, (2) *recognition* and *identification* of the segments (the chunks of speech which go together), (3) *understanding* of the communicative expressions and syntactic structures, and (4) *interpretation* of the message. Listeners require two kinds of knowledge to identify utterances: (1) knowledge of the syntax and morphological elements, which helps them chunk incoming speech into segments, and (2) real-world knowledge.

The process of storing a stream of speech into long-term memory is, at present, thought to be as follows: (1) receiving a message and placing it temporarily in short-term memory; (2) selecting the main ideas (the gist or essence) of what was heard; (3) storing the essence in long-term memory.

This process is not simple. The listener has to be aware not only of the sounds and segments but of the persons speaking, their communicative purpose, and the pragmatic factors involved in the speech act (cultural background, knowledge of the subject being talked about, ''world'' knowledge, and experience).

The learner must retain important elements in short-term memory and then readjust each incoming segment in view of what has preceded and in anticipation of what may come next. How can we help learners acquire the skills needed to *identify, understand*, and *interpret* oral input? We can

1. Teach the phonemic system.
2. Teach necessary morphosyntactic rules and segmentation of subject, verb, object, phrases, and clauses. Write an utterance on the chalkboard; mark off segments with slant lines; say the utterance aloud; ask the learners to repeat immediately after you. For example, Joe/went/to the library/at five o'clock.
3. Repeat an utterance or a brief passage three or more times.
4. Stop at the end of every utterance and ask questions to ensure comprehension.

Before Listening

1. Simplify passages to three levels with simplified questions for each level.
2. Explain difficult vocabulary and cultural allusions in the passage before listening.
3. Give simple, clear, precise explanations of what to listen for through one or two prelistening questions. What do the learners know about the topic?
4. Divide a passage into manageable pieces.
5. Discuss the pragmatic elements in the situation.
6. Have learners make notes about what they expect to hear (based on the title).
7. Make learners aware of redundancy clues (the multiple signals in sentences for plurality, possession, gender, verb aspect, etc.).

While Listening

1. Give learners a list of facts and items they can check as they are listening (things, people, dates, words).
2. Give them maps on which they can chart a route being discussed.
3. Tell them to jot down only the key words as they listen. Have them draw something simple which the passage suggests.

After Listening

Depending on their ability, the learners may be asked to:

1. Take a dictation of the passage.
2. Fill in a cloze test.
3. Answer multiple-choice questions.
4. Answer open-ended questions.
5. Write a two- or three-line summary.
6. Tell whether the language they hear is formal or informal, appropriate or inappropriate.
7. Tell who the speakers are (when listening to a tape), what their attitudes are, what their roles are, where they are, what they are speaking about.
8. Tell what they can infer from what X has said.

THE STRUCTURES AND COMMUNICATIVE EXPRESSIONS

A procedure you will find useful in presenting these for active use (whether or not they have been heard first in a conversation or story) is as follows:

 1. *Motivate.* You may do this by dramatizing a situation, by reminding students of a familiar dialogue or narrative passage in which it was used, by asking them how they would say something in their native tongue.

 2. *Review* briefly familiar language items which you will need in order to present, clarify, or practice the new language item. If you are going to teach adjectives, review appropriate content words; if you are going to teach the simple present, you may wish to review expressions of time; if you are going to teach the present perfect, you may wish to review the verb *have* and also the simple past (in order to contrast the two "tenses"). With communicative expressions, give paraphrases or synonyms: Do you mind? May I?

 3. Use the structure or communicative expression in a normal utterance.

 4. Make sure the students *understand* the utterance. Do this by dramatizing an action many times, by using a picture, by giving several sentences in English with familiar words which help explain the one you are teaching, or by giving them their native language equivalent (as a last resort, however).

 5. *Repeat* the utterance many times. The number of repetitions will depend on the known sounds or sound sequences in the utterance. If you have a large class, walk to various parts of the room so that all students can see your mouth.

 6. *Have the utterance repeated in chorus* by the entire class several times. Give the model before each repetition you ask of the class.

 7. If the sentence is long (six or more syllables), or if the sound sequence is unfamiliar, you may wish to break the sentence into smaller elements for practice. Break it from the end. It is easier to keep the same intonation when you start breaking it from the end. Of course you may vary this occasionally by breaking the sentence from the beginning. For beginners, here is the procedure for breaking a sentence from the end. Let us take "He's going to read now."

a. Say the entire sentence a few times.

b. Say "now." Class repeats "now."

c. Say "read." Class repeats "read."

d. Say "read now." Class repeats "read now."

e. Say "going to." Class repeats "going to."

f. Say "going to read now." Class repeats "going to read now."

g. Say "He's going to read now." Class repeats "He's going to read now."

8. *Engage in group repetition* of the same sentence (half a class, the right side, the left side, the front, each row, etc.). Indicate the group which is to repeat with a hand signal which you have devised and with which you have made your class familiar.

9. *Have individual students repeat* the same sentence. It is a good idea to start with the more able students. In that way, the less able students will have more time to listen to and repeat silently a reasonably correct sentence.

10. If there are errors in pronunciation, *you* say the sentence and engage the class in choral, group, or individual repetition again.

11. Using *familiar vocabulary only, give other sentences* which illustrate the point you are teaching and have the students repeat them. For example, if you are teaching the adjective of color after *be*, say, as you show each item, "The pencil is red. The pen is red. The book is red. The notebook is red." And so on.

12. *Ask questions* which make your students see that the word *red* is a color, that it follows *is*, and that it does not change.

a. Step 12 may be done *after* you place several sentences on the board in the form of a chart. Do not place the sentences on the board unless the students have heard them and can say them with reasonable accuracy and fluency. With younger students, you may prefer not to write sentences on the board at all.

b. The grammatical terms you use in helping your students see the *form* (sound, i.e., phonological or spelling), *meaning, position*, and *grammatical function* of any new item will depend to a great extent on their knowledge of grammatical terms in their native tongue. Grammatical terms are not necessary, and neither are prescriptive rules of grammar. The rule, if any, should be a description of the sounds and arrangements of sounds in the utterance. What we are striving for is (i) automatic and habitual production of the item in speech, and (ii) internalization of its recurring, interrelated, interdependent features so that it can be used in other appropriate communication situations and in increasingly broader contexts.

c. Note a possible chart:

The	Noun	"Be"	Color (or Adjective)
The	pencil	is	*red*
The	pen	is	*red*

13. When, for example, the plurals of nouns are taught, the charts may look like this and be placed next to each other:

The	Noun	"Be"	Color
The	pencil	is	red
The	pen	is	green

The	Noun	"Be"	Color
The	pencils	*are*	red
The	pens	*are*	green

14. After the students are made to see word order, inflections, or whatever the item is that we are teaching, we engage them in *varied* practice.

BASIC ORAL PRACTICE ACTIVITIES

While language may be rule-governed, speakers will still have to develop the habits of using their vocal organs perhaps in completely new ways, quickly and correctly; of adding inflections, prefixes, and suffixes to words; of arranging words in positions and combinations required by English; and of using the registers or varieties appropriate in the particular communication situation. Listeners, of course, will have to learn to recognize and react to the oral signals they hear in a message. Only intensive practice can bring about the competence and performance needed to encode (transmit) and to decode (understand) a message.

Oral drills—about five for each new item— should follow the presentation of the item in a communication situation, its rote repetition, and its description or rule. Most oral drills fall into the following categories: *substitution, expansion* (including embedding), *deletion*, and *transformation*. There are numerous variations of these as we shall see.

Other distinctions are often made among these drills. They may be subdivided into *mechanical* or *manipulative, meaningful*, and *communicative*. (At any level, the three types, including the mechanical substitution drill, can be used with profit.) Here is an example of the distinction made among them:

Mechanical substitution: Teacher: He arrived at *seven* (cue: nine) Student: He arrived at nine. (cue: eleven, etc.)

Meaningful response: Teacher: What time did you arrive? Student: I arrived at nine.

Communicative response: Teacher: What have you done this morning? Student: (time of getting up, leaving for school, etc.). We will have more to say about communicative practice later.

A few other general remarks should be made about oral practice. (Incidentally, drills particularly appropriate in developing reading and writing will be given in subsequent sections although any drill will contribute to the growth and reinforcement of the abilities to read and write.)

1. The utterances used in the drills should be authentic (e.g., those that a native speaker would use; those that make sense; those that are relevant to the students' interests and lives).

2. You should relate the utterances (after the mechanical substitution drills) either with respect to structure and communicative expressions or to the vocabulary area. This will make a real conversation—hence communication—possible more quickly.

3. Substitution drills should *precede* all other types of drills (except for repetition drills) so that students will get into the habit of arranging words in certain positions.

4. You should practice other drills—where feasible—in mini situations, for example, "Be careful." "I will be" or "Take care." "Don't worry, I will."

5. In the drills immediately following the initial presentation, the change to be made should be minimal (only *one* change) and it should be consistent, for example, the instruction might be: "Use the word *never* in each of these sentences." (Each of the sentences would contain the verb *be* or a regular verb.)

6. You should present only the most appropriate drills for the item being practiced. For example, in teaching adjectives, *substitution, expansion, transformation*, and *embedding* (integration) drills would be effective—as well as questions and answers, of course.

7. You should present the drills briskly. This is possible (a) if you have prepared a small card to fit into your hand (leaving your other hand free for gesturing, calling on students, etc.) which contains the cue words you plan to use, (b) if you have given clear instructions, and (c) if you have modeled two examples.

8. Some drills should not be attempted orally unless the timing and pauses are perfect; *I went———the store* (requiring the response *to* or *into*) would give students a distorted aural impression of the sentence. Moreover, it would call for an isolated word in the response that could not be considered a true utterance. If tried at all, students should be asked to repeat the entire sentence.

9. The use of oral reconstruction drills depends on extensive previous practice and good timing. Students should *see* the cues for the sentence you want them to reconstruct: *John/not/eat/yet*. This eliminates the danger that they may develop a form of pidgin English.

10. You can do all drills—especially in the early stages—with five kinds of cues: (a) the spoken word and the object shown simultaneously, (b) the spoken word, (c) the object, (d) a picture or sketch of the object, (e) the written word.

11. You should avoid giving students jumbled words to be placed in the correct order, especially if they are printed in linear sequence, for example, went a park the to basket I with. If you do want to have students place words in proper position, it is more desirable to list them vertically.

12. Before asking students to choose between such contrasting items as verb forms, pronouns, or placement of adverbs of time, I would give them the entire series of utterances I plan to use which they would then listen to and repeat.

13. There should be an appropriate pause between the base sentence and the oral cue so that students do not hear (e.g., in a drill in which they are to transform the present continuous to the simple past) a string of words such as, "I'm going there (yesterday)."

14. In order to avoid possible different responses which may cause confusion, the entire group should not be asked to respond to a cue. (The responses of individuals might, however, be confirmed by a choral response.)

Following are the commonly agreed upon names and some examples of oral pattern practice activities which help students grow in their control of the patterns of language. In doing any drill, you should give the model sentence two or three times and show the students, *by doing it yourself*, exactly what you expect them to do.

Substitution. In this drill, students use another word of the same class in place of a word in the sentence. A noun is replaced by another noun, a verb by another verb, an adjective by another adjective, a determiner (*the, a, some, each, any*) by another determiner.

Let us assume you are teaching the present of *have*. Give a sentence: "I have a pencil." Say in English (at the beginning, you may use their native tongue to make sure they understand the directive), "Now, I'll give you another word. Put it (or use it) in place of *pencil*." (Remember to do at least two examples with them.)

Replacement or Restatement. The students will be expected to replace one element by another, for example, *nouns or names* by a pronoun (*he, she*, etc.); or to restate the sentence using a synonymous expression.

1. Give a sentence: "John has a ruler." The students will be expected to say, "*He* has a ruler." Do not change the object (ruler) in any of the sentences in the drill. In the drills we will describe (except the progressive replacement drill), only one element in the sentence should be changed at one time.

2. Give sentences with *often*, for example. The students will give the same sentences with *many times a week*, for example, "I *often* speak to him. I speak to him *many times a week*."

3. Give sentences such as "I see *the man.*" Students will say "I see him." (Remember that stress changes here.)

4. Give sentences such as "I *have to* go now." Students will say "I *must* go now."

Paired Sentences. In this drill, you will give a sentence and then ask a question. For example, you will say, "Mary likes to study. What about you?" or "What about the boys?" A student would say, "I like to study too" or "They like to study too." This is a good drill for practicing verb forms or adjectives. For example, "Joan is friendly. What about Helen?" "Helen is friendly, too."

*Transformation (*sometimes called *conversion).* The students will be given practice in changing from affirmative to negative or to interrogative and later from present to past or to future, and so on. Give the model sentence and say, for example, "Now we're going to make questions from these sentences." Say "He has a ruler." The student will say, "Does he have a ruler?" (or "Has he a ruler?" depending on the book you are using or the form *you* use in your speech.)

It is not necessary to use words like *negative, past,* and so on. You can say instead, "Let's start each sentence with *no*" or "Let's use *not* in these sentences" (even though you may ask them to use the contracted form of *not*) or "Let's use *yesterday,*" or "Let's use *going to,*" and so on.

Expansion. The students will be given a word or expression to be added to a sentence you give them. For example, "Let's add the word *always* to these sentences." In later stages, they may be asked to place expressions such as *I'm sure, I think,* and *I know before* other sentences.

They may also be asked to make *multiple expansions* (one at a time, however), to noun phrases or verb phrases. For example, say, "I see a boy" (cue *good-looking,* (cue) *with red hair.* Students called upon would give the entire sentence with each new cue added.

With advanced classes, you may ask them to expand a sentence with a word or expression which will necessitate a change in verb form. For example, "Use *yesterday* in these sentences. Make the necessary changes." "I'm eating (I ate yesterday)" or "Place 'The man asked me' in front of these sentences. 'How old are you?' (The man asked me how old I was.)"

Reduction. This drill is a form of replacement drill because you "reduce" a sentence by changing an expression to a word, for example, "I have *the picture*" to "I have *it*"*; "I'm going to the *library*" to "*I'm going there*"; "Come *to my house*" to "Come *here*." Later you can practice substitute expressions: "I'd like one of the books in the window" to "I'd like one of those"; "I see all the people" to "I see everyone"; "I think it's raining" to "I think so." When appropriate, you can give practice in reducing clauses to phrases, for example, "All the people who were in the store" to "All the people in the store."

Directed Practice. A student is directed (asked) to ask another student a question. The second student is directed to answer. This drill needs a lot of help from you at the beginning. It should be done in three stages:

*Notice the change in stress.

Stage I. The teacher says to the first student, "X, ask Y, 'Do you have a ruler to lend me?' " and to the second student, "Y, tell X, 'I have a ruler' or 'Yes, I do.' "

Stage II. The teacher says to X, "X, ask Y if she has a ruler to lend you" and whispers to X, "Do you have a ruler to lend me?" X says aloud, "Do you have a ruler to lend me?" The teacher says to Y, "Y, tell X you have a ruler" and whispers to Y, "Yes, I have a ruler." Y says, "Yes, I have a ruler" aloud.

Stage III. The teacher does not whisper the direct question (i.e., the teacher does not prompt the students).

A student is asked to tell or ask something requiring transformation; for example "Ask him how he came to school."

Integration. Students are asked to put two short sentences together to make one sentence. For example, "I have a dog. It's black" becomes "I have a black dog"; "The woman is in the store. She's my sister" becomes "The woman who is in the store is my sister," or "The woman in the store is my sister."

Progressive Replacement. This drill needs much teacher help at the beginning, but students enjoy doing it after they have learned the trick of it. This is a multiple substitution drill in which a new element is changed in each sentence. The students have to remember what is said in each sentence in order to form the new sentence. Notice:

Teacher	Student
I have a red cap.	I have a red cap.
green	I have a green cap.
He	He has a green cap.
sweater.	He has a green sweater.
Mr. Jones	Mr. Jones has a green sweater.
some	Mr. Jones has some green sweaters.
They	They have some green sweaters.
need	They need some green sweaters.
	And so on.

Translation. Only the teacher who knows the native language of his or her students can engage in this drill because the students should generally not use the native language. If translation is to be done at all, it should always be on a limited structure point, and on one point only. The equivalent is always given; never, of course, a literal translation. Example:

Teacher	Student
(Native language)	I have a few pencils.
(Native language)	I have a few books.
(Native language)	I have a few notebooks.

or

Teacher	Student
(Native language)	I've been studying for an hour.
(Native language)	I've been waiting for an hour.
(Native language)	I've been resting for an hour.

With slow students and especially with structures which contrast markedly with those in the native language, you may wish to precede the type of exercise just described with one in which you give the English and individual students give the native language.

Since many school systems throughout the world include a translation from English to the native language, and vice-versa, on achievement or proficiency examinations, the equivalents proposed above will serve several purposes: They will (1) heighten the morale of students, (2) give you firm assurance that the contrasting features have been internalized, and (3) prepare students for the often dreaded examination. As usual, the key word is *judiciously*.

Question-Answer Practice. There are several basic types of question-answer drills. Moreover, each drill can be done in several ways: (1) The teacher asks all the students a question; one student answers.* (2) A student asks the teacher a question; the teacher answers. (3) A student asks another student a question. (See also Appendix I for paired practice activities.) (4) Pairs of students question each other in chain fashion. This too has several variations:

a. Student 1 asks Student 2 a question. Student 2 answers. Student 3 asks the same question of Student 4.

b. Student 1 asks Student 2 a question. Student 2 answers and asks the same question of Student 3.

c. Student 1 asks Student 2 a question, for example, "Do you have a pencil?" Student 2 answers, "Yes, I do" or "Yes, I have a pencil." Student 3 asks Student 4, "Does he (or she) have a pencil?" referring to Student 2.

Let us examine some basic question and answer drills which can be used effectively in teaching *structure*.

1. Answer *yes* or *no*. "Do you have your book?" "Yes." "No."

2. Answer *yes*. Give a long answer (or a complete sentence). "Do you have a pencil?" "Yes, I have a pencil." A substitution drill can be combined effectively with this question-answer practice.

3. Answer *yes*. Give a short answer. "Do you have a pencil?" "Yes, I do."

4. Answer *no*. Give a long answer. "Do you have a pencil?" "No, I don't have a pencil."

---

*A choral answer may lead to confusion unless the teacher models both the question and the answer.

5. Answer *no*. Give a short answer. "Do you have a pencil?" "No, I don't."
6. Answer *no*. Give a short answer and a long answer. "No, I don't; I don't have a pencil."
7. Answer *no*. Tell what you have (or tell what it is). "Do you have a pencil?" "No, I don't have a pencil. I have a pen." "Is this a table?" "No, it's not (or it isn't) a table. It's a chair."
8. Choose one or the other. "Do you have a pencil or a pen?" "I have a (pen)."
9. Patterned response. You ask a question such as, "Do you have a pencil?" or "May I borrow your pencil?" The student always answers with the sentence being practiced, for example, "Yes, here it is" or "Do you like salad (ice cream, swimming, etc.)?" "Yes, very much."

   At more advanced levels, the patterned response drill can be used to practice changes in word order or substitute expressions. Notice:

   > I'm hungry. So am I (*or* I am too).
   > I'm thirsty. So am I (*or* He is too).
   >   or
   > Do you think she's intelligent? Yes, I think so.
   > Do you think it's going to rain? Yes, I think so.
   >   or
   > Would you like one of these lovely pictures? Yes, I'd like one very much.

10. *"Wh" or information questions.* You or individual students will ask questions with *who, whose, where, how long,* and so on. Other students may be asked to reply with an utterance or with a complete sentence, depending on what you wish to practice.
11. *Free Response.* You may ask, "What do I have on my desk? (or in my hand")". A student would answer, "You have a pencil, a pen," and so on. You would ask, "What do you have on your desk?" or "What do you always bring to school?" or "What do we have in this room?" or anything you are practicing. In this activity, you (or a student) can again use spoken words, pictures, objects, or written words to elicit the response desired.

OTHER COMMENTS ON ORAL DRILLS

Some drills lend themselves better than others, of course, to the items we are practicing. It is important to vary the drill activities and to conduct them briskly in order to prevent monotony. As soon as interest in one type of drill lags, you should either proceed to another type of drill, change the cue, or vary the type of student participation involved; that is, proceed from choral repetition, to chain repetition, to your questioning students, to students' questioning you or each other.

When you start a chain, break it after four or six learners have spoken. Begin the chain again in another part of the room, using the same sentences or, if you wish, changing some part of the sentence but maintaining the same pattern.

Drills should lead gradually to the normal use of language items in real situations. Formulas of the language, as well as rejoinders of all kinds (agreement, surprise, disagreement), should be practiced. For example,

> Does my speaking bother you? No, not at all.
>
> Do you mind if I leave now? No, of course not.
>
> Hello! We thought we'd come to visit you. What a nice surprise. Do come in!

In addition to the dialogues or exchanges in which each speaker in turn makes one statement or where one asks and the other answers a question, multiple responses should be practiced as soon as the students are able to make them. Whereas at the beginning, the stimulus statement can be "That's a nice tie," and the response "Thank you," the second time the response may be "Thank you. I'm glad you like it" or "Thank you. It's new" or "Thank you. It's a gift from my wife" or anything else you have practiced previously in pattern practice drills.

With advanced classes you may devise a code or a format for dialogues which students will follow with little or no prompting on your part. The following (or even a longer list) may be placed on a chart or on the board*:

S (Stimulus)	R (Response)
Q (question)	St or Q (statement or question)
Q and St	Q
Q, St and St	St and St (two utterances)
St, St and Q	St, St and Q

Your advanced students can use any of the above combinations to prepare increasingly longer conversational exchanges within the list of cultural situations given in Chapter 2 and in Appendix II. You may wish to prepare another easily accessible chart with a list of twenty or more topics of interest. Thus students can select a topic and be guided to speak about it utilizing the cues in the chart above to practice the normal forms of conversation of native speakers. Following is a simple illustration of this technique where the topic is a new suit.

1. Is that a new suit?

2. Yes, it is.

***

1. Is that a new suit? It looks very good on you.

2. Do you really like it?

***

1. Is your suit new? I've never seen it before. It looks very good on you.

2. Yes, it is new. It's the first time I have worn it.

***

---

*The words in parentheses need not be on the chart. They are noted here for your use only.

1. I've never seen that suit. Brown is a good color for you. When did you buy it?

2. I bought it last week. Brown is my favorite color. Do you really like the suit?

It is essential that students, particularly those in advanced classes, be given practice in recognizing and using the polite forms and appropriate responses of the language. For example,

Would you like (a cup of tea)? Yes. Thank you.

Won't you have another (sandwich)?

Yes, thank you very much.

No, thank you. I can't now.

May I get you (a cup of coffee)?

Yes, thank you. I'd like one.

I'd be very grateful if you got me (a cup of tea)

Of course, I'll be glad to.

Other items which give the language its authentic "ring" are words like *so, well, then, of course, as a matter of fact,* which many native speakers use to begin their utterances. Systematic practice should be given in these as they arise in the texts you are using. You should make provision to teach them, however, whether or not they appear in the formal instructional materials.

We have talked about *understanding, repetition,* and *practice,* the first three steps in our language learning process. We have also indicated how conscious selection operates. When students have to choose between *he* and *she,* or *here* and *there,* or any other contrasting feature in English in a practice activity, such as a chain drill, they are consciously choosing between one form and the other.

Another technique you may wish to use is the following: Give the students some sentences about a situation and then ask, "What would you say?" or sometimes, "What would you do?" For example, say, "You meet someone in the street who invites you to a party at her home. You've never been to her home. What would you say? What would you ask?" ("Thank you, I'd like to come. Where do you live?" etc.) Additional communication activities will be suggested later in this chapter.

Before leaving the topic of oral drills permit me to express a few words of caution:

1. Try to minimize student errors. This is possible if you (a) give many models; (b) prompt the answers; (c) engage in choral repetition first; (d) call on your more able students first; (e) give the correct response, statement, or answer yourself by saying simply "Listen" or "Ask me the question"; (f) do not expect your students to create sentences or to improvise in the early stages.

2. Correct errors immediately by giving the correct form (except during the motivation stage of your lesson when you may overlook minor mistakes *temporarily;* you will make a mental note of them, of course, and give practice which will eliminate them, later in that lesson or in the next lesson). Merely say "Listen" and give the correct form. Do not inhibit the learners by scolding or overcorrecting.

3. Start the drills, but then give your students every opportunity to ask questions, give answers, and so on. Remember that they are the language learners, not you.

THE LEXICON—SPECIFIC NOTIONS

The importance of communicative meaning has gained increasing currency in the last few years. Messages between speakers and listeners, in other words, *communication*, must include meaningful words, a content of shared referents, shared experiences, and shared cultural concepts.

At the beginning level we should concentrate on the function (structure) words and the more frequently used vocabulary items which are needed to give practice in the basic communicative expressions, structures, and sounds of the language. Precedence, however, should be given to the vocabulary which is intimately related to the environment and experiences of the learners. While our major concern may seem to be with sounds and syntax, a store of content words from everyday life situations can make practice of the communicative functions and structures much more interesting to the students.

A question frequently asked is "How many new words can be taught in one lesson?" As is true of other questions related to teaching, there is no one answer. Children of eight or nine may learn four or five new words; children of ten or eleven may learn seven or eight; secondary school students may learn fifteen to twenty; while highly motivated university students may absorb thirty or more words.

Several premises and comments related to the teaching of vocabulary follow:

- Not all of the words students hear during any lesson need become a part of their active vocabulary (for production) during that lesson or even in later lessons. Some words in the new language (and in our native language) will remain passive (for recognition only); that is, we understand them when we hear them or read them, but we don't use them ourselves in speaking or in writing. The vocabulary for active use should be systematically presented and practiced.
- Vocabulary should always be taught in normal speech utterances.
- New vocabulary items should always be introduced in *known* structures and with familiar communicative expressions.
- Whenever possible, the vocabulary items should be centered about one topic. Words about food should be given in one lesson; words about clothing in another; words about weather in still another; and so on. All the words around a center of interest (food, clothing, recreation, etc.) should *not* be taught at one time or at one level. Other words within the same center can always be added when they fit logically with the other sociocultural topics being studied or when they are met in reading.

    In the beginning stages, the same context (situation or topic) should be used with a new word so that students will learn to associate the word with the situation in which it is usually used. For example, "What *mark* did you get on that test?" "The teacher gave me my *mark*."

- Whenever a familiar word is met in a new context, it should be reviewed again and practiced. A review or mention of the known meaning of the word should be made so that the students will understand the contrast or the similarity. If possible, only one context should be taught at one time.
- Vocabulary items should be taught in the same way we teach everything else. We give our students an understanding of the meaning in many ways. We dramatize; we illustrate using ourselves and our students; we show pictures; we paraphrase, we give the equivalent if necessary; we use any appropriate technique.
- Vocabulary should be practiced as communicative expressions and structures are practiced—in substitution drills, transformation drills, questions and answers, and other relevant tasks.
- Vocabulary items should be reintroduced many times with all the structures and in all situations in which they can logically be used.
- Students should be encouraged to learn and use nouns, verbs, adjectives, and adverbs which contain the same roots. We can help the learner prepare four-column word charts. For example,

Noun	Verb	Adjective	Adverb
difference	(to) differ	different	differently

We give extended practice in their use in order to reinforce position (slot, grammatical function, and meaning).

Prefixes and suffixes should be presented and practiced systematically. Attention must be given to changes in the spelling of some prefixes (*in-*, *il-*, *ir-*, *un-*, etc.). Use a four-column chart to teach prefixes.

Noun	Verb	Adjective	Adverb
ability	to be able	able	ably
inability	to be unable	unable	—
legibility	to be legible	legible	legibly
illegibility	to be illegible	illegible	illegibly

A FEW ADDITIONAL WORDS ABOUT COMMUNICATION ACTIVITIES

Since many teachers feel that oral practice activities leading to communicative competence are at the very heart of the language learning process, it may be useful to summarize some of what has already been said and to pinpoint activities which may be considered more properly communicative. First of all, what are some of the responsibilities of the language teacher in this regard? Let me note several:

1. *To know* intimately the students and the community in which they live in order to relate new language and cultural material to the probable experiences and interests of the students.

2. *To broaden* the students' experiences through discussion of music, art, hobbies, and other areas of interest in the school curriculum or in the community.

3. *To enrich* the students' vocabulary not only through studies of antonyms, synonyms, cognates, and words of the same family, but also by giving them—from the outset—the words and expressions they will need to talk about their communities and their backgrounds, for example, stores, farming, dating.

4. *To teach* as quickly as feasible the formulas or "routines" of English— phrases like *By all means* and *How do you do*, and to create situations in the classroom in which the use of such formulas will be appropriate.

5. *To present* all new vocabulary, communicative expressions, and structures in easily demonstrable situations or in a meaningful, self-explanatory context and to make sure that students understand them and can integrate them in listening, speaking, reading, and writing tasks.

6. *To exploit* every language learning activity so that it will reinforce and facilitate communication.

7. *To proceed* from tightly controlled drill to freer, more authentic creative expression from the very first day of the language program. For example, if names have been taught:

Teacher: What's his name?

Student 1: I don't know (or I don't remember).

Teacher: Ask him.

Student 1: What's your name?

Student 2: It's . . ..

8. *To reintroduce* communicative expressions, structures, and vocabulary of high frequency as often as possible after their initial presentation in as many appropriate situations as feasible so that students will be able to recall them with ease when needed for communication.

9. *To add* to textbooks authentic, meaningful language activities and short, two- or three-line dialogues for frequent dramatization.

10. *To suggest*—or encourage students to suggest—alternate sentences in the dialogue utterances so that they will not always expect the responses they have learned in the original dialogue, for example, depending on the class, your rapport with the students, and their rapport with each other. Student 1: What did you do last night? Student 2: I went to the movies. A possible alternate sentence might be: I can't tell you yet. It's a surprise. The students can be as creative as possible, but they should be helped to avoid giving offense.

11. *To modify*, if necessary, the sequence and order of materials in textbooks so that questions of all kinds and the pronouns *I* and *you* are introduced and practiced very early.

12. *To remember* that understanding the meaning of any utterance depends upon knowing its single elements of pronunciation, of grammar, of vocabulary, and of culture. While, very often, the first understanding of a dialogue or reading passage may be global, teachers must eventually make provision for teaching and practicing most of the single elements within the material. The learning of dialogues and reading passages, for that matter, should generally proceed in two parallel streams. First, in order to engender motivation, a global understanding of partially unfamiliar but authentic material may be asked for. I consider Stream I the one of greater importance. In Stream II, I would provide for systematic, ordered presentation of the individual elements within the longer live material. How boring it would be for us and for our students if we waited to introduce authentic, real-life material until students had mastered all the individual items within it!

13. *To help* the students note the integration (or meshing) of the communicative function, its purpose or intention, the grammatical structure, the elements in the situation (people, place, time, and topic), and the specific notions in the message. Remember that the utterances in the message containing the elements noted above are called *exponents*.

14. *To enable* the learners to change from informal to formal language by effecting a change in some element of the situation (the age of the speaker, the role or status of the person being addressed, the place—beach, place of worship, library, etc.—where the speech act is occurring), the topic (recreational, scientific, commercial), and the mode (oral or written). Language registers can be tentative, colloquial, informal, consultative, or formal. Some writers also add the register *frozen* (e.g., the linguist Martin Joos). Oral communications are generally less formal than written ones.

15. *To remind* the learners that most people "switch codes" many times during the day depending on the elements in the situation. (Who are they talking to? What about? Where? Why?)

16. *To present* new communicative expressions. You may dramatize, for example, "Please open the window," and then say, "Now listen to another way: Would you mind opening the window?" (with gestures).

Let us assume you have presented "Could you buy me . . .?" Draw stick figures on the chalkboard. Over one figure is a bubble which reads, "Could you buy me . . .?"; over the other figure is a bubble reading "Of course." Point to the first figure and as you do, pick up a newspaper from your desk and say, "Could you buy me a newspaper?" Use any available picture or object.

The activities I have mentioned are primarily listening-speaking activities. It goes without saying, however, that reading and writing activities—also communication skills—lend themselves very well to the further stimulation of listening and speaking.

Often you may wish to read a passage several times and have students reproduce orally what they remember of it, or you may ask them to predict the outcome, particularly if it describes a brief, humorous incident.

Letter writing or composition writing should, of course, be preceded by a discussion of ideas to be included in the letter or composition and by class discussion of a possible logical informational sequence for the ideas suggested.

Let me say that, *ideally*, communication implies the absence of external controls or stimuli. I feel that this is an unrealistic expectation in our secondary schools or even at the university level for students who are not working for a degree in English. Teachers must be prepared with audiovisual aids, everyday situational topics, themes of interest, and suggested formats for eliciting longer sentences or multiple responses.

Communication is at the very core of success in language acquisition but more important in interpersonal relationships—in communion with others. It is our responsibility to make sure in every way possible that learners will not only have *something to talk about* but that they will also develop the increasing desire to do so whenever the opportunity arises.

Let us turn to some language learning activities which will hopefully lead to verbal communication. I shall omit questions and answers. Students may be asked to

1. Develop a new, brief dialogue using utterances from two or more previously learned dialogues. For example, the new dialogue, "Where did you go yesterday?" "I went shopping for a hat," may be adapted from the following two dialogues: "I went shopping for a hat yesterday," "Did you buy one?" and "Where did you go yesterday? I didn't see you." "I had to go to the library."

2. Dramatize a dialogue with varying emotions, for example, "Look at my new coat!" (excitedly, angrily) or "What a funny joke!" (humorously, sarcastically).

3. Dramatize a telephone conversation—when the person called is there and when the person is not there.

4. Take part in role-playing activities (older students especially). For example, A student applies for a job giving his or her name, address, date of birth, experience. The same student may be called back for a further interview. The "employer" may make numerous errors of fact, for example, "Ah, you're Mr. . . ." The applicant would then have to say, "No, I'm not. . . . I'm . . ." or "My name's . . .."

5. Describe hobbies and activities and how they do or make something—stamp collecting, fishing, cooking.

6. Talk about a film or television program. Several students may contribute one sentence each to the description.

7. Describe a picture, a set of pictures, or a wall chart. (A series of pictures will be found in Chapter 4.)

8. Summarize what a previous speaker has said.

9. Develop increasingly sustained conversation for each of the situations you create, situations such as going to the post office, the market, or a tourist agency, by means of pictures or a magnet or flannel board.

10. Tell you and their classmates what they did on a holiday, before they came to school, or after they got home yesterday.

11. Perform some actions in the classroom. You or another student may ask, "What is he (she) doing?" or "What has he just done?" "What do you think he'll do now?" or whatever you are practicing.

12. Prepare (in groups) a short talk on some aspect of culture. They will give the prepared talk and then answer questions (asked by you or their classmates) about what they have said.

The Reading Process

Recent research and hypotheses about the complexity of the reading process and some implications for the classroom (at whatever level) should be of interest to all of us. Allow me to note several.

1. The reader's *background knowledge* must interact with his or her innate *conceptual abilities*, as well as with his or her *mental processing strategies*, in order to ensure comprehension of a text. The three basic factors learners must possess and develop are background knowledge in the first or second language, innate conceptual cognitive abilities, and processing strategies.

2. The role of background knowledge has been formalized as *schema theory*. According to recent research, no text, either spoken or written, carries meaning by itself. It does, however, provide direction for learners or readers as to how they should retrieve the knowledge already stored in their memory, or how they should construct meaning from their own previously acquired knowledge. This knowledge could include, for example, language learned (L1 or L2) and knowledge from con-

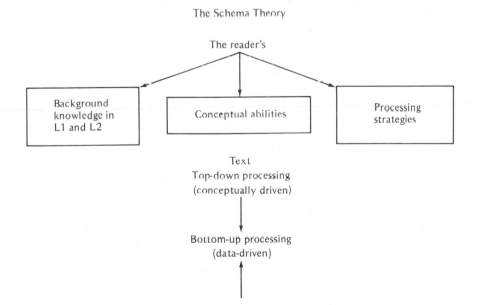

The Schema Theory

tent areas (math, history, etc.), from reading materials in the first or second language, and from reasoning and making inferences from the data in the text. These knowledge structures are called *schemata*.

3. In order to interpret the reading, new input information and existing schemata must be compatible and congruent to some extent; that is, elements from a previously internalized schemata would contain features found in the new schemata.

4. There are two basic modes of processing information: *bottom-up* and *top-down* processing.

5. In paragraphs or longer texts, schemata are hierarchically organized from most specific at the bottom to most general at the top. The topic sentence—generally the first sentence in the text—gives the reader an immediate clue to the major idea or concept in the paragraph. The reader will thus be able to fit the comments, details, and explanations found below the topic sentence to the subject being discussed. Top-down processing occurs as the mind (the mental organism) makes general predictions on higher conceptual levels and then searches the input for information to fill in the partially satisfied higher-order schemata. Top-down processing is called *conceptually driven*. Bottom-up processing is called *data-driven* since it occurs through the reader's recognition and perception of details and comments in the text.

6. Bottom-up and top-down processing should occur on all levels simultaneously. Top-down processing facilitates the assimilation of concepts and ideas if they are anticipated or consistent with the reader's conceptual expectations.

7. Bottom-up processing ensures that the reader will be sensitive to novel information, whereas top-down processing helps the reader resolve ambiguities, that is, select among alternative possible interpretations of the material being read.

8. The appropriate schemata must already exist and be activated during text processing (reading or listening).

What are some implications for teaching resulting from the above? I will merely outline them, as some will be familiar to you.

1. Prereading activities should have two purposes: (a) to build new background knowledge and (b) to activate existing background knowledge. These goals can be effected in several ways: (a) Teach about the topic of the text in L2 or L1 if necessary; (b) view and discuss movies, slides, filmstrips, or pictures; (c) look at the title and first paragraph and invite students to generate questions about the topic, asking you or other class members for responses or comments; (d) discuss new or difficult vocabulary with the students, giving numerous examples of its use in authentic contexts; (e) place the new words or concepts on the board and give several examples of them: (f) provide key word/key concept activities such as word association tasks (antonyms, synonyms, definitions, connotations, circumlocutions, paraphrases); (g) at the beginning and intermediate levels, give picture cues; and (h) intersperse questions on the text throughout the reading.

2. Other suggestions have been made to facilitate the reading process so as to permit eventual fluent reading. Here are a few from various sources.

a. Students in groups should discuss the title, language, difficulties in the first paragraph, and illustrations (if any).

b. Learners should attempt to determine the communicative intention of the writer. Is he or she *describing, comparing, defining, generalizing,* or *classifying?*

c. The teacher must help make the author's message comprehensible, accessible, and acceptable, using the techniques above.

d. Narrow reading, that is, reading about the same topic in a number of articles or texts, will enable the learners to become familiar with the vocabulary and with the concepts.

e. Learners' expectations, generated by preliminary discussion and other prereading activities, should be met. Have they been substantiated or violated in the text?

f. An innovative related theory is *frame theory,* similar to schema theory in some ways. Frame theory includes the study of background knowledge, the processing of information, and mental reasoning. We select from our memory store the frame which is closest to the situation in the text. The learners' and our knowledge is linguistic (phonological or morphosyntactic), extralinguistic (sociocultural values, attitudes, objective and subjective experiences), or metalinguistic (the reader can distinguish from his or her knowledge of L1 one kind of text from another, e.g., narrative, scientific).

g. Use a language experience approach in which you help learners create their own brief texts based on a real experience.

h. Material which is culture-specific will cause problems unless learners are given relevant cultural information.

I. Materials must be selected carefully if learners are to cope with them.

j. The learner needs motivation, the occasion to read, and material that is pleasurable to read.

In addition to predicting and processing reading material, there are two techniques the learners should be taught to use reasonably well before being launched into intensive or extensive reading: skimming and scanning. In skimming, the learners read through the material quickly (after prereading activities have been engaged in) in order to get the gist, the essence, a global comprehension of the passage. They should not look up any words or stop to ask the meaning of a word. I am assuming that difficult or special vocabulary or cultural allusions were clarified in the prereading phase. Several individual learners are asked to give one or more sentences which will give evidence of their global comprehension.

Learners can also be asked to scan the reading material (a text, a newspaper, a magazine) to find specific detailed information. For example, in looking at television or radio listings in a newspaper, you can ask, "On what channel (station) is 'The Suspect' on Tuesday, the . . .?"

Skimming and scanning, particularly when timed, will enable learners to become more fluent readers. It is important that you keep a record of the time they take to complete skimming and scanning activities and that you decrease it when you feel they are ready to cope with the increased speed that will be necessary for fluent reading.

READING AT ADVANCED LEVELS

Whether we expect learners to read material for special purposes (academic, scientific, technical, etc.) or for comprehension and enjoyment of a literary text, we must still ascertain whether they have internalized a basic core of English and whether they have a good grasp of the language system, of language use and usage, and of language and study skills for unlocking the meaning of the texts. Generally speaking, teaching English for specific purposes may be simpler. Books and articles usually contain numerous labeled illustrations and diagrams as well as a redundancy of lexicon and structure.

You will still have to clarify vocabulary items and place special emphasis on word order, morphological features (inflection and derivation, in particular), deictic features in the text (what pronouns refer to in preceding or following sentences), and cohesive devices (words like *first, next, then, in addition*) in the text. Such words become extremely important when a process, for example, is being illustrated.

Tasks which will help learners include skimming, scanning, giving synonyms and antonyms, outlining after taking notes on the material read, taking a cloze test in which they have to fill in morphological items, reordering facts, stating the referent of a part of speech (e.g., Pronoun X on Line O). If the books belong to the learners, it may be desirable to number every fifth line of the text in the left margin for ease in scanning. Other language development skills and group discussions (with groups of three or four students) that should precede the activities listed above are the following: (a) transferring the text material to a grid, (b) completing a questionnaire, (c) outlining, (d) summarizing, and (e) giving oral, sequential reports before the entire class in order to receive feedback.

We have already touched upon the learners' need to be familiar with the language system, its use, and reading and study skills. Whereas the language system and its use remain the same, the reading and study skills may have to be modified, depending upon the genre. Are we reading a poem, a short story, a play, a novel, a biography, or an autobiography? The criterion for selection (if you have a choice) is that the text must be capable of arousing emotional reactions in the learners. The focus will be on the theme, the plot, the characters, and the narrator's point of view. Some questions that you might want to explore with the students are the following: Are there conflicts in the plot? What brings about the climax? Does the main character change because of the events? What is the narrator's point of view? Why do you think this work has become a classic? (Point out the universality of the situation over the centuries if such is the case.)

What are the broad steps in the study of a piece of literature?

1. Before reading: introducing the topic, clarifying the difficult (new) vocabulary and cultural allusions, predicting what may happen

2. First reading by the teacher

3. Skimming

4. Reading a passage intensively

5. Answering direct and inferential questions

6. After reading: writing a summary and answering questions (Would you have acted in the same way? Why? Why not?)

Some tasks would include finding synonyms and antonyms, as well as finding and analyzing collocations (e.g., nouns and adjectives which are generally found together in a literary text).

To develop the students' capacity for imaginative, creative thinking, after the analysis of the literary text, ask questions such as: Did any character in the work stir a response in you? Why? Did you find anything in the work that you could call beautiful, ugly, or repulsive?

SOME DETAILED TECHNIQUES*

1. For judging recognition and comprehension of vocabulary:

   a. Choosing from among three or four words the one that has the same meaning as the one given

   b. Choosing from among three or four words the one that has the opposite meaning of the one given

   c. Indicating whether pairs of words are synonyms or antonyms

   d. Giving the negative prefix of a list of words

   e. Completing a sentence with the correct negative word

   f. Completing tables of words, for example,

Noun	Verb	Adjective	Adverb
ability	to be able to	able	ably

   g. Choosing a sentence from among three which illustrates the same use of the italicized word, for example, He *spared* the prisoner.

     i. I cannot spare the money now.

     ii. Use the food sparingly.

     iii. We must spare the women.

   h. Using contextual clues, indicate the synonym (from among three given) of the italicized word in a sentence.

   i. Using words in original sentences.

2. For judging and giving practice in sentence structure:

   a. Using the appropriate preposition in a sentence, for example, He lives _____ Main Street.

---

*Some of these methods were suggested in an article by William Norris in *English Teaching Forum*, September 1971, pp. 6–13.

    b. Completing a paragraph using appropriate words. (Every fifth or sixth word can be deleted. These may be nominals, prepositions, conjunctions, etc.)

3. For judging sentence comprehension:

    a. Completing a sentence using one of four words given, for example, He's used to a spacious house. This place is too _____ (*large, cramped, old, modern*).

4. For ensuring comprehension of the entire selection:

    a. Giving an outline of the text when sentences are given out of order.

    b. Using comprehension questions.

        i. Indicating whether a statement is true or false.

        ii. Choosing the correct word to complete a sentence.

        iii. Asking *wh* questions.

        iv. Formulating *wh* questions, either when specific parts of the sentence are italicized or when they are not.

        v. Asking questions with *or*.

        vi. Asking questions which will force students to make inferences, for example, How do you think _____ felt about that? Why?

        vii. Asking questions to elicit the students' viewpoint, for example, What do you think should have been done?

THE STAGES IN READING GROWTH

We have talked about the process of reading. Let us talk now about the stages in the teaching and learning of reading. There are several stages, and they should be followed wherever possible.

Stage I. Students read material they have learned to say very well* or material they have memorized. This may be a dialogue, a series of action sentences, a simple story of an experience the class members have had and which they have discussed, or model sentences containing some of the structures taught.

    You will have the students say the known material without looking at it. Then you will read the material aloud as the students look at it. They can read in chorus after you.† Next, you may ask groups and individuals to read it.

Stage II. You and/or a group of English teachers in the school combine the known words and structures to make a different dialogue or paragraph. The students are helped to read this newly organized material in which all the elements are familiar to them.

Stage III. The students start to read material in which some of the words and struc-

---

    *This might not be true for students whose only immediate interest is the translation of scientific material, for example.

    †The number of times this is done depends on the students' age, ability, and so on.

tures are unfamiliar to them. A committee of teachers can write this type of material, or existing texts with a low vocabulary and structure level, but at an interest level in harmony with the age of the students, may be used. Experimentation has shown that students experience little or no difficulty when one new word is interspersed among about thirty familiar words. Often grammar texts contain paragraphs and selections which are suitable for reading at this level. A detailed technique for teaching reading at Stage III will be explained below.

Stage IV. Some people recommend the use of simplified classics or magazines. There are others who object to the use of simplified texts on the grounds that they do not convey the style or the spirit of the author. I have found excellent simplified books on the market, however, which can be used to great advantage with students who are still not advanced enough to read the originals. The technique used for teaching this simplified or adapted material will be the same as the one for Stage III outlined below.

Stage V. Unlimited material. The whole world of books should be open to your students.

When do learners reach Stage V? Some may never reach it, as they would not reach it in their native language. Some may reach it after a six-year program in junior and senior high school. Some may reach it after one or two years of university training. All the factors in learning which we have stated several times must be considered in discussing the mastery of this skill, as of any other.

A PROCEDURE

You may wish to use the following procedures in teaching reading at Stages III and IV:

1. Divide the reading for the day into two or three sections so that you can vary your techniques.

2. Motivate the reading. Relate it to the pupils' own experiences, or if the reading is part of a longer story, relate it to the longer story.

3. State the purpose of the reading. "What do you think will happen? Let's find out" or "Let's read more about. . . ."

4. Deal with any difficulties in the first portion. Place (or have placed beforehand) the new words on the board. Say them; have the students say them after you. Explain them in the ways we have mentioned. You may even wish to give a short summary of the reading portion, weaving in the words on the board. (This is the most interesting way.)

5. After the difficulties have been clarified, you may do several things: You may use Technique A (below) for the three portions of the day's reading; or you may use Technique B for the three portions; or you may use ABA or BAB. When you first start Stage III reading with your students, it is desirable to use A for most of the reading.

Technique A. Read each line aloud and ask simple questions about each one. Make sure the answer is on the printed page.* At the end of the paragraph, ask for a summary (with various students contributing ideas). Use of the exact words of the text will minimize the possibility of errors. If the summary is difficult, ask questions to help your students summarize.

Technique B. Read the portion aloud; then ask the students to read it silently. (Time the reading.) After they have read, ask them questions; or have them complete sentences which you have placed on the board (use multiple-choice or cued responses); or ask them if statements you make are true or false (if they are false, they are to give the true answer); or ask for a summary.

6. Ask for a complete summary of the day's reading.

7. Now you may want to do one of several things:

a. Distribute four or five sequential questions you have prepared. Have one student read a question, another answer it, and another place it on the board. When all the answers are on the board, correct any mistakes with class cooperation† and *then* read them. The students can read them in chorus after you.

b. Read the selection, one sentence at a time, and have the class read in chorus after you. The importance of reading aloud in order to teach word stress cannot be mentioned often enough. This is particularly true when dealing with words which are spelled the same but may have different grammatical functions in the utterance, for example, *désert* (noun), *desért* (verb); *cóntract* (noun), *contráct* (verb).

c. Have the new words (see Step 4) used in other sentences.

d. Do word study drills with the students, for example, Find a synonym of . . . in Line 1. Make a noun from the word. . . .

e. Have the students formulate questions about the story which they will ask their classmates to answer. (Place question words—*who, what, when, where, how, how much,* and so on—on the board to help them, if necessary.)

One other word should be said about reading. You may wish at the intermediate or advanced level to assign supplementary reading to your more able students. Suggest books in their areas of interest and give them sufficient time to read a book. (You may wish to assign different parts of the same book, or books with different points of view, to several students.) Give them the opportunity to tell you and their classmates what they have read. Make the supplementary reading the stimulus for discussion and free communication.

---

*The question of having books opened or closed is also controversial. If time permits, have students close their books while you read the first time. Have the books open during your second oral reading. (Vary your techniques.) But remember that *reading* means looking at printed material. Reading should be distinguished from practice in listening comprehension.

†See the procedure for correction in the next section.

Writing

The fourth and last of the communications skills we help develop in our students is writing. When we say *writing*, we mean primarily the carefully guided marks on paper that we assist our students in making unless we are teaching a course in creative writing or advanced composition.

We lead them through several stages over a long period of time—the length depending, as usual, on their age, interests, capacities, needs—to a freer stage where they are able to write a composition or essay on a topic of interest.

Specialists in the field of second language teaching and learning usually recommend that in secondary schools this freer type of composition be deferred until the middle of the third year. At the university level it may well come in the middle of the second year.

Naturally, the type of writing system (alphabet, picture) which exists in the native language is an important factor in determining the ease of speed with which students learn to write. Some students may have to learn an entirely new writing system.

SOME OF YOUR RESPONSIBILITIES

Progressively, and in small steps, you should teach students

1. The sound-spelling correspondences
2. The mechanics of writing (punctuation, capitalization, spelling)
3. Letter writing, formal and informal (greetings, endings, other mechanics)
4. Practical, functional writing needed for note taking, outlining, summarizing
5. The organization and expression of an idea which will convey its desired meaning and permit the reader to understand the message
6. The differences (where such exist) between speaking and writing, between informal and more formal styles of writing, and between modes of discourse.

In English, for example, we generally contract and elide sounds in speech but we do not necessarily do so in writing. The vocabulary we use may differ depending on the message we are attempting to convey and the person(s) to whom we are addressing the message. (These variations have been termed *registers*, as you know.)

There are two major types of writing, both overlapping: practical and creative. Practical writing is found in letters as well as in outlines, summaries, and a series of notes; creative writing is found in literature. Many of your students will never write creatively, as they would not in their native tongue, but creativity, where observed or suspected, should be encouraged and carefully nurtured. *All* students can be taught to express their ideas clearly and correctly.

Students should be helped to recognize and to use different modes of discourse. The mode may be narrative, expository, critical, or a combination of these.

Any of these modes may be found in letters, dialogues, poems, essays, or plays.

Writing has been characterized as written thinking. Students should be encouraged to express their ideas, experiences, thoughts, and feelings. Any free or creative writing they are required to do should have a content in harmony with their evolving interests.

The ideas may be suggested by you directly but, better still, they should result from many experiences and oral discussions which you will provide. When this is feasible, students should listen to recordings of music, plays, or speeches. They should look at and discuss works of art; they should examine pictures for details of color, shape, and form; they should view films, slides, and filmstrips; they should read material in many fields of interest; they should listen to talks and lectures by guest speakers. They should work with peers in pairs and groups, adding to each others' ideas and revising them constantly.

A FEW GENERAL CONSIDERATIONS

Before discussing several types of writing activities which give practice in correctness and which help lead to creativity, let me mention a few general considerations.

- Little or no writing should be practiced in class.* Class time should be devoted to listening and speaking, that is, to activities which the students cannot do by themselves outside of class. (It goes without saying that with students who are not accustomed to alphabet writing, some class time may be devoted to the holding of paper, pen, and pencil and to the writing of the alphabet. This need be done only when writing is introduced, however.)
- Occasionally dictations and simple aural comprehension exercises should be done in class. Procedures for giving these will be explained below.
- Writing should reinforce the structural and lexical items which have been taught, as well as the listening, speaking, and reading skills.
- All writing done by students, whether at home or in class, should be corrected as quickly as feasible.
- The correction of written work need not be a heavy chore for the teacher. The next section offers some suggestions for checking written work.

CORRECTING WRITTEN WORK

Homework

1. Permit students who have not done their homework to tell you so *before* you start your regular lesson.

---

*Any writing of rules—paradigms, charts, dialogues, and so on, from a chart or blackboard— should be done during a *specific* period of time (preferably toward the end of the lesson). Anything else slows down the lesson considerably and may lead to behavior problems.

2. If you wish, with young students, assign the first person in each row to check whether homework has been done.

3. If chalkboard space permits, send two or three (or more) of your more able students to place a designated segment of their completed homework on the board.

4. When all the work has been placed on the board, ask another able student to go to the board and to ask his classmates questions such as "Is there an error in Line 1?" "Who sees a mistake?" The student will cross out the incorrect word and write the correct word above it. While this is being done, you may walk around the room to make sure the students are correcting the work in their notebooks.

5. When the work has been completely corrected, ask still another student to read it from the board.

6. If time permits, have several students read the corrected work from their notebooks.

Dictation and Aural Comprehension Exercises

1. Use Steps 3, 4, and 5 above, or

2. Have students exchange papers with their neighbors. Follow the procedure for correction outlined above.

Free Compositions

1. Ask your students to leave a one- or two-inch margin on the left-hand side of their papers.

2. Have them divide this margin into four columns. The first will be Sp (spelling), the second P (punctuation), the third Str (structure), and the fourth V (vocabulary).

3. When you collect the compositions, perhaps once every two weeks, merely *underline* the error and *place a check* on the appropriate line in the appropriate column. See the accompanying figure.

Sp.	P.	Str.	✓	Composition
✓		✓		*My freind he comed to my*
	✓			*house yesterday. He said do you*
✓	✓	✓✓		*need to come to movie. She's a*
	✓	✓		*a good picture. We could to go*
✓				*now and be bak in time to get*

4. You may wish, on a ten-point scale, to deduct one quarter-point for each error, or you may deduct one half-point for structure and one quarter-point for vocabulary, and so on. You may prefer, if ideas are important, to give two points for ideas. (If you think four ideas are necessary, give one half-point for each.) In later stages, and if you have given practice in word study, you may also wish to give one or two points for richness and variety of vocabulary.

5. Have the students rewrite the composition and return the original and corrected copies to you, within a reasonable time.

Guided Writing Activities*
What are some of the guided writing activities which lead to correctness and ease in writing? Students may

    1. Write out in full the pattern practice sentences they have practiced orally. Say, for example, "Use the words in the list to write sentences like Sentence 1."

I went to the store.
I went to the library.

    2. Write out in full a number of pattern practice sentences using elements from each group. Say, "Write ten sentences using any word from each column." (It is important to choose words carefully so that the combinations will be logical.)

I	bought	a	pen.
John	wanted	a	pencil.
Mr. Jones	found	a	notebook.
The boy	paid for	a	ruler.

When your students reach the stage of conscious selection, prepare columns which will force them to choose appropriate items from each of the columns, for example, "Make five sentences using these words":

The boy	drank	the bread.
The old woman	ate	his dinner.
The man	threw away	the milk.

    3. Change the sentences in a known dialogue, short paragraph, or series of action sentences in the following way:

a. Change the subject. (The name of the person or pronoun.)
b. Change the subject and verb to the plural.
c. If the subject and verb are plural, change them to singular.
d. Change by adding *yesterday* or *later* or *tomorrow*.

    *For other suggestions, see Chapter 5.

e. Change the point of view of the paragraph, for example, "I went to the movies. I liked the film. The hero was excellent" to: "I went to the movies. I didn't like the film. The hero was terrible."

4. Add to a known related dialogue using newly learned structures and vocabulary.

5. Answer a series of specific questions on any activity or on a reading passage. (Wherever possible, the questions should be in a logical sequence.)

6. Complete a series of related sentences. The completed sentences will constitute a short composition. For example,

I went. . . .

. . .went with me.

The music was. . . .

We heard. . . .

After the concert, we went to. . . .

7. Write a summary of material which has been read.

8. Write an outline of material which has been read.

9. Write a letter (after the appropriate form has been taught and practiced) in which students expand the ideas you have given them. For example, "Write a letter to a friend. Tell him or her about the subjects you are studying, the ones you enjoy, your plans for the future. Ask about his or her plans."

10. Write an original ending to a story which the students have read.

11. Write an ending to a story they have not yet completed reading or hearing.

12. Write simple dialogues using (recombining) known structures.

13. Complete a dialogue after the first few lines have been given.

14. Prepare a narrative paragraph from a dialogue. This activity, as the next, will require much teacher guidance and patience. (Many similar sentences should be changed to indirect discourse and linked together with appropriate connectors over a long period of time in preparation for this activity.

15. Prepare a dialogue from a narrative paragraph.

16. Reconstruct a dialogue from one or two words given in each utterance.

17. Reconstruct a passage in which every fifth (or sixth) word has been omitted (a cloze procedure).

Other writing activities—many of them combined with listening, speaking, and reading activities—will also be found effective in preparing students for the freer writing which we hope many of our language learners will be able to engage in. You may find one or more of the suggestions below helpful to your students.

Ask the entire class, small groups, or individuals, as the need arises, to

1. Combine clauses or sentences using connectors such as *and, but, although, unless.* (Two sentences only should be combined at first, then three, then four, etc.) Needless to say, you should give extensive practice with each connector before students are asked to choose from among them.

2. Use connectors between sentences or paragraphs such as *on the other hand, nevertheless, however, furthermore, similarly,* and so on.

3. Transform base sentences to note the different stylistic effects possible through various transformation rules.

4. Proofread paragraphs you will compose or that students have written containing mechanical errors, inappropriate vocabulary items, or incorrect structure. (These may be shown on a wall or screen or they may be duplicated for distribution.)

5. Take dictation. (A procedure will be suggested below.)

6. Take notes on a reading passage. Learners will need extensive help in determining what the key words are.

7. Do a listening comprehension exercise in which the answers are to be written. (A procedure will be suggested below.)

8. Add an explanation or appropriate details to a statement that you give.

9. Place a series of sentences in a logical sequence. This may follow reading and oral discussion.

10. Study a model paragraph several times in order to note the central thought, the connecting words, the transitional sentences, the details explaining the topic sentences, or the sequence of steps.

11. Supply the missing words in a model paragraph which has been studied.

12. Paraphrase a model paragraph substituting not only individual words but also structures and phrases. (These words may be supplied by you, or the students may be expected to recall them from previous learning activities.)

13. Write a paragraph based on a model but on a different topic suggested by you (using the same organization and structures).

14. Memorize carefully chosen sentences or brief paragraphs.

15. Reconstruct a paragraph using key words which you will supply.

16. Rewrite a paragraph using a different register or style (more formal or colloquial, etc.).

17. Learn symbols for numbers, punctuation, weights, measures.

18. Learn frequently used abbreviations.

You might want to try the following writing activities:

1. Give students a polysyllabic word such as *architecture*. Have them make as many shorter words as they can from it.

2. Write (or have written) paragraphs which contain no punctuation marks. Ask learners working in pairs to write them in.

3. Write (or have written) paragraphs with morphosyntactic errors. Have them corrected by students working in pairs.

4. Have students keep journals about incidents that happen during the day and their reactions to them.

5. Have students write movie, television, or book reviews.

6. Ask students to write resumes about themselves (including their skills, special talents, likes, and dislikes, and a short biographical sketch).

7. To develop imaginative thinking, write three "emotional" words on the board, for example, *love, hate, joy*. Have students list specific ideas which these words suggest to them.

8. Have a group write a brief story in informal or colloquial language (slang). Have another group transpose it to more formal language.

9. Supply a brief thought-provoking sentence, for example, "I wish I had known about it." Ask each student to write for three minutes and then pass the page on to another student who will add to it for three minutes (five students can start working on the same sentence).

10. Have students answer an ad describing an interesting job offer.

11. Have students brainstorm in order to write words under any category from "things in a kitchen" to "being poor."

Freer Writing

As noted above, this is a much more difficult activity. Students normally need a great deal of help before they can be asked to go home and write a composition. As we all know, such an assignment often causes panic even when writing in one's native tongue.

The following prewriting steps are essential:

1. Select a topic. (The students may help suggest a topic based on something of interest which has occurred or is about to occur.) Place the title on the board (top center) and divide the board in thirds.

2. Engage in oral discussion of the topic. Have students give several ideas that should be included. (Have an able student under your direction list these on the left third of the board as they are suggested.)

3. Discuss with the students a *logical* sequence of ideas. Have the ideas listed in Column 2 (with adequate space between them) in the sequence in which they will be written.

4. Next to each idea, write in Column 3 the communicative expressions, structures, idioms, and vocabulary items needed to write about each. Some items will be suggested by the students; some may have to be supplied by you.

   a. Pronounce the new words.

   b. Give numerous examples of each structure or communicative expression.

   c. Give brief pattern practice when time permits (I enjoy boating; I enjoy fishing; I enjoy swimming; etc.) using pictures, words, and so on. (The important thing is to get to the writing.)

5. Have individual students compose a few sentences about each idea. When this has been done, you may wish to ask the students to write the first paragraph. As the students write, you may quietly look at several papers and ask one or two students to read to the entire class a paragraph which you consider a good model.

Give the students several days to write the composition at home. Tell them not to expect the corrected material before a week. After the compositions are corrected in the manner indicated earlier in this chapter, or any other you prefer, ask the students to make the corrections and return the compositions to you.

Before leaving the subject of writing, there are some additional matters which should be mentioned:

1. In order to assist your students in developing a rich vocabulary and more ideas, you may wish to reinforce through writing some of the techniques we mentioned under reading—broaden their experiences by having them listen to music, look at paintings, or discuss ideas found in books. Give them practice in paraphrasing sentences. Give them synonyms for simple, overworked words like *said* (exclaimed, stated, observed, cried, shouted, etc.).

2. Give, at least once a week, *short dictations*, first on familiar material and then on combined new and familiar material. After you have motivated your students and explained all of the difficulties, dictate the material at *normal* speed. Then dictate the material again but more slowly and in logical breath groups. Have students write during this second dictation. (One or two students may write on the back or side board or even on the front board.) Say the material again at normal speed. Give the students one or two minutes to look over their papers before correcting the material in one of the ways suggested previously.

Some teachers prefer to indicate punctuation marks during the second or third readings. Others feel that students ought to learn to write punctuation marks by listening to the rise and fall of the voice.

The skill of transferring spoken intonation to written punctuation marks has to be specifically taught and practiced. Transfer of learning does not normally occur automatically.

If you have time and appropriate facilities, you may wish to prepare copies of paragraphs for dictation* leaving blank spaces in various places. Then students (at the second reading) will write on their separate answer paper only the words that are missing.

3. *Aural comprehension* exercises also provide excellent practice in understanding and writing. The paragraph chosen for this activity should be short and, if possible, should represent a complete idea about which you can ask four or five questions, the answers to which can be taken word for word (or nearly so) from the paragraph.

The procedure for conducting an aural comprehension activity is as follows:

a. Motivate by giving a brief summary.

b. Clear up any difficulties.

c. State your aim and the procedure you will follow.

d. Read the paragraph through twice at normal speed.

*This is generally termed *spot dictation*.

e. Read a question twice. Give the students the opportunity to write the answer. (One or two students may write on the board.)

f. Continue until you have given all the questions.

g. Read the paragraph again at normal speed.

h. Read the questions again at normal speed.

i. Give the students one or two minutes to check their own work.

j. Correct the material in one of the ways suggested before.

4. *Dicto-comps*, as the name implies, are a combination of dictation and composition. Here is a possible procedure:

a. Select two or three sequential paragraphs on a topic of interest.

b. Motivate the topic by relating it to a familiar experience.

c. Clarify any difficulties by writing words and expressions on the board. (You may leave the words on the board, particularly the first few times you use the technique.)

d. Read the paragraphs aloud four or five times.

e. Ask your students to reconstruct the paragraphs sequentially using the words they remember in them. (Permit them to look at the words on the board.)

f. For checking, either distribute a sheet on which the paragraphs appear or use a device to show them on a screen. If the paragraphs will be used later, you may wish to write them on a chart which can be used for such activities as choral recitation, structure and word study, and especially, as a model for the composition of paragraphs on a related theme. For example, a dicto-comp on a trip to the mountains can be rewritten (with new words given, of course) as a trip to the seaside.

5. A cloze test that can be given in several ways: (a) Any class of word can be omitted. (It is best not to indicate the first letter nor the length of the word by dashes. This would inhibit learners who cannot recall an appropriate word beginning with the letter or containing the number of letters asked for.) (b) Concentrate on one word class only, for example, definite articles, subordinators, adverbs, or verbs, or on aspects. (c) Omit every fifth to seventh word.

It is important to underscore again that any of the procedures noted above can and should be modified according to your students' needs and interests. For example, in saying the dictation the second time (in logical breath and writing groups), you may have the students say the words aloud *before* writing them. Listening to you, followed by their oral repetition and feedback, will undoubtedly be of help to them as they write the words.

No procedure given in this book or in any other book should be considered immutable. As we said above, needs, modalities of learning, and the interests of *your* students should always be taken into consideration in selecting and conducting any activity.

WRITING BEYOND THE SENTENCE

If we were to sum up the important characteristics of writing beyond the sentence, that is, of paragraphs or longer essays, we would have to include both the concepts of *coherence*—what used to be called informational or logical sequence—and of *cohesion*. Lexical items which produce coherence and cohesion in English are many, as are the activities which exemplify and reinforce them, such as (1) telling a story and asking for a summary in the sequence in which it was told. Questions like "Then what happened?" and "What happened before that?" help learners to develop coherence; and (2) asking learners to explain a recipe or instructions about how to put an object or a toy together. This will also force them to adhere to a logical sequence.

Cohesive devices are numerous and can be practiced in multiple-choice activities and in cloze procedures or pointed out in reading or listening activities. Following is a brief list of terms used to produce cohesion. These connectors can be used to link clauses, sentences, or paragraphs to indicate

Addition—and, furthermore, moreover, in addition

Cause and effect—because, since, so that, in order to

Condition—if, provided that, unless

Contrast—but, although, however, on the other hand, even though

Exemplification—for example, for instance, such as

Restatement—in other words, namely

Time—when, before, after, while, then

Conclusion—to sum up, in conclusion, to put it briefly.

Developing Cultural Insights

And now, what are some of the ways in which cultural insights can be provided? Any one of the techniques noted below and, preferably, a combination of them should be used. They are listed in no particular order. Some are possible at every learning level. Some, such as the reading of literary masterpieces, will be possible only at the fourth or fifth level, if at all.

1. The classroom should reflect the culture of the English-speaking world. (This is possible, we realize, only when one or more rooms in the school are set aside for language instruction.)

a. At the beginning levels, parts of the room may be labeled in English.

b. Maps and posters of English-speaking countries should be attractively displayed.

c. A bulletin board should include newspaper or magazine clippings of current events (taken from either English or native language sources), advertisements, comic strips, proverbs, pictures, songs, and music.

d. A display case or a table may contain objects related to English culture such as a collection of dolls, money, stamps, menus, costumes, and other artifacts.

e. A library corner should contain books and magazines in English at the reading and interest levels of the students. Books in the curriculum areas used in English-speaking schools are of particular interest to students. There should also be books about English-speaking countries written in the students' native language. Wherever possible, a piece of literature in English and its equivalent in the students' native language should be provided.

It is also informative to have books written by nonnative English speakers. What is their view of us? Why? If it is unfavorable, could it be changed? How?

Newspapers, where available, can be a source of study for format, style, point of view, attitude towards others.

The magazines should be on sports, adventure, science, romance, and anything else that is of interest to the students and which will motivate them to learn the language while developing cultural awareness.

f. A record player and records of contemporary music or folk songs should be available for frequent use.

2. Individuals and groups of students should carry out projects related to English-speaking culture which will then serve for class reporting and discussion. The projects may include the collection or creation of

a. Maps—physical, economic, geographic—showing the relation of English-speaking countries to the one in which you are teaching; the location of important cities, monuments, and places of interest; regions where natural resources are found or certain foods produced; and areas which are the setting for well-known literary masterpieces.

b. Itineraries for actual trips to pertinent places of interest in the community or for trips to English-speaking lands.

c. Floor plans of houses and other buildings—with appropriate labels.

d. Menus of food eaten on special occasions.

e. Calendars indicating special holidays.

f. Question-answer games or quiz programs.

g. Word study materials [English words and expressions in the native tongue, native words and expressions in English, common word origins (where feasible, of course)].

h. An English language newspaper.

i. A scrapbook (current events, art, science, etc.).

j. Filmstrips or picture series.

k. A play reading.

l. An original skit or playlet.

m. A book fair.

n. Forms, documents, and other pertinent materials related to commerce and industry between English-speaking countries and the country in which you are teaching.

3. The culture of English speakers may be studied and experienced in:

a. An assembly program (songs, dances, backdrops, talks).

b. A festival to which community members are invited.

c. Songs and dances which are heard and learned.

4. Audiovisual equipment and the language laboratory should be used for:

a. Listening to recitals or readings by contemporary authors.

b. Viewing filmstrips, videotapes, and films on any aspect of English-speaking culture.

c. Listening to spoken descriptions of museum materials as students view works of art or artifacts.

d. Seeing short films or videotapes of interviews with people in the news.

e. The use of video is highly recommended, but unfortunately it is not generally available overseas.

5. Masterpieces of literature should be read and studied (adapted when necessary), since a real work of literature reflects, as perhaps no other art form or material, the character of the people, the situations in which people interact, the historical or geographical rationale for their behavior, the values to which people are attached—in short, the entire gamut of the values, customs, and beliefs included in the term *culture*.

Moreover, the study of a literary masterpiece permits discussion of linguistic style and aesthetics and perhaps of language registers, dialects, and idiolects which no other art form can exemplify as well.

Although this is a controversial issue, I am convinced that a good translation of a masterpiece is better than not exposing students to English literature at all.

6. The possibility of correlation with other areas in the curriculum should be explored continuously. For example, the relationship between the study of the native tongue and English can be emphasized through the study of plays, stories, and films which are translated and shown in your country or in the English-speaking community.

The music department in your school, if one exists, will be delighted to cooperate with you and your students as they learn about any outstanding composers and their works or as they learn the songs and dances of the English-speaking world. The social studies department will welcome your support in discussions of the interrelationships of governments in world economy, production, imports, exports, and so on. The impact of geography and history on the culture of any society would be a fruitful field of correlation between the social studies and English departments.

7. Resource people should be invited to speak to the class on cultural topics. If the talk is in English, it would be desirable to ask the speaker to explain important words or to show visual materials to clarify his topic. His delivery (gestures, distance maintained, facial expressions, use of certain expressions, intonation) will still be helpful to the students whether or not they understand everything. You can videotape the presentation, if possible.

If the visit is preceded by a letter of invitation and followed by a letter of thanks, the authentic formulas used in letter writing (including the writing of dates, numbers, salutations, closing remarks, etc.) will be another example of cultural knowledge the students will acquire.

8. A pen pal project should be initiated very soon after the students learn to write. The first letter need not be elaborate but may simply indicate: "My name is so and so. I'm sending you a picture. I go to X school. Please write to me." Appropriate headings and closing should be used, of course. Sources of pen pals are International Friendship League, 40 Mt. Vernon Street, Boston, Massachusetts; Letters Abroad, 18 East 60th Street, New York, New York; World Pen Pals, University of Minnesota, Minneapolis, Minnesota.

9. Teachers of art, science, and social studies may give brief lectures in the native language. You can then engage the class in oral activities in English related to the topic.

10. Last, but most essential, you can give a twenty-minute illustrated lecture in English on any cultural topic, followed by questions and a summary.

Summary

In summary, I would like to emphasize again several premises on which the development of communication is based:

1. The sequence in which the four skills are taught is listening, speaking, reading, writing. The first approach to language should be through the ear. Students should be asked to read only the material they can say with *reasonable* fluency.

2. The principal aim of any lesson may be the development of only *one* skill, but there will be necessary overlapping with other skills. For example, we usually speak after listening or reading. We may write as a result of listening or reading.

3. Since it is impossible to teach all the sounds, communicative expressions, or structures at one time, we should hold our students to a higher degree of correctness *only* for those features of language which we have practiced intensively. Let us assume we have practiced intensively only the sound /I/. In teaching "What's this," we should expect only reasonably good imitations of "What's" and of /ð/ and /s/, but a more correct production of /I/.

4. Within each of the skills, attention must be given to the sound system, communicative functions, the structure system, and the vocabulary.

5. In the beginning stages of language learning, the teacher's role is to have the students reproduce correct responses which he or she has modeled and to help students make carefully cued substitutions or transformations. Creativity or improvisation before the students are ready will cause unnecessary errors which necessitate an expenditure of time for correction and eradication and will result in frustration.

6. As soon as possible and with every technique or tool at our command, our students must be made to feel and see the relationship between each of the separate language features and each of the separate skills within the total act of communication. They should be enabled to understand and to use in English the normal forms of speech they would use in their native tongue. They should, in addition, be enabled and motivated to develop further the basic skills of reading and writing which we have initiated.

7. No skill is developed without continuous and intensive practice. No skill can be maintained unless it is used frequently. The planning for continuous and intensive practice in which the material which has been taught is constantly *reintroduced* and *consolidated* with known material is one of the major responsibilities of the teacher of English as a second or foreign language.

8. Communicative competence—the primary objective of the majority of English as a second or foreign language programs—will result from our efforts to give learners opportunities for practice which will ensure accuracy, fluency, and appropriateness in a variety of social situations.

9. Since language reflects the culture of English speakers, students should be given insight into habits, customs, and values which are similar to or different from their own. It is imperative, however, that they appreciate that *all* people have culture and that there are no ''good'' or ''bad'' cultures. It is essential that the learners retain pride in their own cultures as they move toward acceptance of the language and culture of native English speakers.

10. Cultural insights are acquired incidentally as students dramatize conversations, using not only different varieties of language but also the appropriate gestures, expressions, and distances which duplicate those of a native speaker. They are acquired also as a result of the learners' group activities and your direct teaching of the values, beliefs, art forms, and literature of English speakers.

Most important is that learners develop an appreciation of *cultural pluralism* and *global understanding*. No one of us can be ''an island unto himself.'' We each need the cooperation and humanity of our fellows to remain human.

For Review and Discussion

1. With a partner or a group, discuss several ways of approaching different facets of the language system (e.g., communicative functions, structures, specific notions).

2. What are the six basic steps needed to present and practice a language item? With a group of five others, prepare microdemonstrations of each successive step using the same language item.

3. Explain several ways of presenting and giving practice in the sound system.

4. Give microdemonstrations (preceded and followed by discussion), teaching one sound or two contrasting sounds.

5. What four steps are needed to comprehend an utterance or a passage?

6. What is the difference between short-term and long-term memory?

7. List several techniques which will help learners interpret (decode) oral input or a written text.

8. Give the basic steps in presenting a language item—from motivation to free communication.

9. What are the four elements of a descriptive rule of grammar? With a partner, select two grammatical (morphosyntactic) items and explain what you would elicit from your partner about each.

10. In a group, discuss at least ten recommendations about practicing oral drills you would make to new teachers.

11. What are the differences between a substitution and a replacement (restatement) drill?

12. With two other learners, demonstrate the three steps in a directed practice activity.

13. How does your school district feel about the use of translation? How do you feel about it? Does a translation question appear on end-of-term (or course) exams?

14. With a group, prepare a stimulus-response format for student interaction and a list of twenty topics that would be of interest to your students.

15. How and when would you correct student errors?

16. How would you present specific notions needed for production?

17. Share some communicative activities which have worked for you with other teachers.

18. Explain the schema theory in your own words.

19. List some techniques for ensuring reading comprehension.

20. Prepare tables of words (noun, verb, adjective, and adverb) and with a partner use each in sentences which clarify their meaning.

21. Discuss the differences between skimming and scanning in reading.

22. How would you teach reading at Stage III?

23. What must students know to read texts for English for special purposes or literary texts?

24. What are your responsibilities in teaching writing?

25. How could you correct written work (homework or a composition)?

26. How would you give a cloze test?

27. List ten ways in which you could develop cultural insights and cultural pluralism.

4

Materials and Techniques
of Instruction

Let us begin this chapter on teaching aids by reaffirming our belief that the teacher is the single most important factor in the teaching-learning process. There can be no question that given students with some interest in language learning, it is what we as teachers do—promoting a friendly environment in the classroom, creating and organizing materials, overcoming shortcomings in our textbooks, stimulating and maintaining interest through varied practice activities, emphasizing certain enjoyable aspects of language learning while minimizing other features—which will determine their growth toward communication.

In many instances, the desire to learn a new mode of communication can be fostered even in students who do not have a strong initial interest in language study. By the same token, alas, many students who approach the study of English with enthusiasm are often deflected by teachers who follow the textbook slavishly or who follow, in a mechanical manner, some of the learning steps we have outlined above.

There are so many devices and approaches which can supplement the textbook and often even the teacher's voice that it seems a pity for the alert teacher not to make use of them. In this section, therefore, I will indicate some of the materials and techniques which will help bring motivation into the language learning classroom. Let us start with *materials*.

Some Materials of Instruction

THE PICTURE FILE

Every classroom should contain a file of pictures which can be used not only to illustrate aspects of the sociocultural topics listed in Chapter 2, but also to give interesting, meaningful practice in the sounds, communicative expressions, structures, and vocabulary of English.

The file should contain three kinds of pictures: (1) pictures of individual persons and of individual objects, (2) pictures of situations in which people are "doing something" with objects and in which the relationship of objects and/or people can be seen, (3) a series of pictures (six to ten) on one chart. You may wish to create several of these charts, for example, one for count nouns (e.g., the objects in the classroom), one for mass nouns (e.g., food), one for count and mass nouns placed at random, one for words illustrating difficult consonant clusters without regard to count and mass, one for work activities, one for verbs which cannot add *ing*, one for verbs like *seem*, and many with four scenes depicting four situations which will enable pupils to create a sequential dialogue or an oral (and then written) narrative paragraph. An example will be found in Appendix II.

The file should contain *more than one picture* of individuals and of objects. This is necessary so that students will not assume that your finger touching the fender of a car, for example, indicates that *car* (the word you are teaching) and *fender* are synonyms. Many pictures of cars, pens, boys, women, or whatever you are teaching and, in addition, a sweeping movement of your hand over the entire picture will ensure the proper association of word and object or person.

What criteria should guide us in choosing or drawing pictures? Pictures should be large enough to be seen by all students. The pictures of individual objects or people should be as simple as possible. Some of them should be in color for later use when adjectives of color are presented. The pictures should have no captions* of any kind since you will want to use them at times to have students recall the association of word and object. Situational pictures should not have captions either. The same scene may serve as the basis for various oral discussions.

Some Uses

The pictures can be used in numerous ways. Individual pictures may be used of course to introduce and to test vocabulary items. Individual pictures can be used in pairs. For example, pictures of a boy and a bicycle can be used to teach structures such as:

> The boy goes to school by bicycle.
> How does the boy go to school?
> The boy is riding a bicycle.
> Does the boy go to school by bus?
> No. He usually goes by bicycle.

To give more varied practice, pictures of boys, girls, men, and women can be placed one behind the other, and pictures of means of transportation can also be stacked. With a student assistant who will help you flip the pictures, *double* substitutions can be made, for example,

---

*A caption, title, or brief description for your own use on the back of the picture will be helpful.

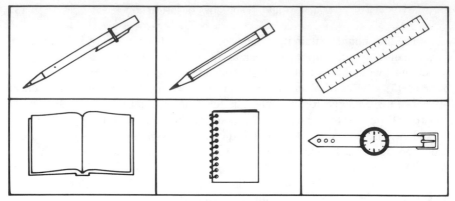

Count Nouns Chart

Mass Nouns Chart

Work Activities Chart

The girl goes by bus.

The woman goes by train.

Three individual pictures (or stacked individual pictures on rings) can be used in the same fashion, for example,

The boy went to the library by bus.

The girl went to the hospital by car.

The man went to the United States by plane.

The further use of individual pictures for testing purposes will be discussed in the next chapter.

Situational pictures are excellent for eliciting "real" language, "What do you see?" "What are they doing?" "Are they sad?" "Would you like to do that?" and any other structure (of age, weather, clothing, action) to which the picture lends itself can be practiced. If possible, situational pictures should be used to stimulate ideas for the freer compositions we discussed in the previous chapter.

Another very good use of situational pictures which you would have to create (very simple line drawings are all that is needed) would be the practice of complex sentences with *before, after,* and *while.* The pictures could show individuals doing something (eating, dressing, going to school or work, etc.). Each should contain a clock with an hour clearly marked. You can then practice patterns such as:

(He) (always) (eats) before (he goes out).*

(He) (ate) before (he) (went out).

Did (he) (go out) after (he ate)?

What did (he) do after (he ate)?

Another set could illustrate *while,* for example,

(He) was working while (she was sewing).

What was (she) doing while (he was working)?

A *series of pictures on a chart* will be extremely helpful in giving extensive practice in numerous structures with a limited *known* vocabulary. You may add variety to the "sameness" of the chart by pointing to the pictures in the order in which they appear, by pointing to them at random, or by having a student point to them in sequence or at random while you call on classmates to respond. You may also add other appropriate utterances.

Let us take as an example the chart containing pictures of a pen, a pencil, a ruler, a book, a notebook, a watch. Notice some of the possible patterns which can be practiced using the same chart at all levels of language learning. Please remember that you always give the pattern sentence several times first. The pattern should always be one which can be used logically with each picture on the chart.

---

*Notice that patterns indicating verb endings allow students to practice the three sounds /Z/, /S/, /IZ/.

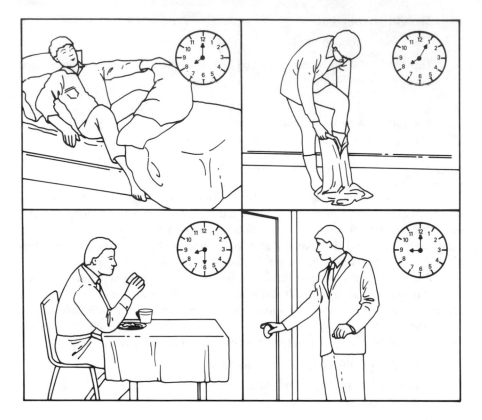

What's this? It's a (pen)*

This is a. . . . (If the students are *touching* the pictures.)

That's a. . . .

Is this a . . . ? Yes, it is.

   No, it isn't. It's a. . . .

What do you have?

   (I) (have) a. . . .

(Do) (you) have a . . . ? Yes, I do.

   No, I don't.

I have a . . . , a . . . , and a. . . .

Show us the. . . . That's the. . . .

May I have the (books)?

Where is the . . . ?

Where are the . . . ?

*Parentheses indicate that other words may be substituted.

I'd like several   I'm sorry. I don't have any.

How much is a . . . ? It's . . . cents.

I have a (new). . . .

My . . . is (new). I've just bought it.

The . . . is (on) the (desk).

The (girls) have a. . . .

There('s) a . . . (on) the (table).

I'm going to (buy) a. . . . Do you need one?

Please give (me) that. . . .

I'm buying a . . . now.

I (always) use a. . . .

Do you have any . . . ?

I have (some). . . . Do you?

I (bought) a. . . .

(He) gave (her) a. . . .

(This) . . . is (mine).

Did you (buy) a . . . ?

Let's not (buy) the (pens). I don't have enough money.

Don't (buy) a. . . .

The . . . is (new), isn't it?

The . . . isn't (new), is it?

I can (buy) a . . . , can't I?

I'm sure the . . . is (new).

If I had a . . . , I'd. . . .

If I had had a. . . , I could have. . . .

I'd like to (buy) a. . . .

May I see a more expensive . . . ?

Thank you for (bringing) the. . . .

And we could continue! Surprisingly enough, students do not get bored with the same vocabulary. If the pace is brisk, if the procedures are varied, and if they are saying correctly the new structures you are teaching, they will find pleasure and comfort in the familiar words.

Pictures can also be used to play games, to illustrate stories, and to do numerous other activities which will certainly occur to you as you use them.

Next to the pictures of objects, write other possible responses such as "I'll be happy (pleased) to" and "Sure, I'll be right back." And for regrets write, "I'm sorry. Not now. I'm watching (a soccer game, an auto race, etc.)." (Use whatever your students are interested in.)

On successive days, add sequence sentences to the requests and to the responses, for example, (to the request) "Can you go to the store," or (to the response) "I can go in a half-hour." Later on, the students can create their own requests and their own "happy" or regretful responses.

It is interesting and profitable to put a list of familiar verbs on the board (or have a learner write them or sketch them as other individual learners suggest them). Engage the class in paired practice. Depending on the learners' linguistic competence, the response could be "I like to study also" or "I do too."

Negative forms can be practiced with the same list of verbs (at least ten): "Harry doesn't like to. . . ." "I don't either." "Joe doesn't either." "Harry and Joe don't either." (Use names of classmates.)

Later in the week or the semester, learners can practice responses such as "Neither do I, and neither does Joe." "Neither do Harry and Joe."

Still later, with newly acquired or familiar learned items, learners working in pairs can create logical, meaningful sequence sentences appropriate to the situation, for example, "I don't like to swim either. I nearly drowned a year ago."

Learners can create situations using the verb list and others they may recall. Encourage sequence sentences and multiple responses.

CHARTS

Simple charts showing various grammatical relationships are extremely valuable. The use of verb tenses and verb phrases can be illustrated graphically by simple lines on a chart as below:

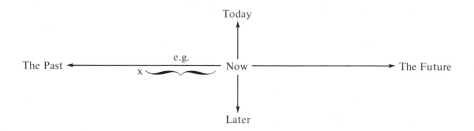

As you introduce a new verb phrase, point to a place or places on the chart in order to clarify the concept of time. You can also use lines, crosses, or any mark to show the time relationships involved, for example, Did an action started in the past continue into the present? (A bracket or brace would be appropriate.)

You will find other charts useful adjuncts many times during the year. Among these could be charts containing question words, prefixes or suffixes, and the Viëtor (vowel) triangle (See p. 59.)

FLASH CARDS OR WORD CARDS

Cards with individual words (either printed or handwritten) can be prepared and filed within the same categories and in the same order as the individual pictures. The cards should be about twelve inches long and four inches wide.

Younger children can be asked to match cards and pictures as soon as they can read. They can also match the cards with words written on the blackboard or on a large piece of cardboard.

The cards can serve as word cues in the oral substitution drills outlined in the preceding chapter. They can be used for review purposes ("Make your own sentence using this word") or in playing games. Many other uses will occur to you as you use them.

THE POCKET CHART

This simple teaching tool is an excellent device for dramatizing word order. It is easily made by taking a piece of cardboard or stiff paper (about two feet in length by about one foot in height) and pinning (stapling or gluing) to it two narrow pockets about two inches high.

Let us assume that you want to teach inverted question word order with the sentence "John is here." You will need six cards. One will say *John*, the second *is*, the third *here*, and the fourth *Is*; the fifth will contain a period, and the sixth a question mark. You will show *John is here*. The students will hear it and say it. Then you will remove *is*, move *John* to the new slot, place *Is* before *John*, and replace the period with the question mark. You can do this in the twinkling of an eye, of course.

Younger children particularly will enjoy going to the pocket chart themselves and making questions from statements, placing *not* or *don't* in sentences, or later changing questions to indirect questions or statements. For this last type of change, you would use the two pockets as follows: The question, for example, *Where is he?* is in Pocket 1. When you place or uncover *"Do you know" "I'm not sure,"* in Pocket 2, you will dramatize the change in word order in the second sentence by moving words from one slot to another.

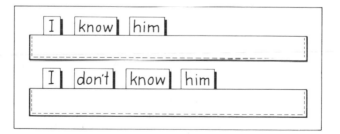

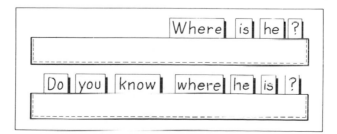

It may be desirable to have younger students make small individual pocket charts so that they can "manipulate" sentences at their seats as you or a student does so at the large pocket chart in the front of the room.

Basic words (forms of *be, do,* and *have*, frequency words, pronouns, names), punctuation marks, and so on, can be kept on individual cards in clearly marked envelopes for easy reference and for quick changes.

THE FLANNEL BOARD*

This inexpensively made device is excellent as still another way of presenting and practicing vocabulary and structures—expressions of place, for example. With younger students, it is useful in playing games or in dramatizing stories. All you need is a piece of the cheapest flannel glued, pinned, or thrown over a piece of wood or heavy cardboard about two feet long by two feet in height. (As a matter of fact, you may wish to make the pocket chart and flannel board of the same size, placing one on each side of a board or cardboard.)

Pictures or cutouts with a small piece of flannel glued to the back adhere easily to the flannel and permit the illustration and teaching of many concepts or structures. Let us assume that you want to teach some prepositions. You may do this with cutouts of plates and utensils. You or a student may place a plate in the center, a fork to the left, and a knife and spoon to the right. You can teach many function words and structures, such as:

The plate is in the center.

Put the knife (above) the plate.

Put the (plate) in the (upper) (righthand) corner.

Please remove the (plate).

You may teach *on, next to, under, above,* and so on, with a small piece of flannel cut out in the shape of a table and another piece of another color which can be placed on, under, etc., the table.

A use of the flannel board which has been popular in many countries is one in which I cut out the figure of a person from another piece of flannel: the head, ears, nose, mouth, eyes, neck, arms, body, legs. We've named it *Poor Jim*. Poor Jim serves to practice the names of parts of the body, words like *right* and *left*, and names of illnesses. (When a student points to "Jim's" stomach, for example, a classmate could say "Jim has a stomachache," if that is the pattern being practiced.) By pointing quickly to the figure, you can give students practice with other expressions such as sore throat (arm, leg).

Fairy-tales are more enjoyable for young students when some of the characters are placed dramatically on the flannel board and moved around as need be. (Try doing this with "Goldilocks and the Three Bears" some day, even with adult students.)

Another amusing way in which the flannel board can be used is as follows:

*A magnet board can be used in the same way.

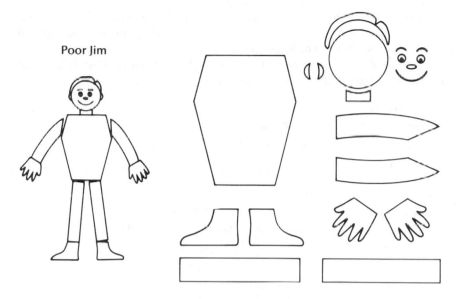

Poor Jim

Make a cutout of a house or a room or anything which lends itself to the game. Let us assume you have made a house. Two students will go to the flannel board. One removes the window and says, "This is a funny (peculiar) house. It doesn't have a window." The next student quickly replaces the window, removes the roof, and says, "Oh, yes, it has a window, but it doesn't have a roof." Two or three pairs of students may play this game during a class period.

GAMES AND SONGS

There are all kinds of language games and songs ranging from very simple to difficult, which help give practice in language while keeping the class lively and interesting. The type of song you teach to your class will depend on the age, interests, and learning level of the students. Songs for children, for example, should contain a repetitive motif where possible. Songs for intermediate levels and/or older students may have love, patriotism, home, or holidays as themes. Ideally, the songs should reflect the culture of English-speaking people both musically and thematically, but if you, someone in the music department of your school, or a creative student can put English words to favorite melodies from your students' countries, by all means do so. These new English songs with melodies familiar to the students can be used most effectively.

Following are ten games which will start you on the road to collecting and adapting others for your classes.

The Curious Owl. Student 1 will ask Student 2 a question, for example, "How old are you?" Student 2 will answer. Student 3 will ask Student 4, "How old is he (she)?" referring to Student 2. Student 4 will answer. Student 5 will begin again with "How old are you?" to Student 6.

I'm Thinking Of. The teacher or student (game leader) will choose an item (number, name, date, month, time, sport, activity, etc.) from among those items the class has been studying. The teacher or leader will whisper the item to another student so that there will be someone to verify the answer. The teacher or leader will call on individuals in the class to guess the correct item.

> Individual: Is it . . . ?
> Teacher or leader: No, it's not. . . .
> Teacher or leader: Yes, it is. It's. . . .

Add-on. This is played with a picture, a real object, or verbal cues.

> Student 1: I see a living room.
> Student 2: I see a living room and a kitchen.
> Student 3: I see a living room, a kitchen, and a bathroom.
>   or
> Student 1: I like milk.
> Student 2: I like milk and pie.
> Student 3: I like milk, pie, and cake.

Oh, No, Not I. The teacher or a student makes a statement using such phrases as "I hear that," "I understand that," "I see that," "I have heard that." What the teacher "heard" should be a statement which the student to whom it is made will want to deny. That student will say that someone else is responsible.

> Teacher: I understand that you came late this morning.
> Student 1: Oh, no, not I. I didn't come late. He did.

> Note that:

1. Responses can be varied and expanded in many ways depending upon the knowledge of the students, for example, "I always come early (on time)" or "I'm *never* late to school" or

> Teacher: You're very sad, aren't you?
> Student: No, I'm not sad. I'm very happy, but I think . . . is sad.

2. Your knowledge of the students can be used to inject humor into the practice without hurting the sensibilities of anyone.

Simon Says. Directions are given by the teacher or a student leader, for example, hands on your head, pencils on your desk, hands on your tie, hands behind your back. When the directions are preceded by *Simon says*, the students are to carry them out. When *Simon says* does not precede the directions, the students should remain motionless.

It's More (Less)

1. *It's More.* To a list of prices or hours, students will be expected to add an amount set by the teacher or a group leader. For example, write on the chalkboard "7 A.M., 8 A.M., 9 A.M., and so on." Have students add a quarter-hour or a half-hour to a basic sentence such as "I usually leave home at seven." The students will change it to "I usually leave home at a quarter past seven."

2. *It's Less.* Same as above, except that students will deduct an amount.

Opposites. Two teams are formed. The first person in Team 1 says a word. The first person on Team 2 has to say the opposite word. If he or she cannot, the team loses a point. (The same can be done with synonyms and with words of the same family.)

What Is It? (or Who Am I?)

1. *What Is It?* A description is given, for example, "It has four legs. It's made of wood." Students on teams have to say, "It's a chair (a stool, a table)."

2. *Who Am I?* A job description is given: "I cut meat." A student has to say, "You are (you're) a butcher."

Twenty Questions. One student is sent out of the room while the others decide on an object, person, or animal. When the student returns, he or she asks questions such as "Is it in the room?" "Is it big?" "Is it red?"

Charades. A proverb or a familiar concept of some kind can be acted out by a member of one team. Members of the other team have to guess what the concept is. They make statements identifying the concept, for example, "The book is difficult." "The boy is tall and handsome." "A stitch in time saves nine."

REAL OBJECTS

A corner of the room and a large box should contain anything you can gather together to illustrate vocabulary items or cultural concepts. Newspapers, menus, flags, maps, ticket stubs, cans, bottles, boxes, pieces of different kinds of cloth (wool, silk, cotton, nylon), artificial flowers, dishes, silverware, all form part of the "baggage" of the interested and interesting teacher and contribute to the "cultural island" we will talk about later.

THE RECORD PLAYER AND CASSETTE PLAYER

Songs, dances, stories, plays, and other language learning materials can be found on records and tape cassettes. Newer English textbooks are often accompanied by recordings of dialogues and of many practice activities. Some include pauses for student repetition.

The record player or cassette player may be used within the classroom lesson to accustom students to a voice other than yours, to provide concerted drill, and/or to introduce songs and dances. You may also plan to have the class or groups of students listen to a story or play or to portions of the English textbook *after* the regular English period.

THE LANGUAGE LABORATORY

Where tape recorders exist, you should make every attempt to use them extensively. If tapes have been made of the textbook lesson, they will be invaluable in giving the additional practice needed to reinforce the material you are teaching in the classroom.

Tapes have the advantage of maintaining the same intonation, repeating endlessly without tiring, providing a uniform length of pause for student repetition. These characteristics may not always be true of the teacher who has to teach many different classes a day.

Many kinds of supplementary materials can be placed on tapes: pronunciation drills where contrasts are featured, sentences of varying length to teach rhythm, sentences illustrating basic intonation patterns, dialogues and stories for listening and repeating, oral practice activities where students manipulate a sentence to create a new one, dictation, aural comprehension exercises, and tests.

In addition to tapes of the textbook lessons themselves, you can use commercially prepared taped stories, plays, dialogues, or drills to enrich the work you are doing.

You will find the tape recorder effective also in showing learners the progress they are making in learning English. At the beginning of the semester you can ask intermediate students to record a short passage. At the end of the semester they can record the same passage again.

For easy identification, each student should give his or her name before starting to read. The number on the tape counter should be noted in a book. Enough tape should be left after each student's reading to permit him or her to re-record next to the original performance. In this way, the progress or sometimes, unfortunately, the lack of it will easily be apparent.

Many excellent books have been written about language laboratories so that I will not duplicate here what has been said so eloquently elsewhere.

USING COMPUTERS

There is no question that computers have a significant role to play in the teaching-learning process. Although still in a comparatively early stage, computer-assisted instruction (CAI) is already being seen as a work saver and an effective learning strategy.

It is interesting that some of the important advantages of CAI are not those that you would expect from a machine. The computer is patient and nonjudgmental and, as such, puts even the most nervous or wary language learner at ease. The student who is not willing or able to respond naturally and calmly in the classroom will often sit for hours before a computer screen, smoothly responding to the same questions asked in the classroom.

I am sure you have heard about the interactive nature of computer-assisted instruction. Two kinds of interaction are possible with CAI. The first is between the student and the computer. Depending on the software (programs you use on the computer), the computer can respond in many ways to student input. The feedback is immediate. While not all programs have this built-in feedback mechanism, material from Regents/ALA not only indicates errors but also guides the student in their correction. For example, when a student misspells a word in the Regents/ALA *Reading Mastery* program, the computer actually looks at each character, erases the incorrect letters, leaves the correct letters in place, and instructs the student to try again. So the sequence would look like this:

> Dinner is on the -----.
> Dinner is on the tabel.
> Dinner is on the tab--.
> ***Try Again***

This duplicates one of the most valuable skills of a teacher, the ability to help a student analyze a problem and correct his or her own error. Other programs simply indicate that the student's answer is incorrect and expect the teacher to explain the cause of the error or the principle involved.

The second kind of interaction fostered by computer-assisted instruction is the interplay among two or more students as they work with the computer. A group of students working with a program without a teacher can discuss answers, make educated guesses, and instruct each other without shame or fear. One doesn't have to worry about the students teaching each other incorrect responses because the correct answer will flash on the screen at a keystroke.

The amount and variety of software available for the language classroom is staggering. Courseware (a set of software) can be used with an entire class as a homework assignment or provided to special individuals for enrichment or remediation.

Courseware can deliver instruction in the form of tutorials (individual instruction at the learner's own pace), drill and practice (repetitive exercises), simulations, games, and tests. Drill and practice has been much maligned for not taking full advantage of the computer's capabilities; however, it has always been vital in the language classroom. The computer is particularly well suited for drill and practice. Giving the task of conducting drills to the computer frees teachers to do what they were trained to do, motivate their students and present new material.

Adventure games (a kind of simulation in which the student participates in a narrative by making decisions that affect the plot) are particularly helpful for language learners. They are successful with language learners because students construct appropriate responses in order to find out what happens next. There are also computer simulations that allow a student to move safely through a new situation or historical reenactment as a participant and an observer at the same time. These allow a student to make purchases, do banking transactions, or apply for a job, all without risking embarrassing mistakes.

Games have their own built-in motivation. We all know that teaching idioms is not the most inspiring task for student or teacher. However, if you can do that job using a computer game, your job is easier and the students will thank you for it. One problem with using these games is that not every student likes games. Some serious-minded students who would react against traditional language games in the class-room will react negatively to computer games.

With most courseware, there is also a management component, that is, a facil-ity for creating a customized lesson plan for each student and keeping track of stu-dent responses. The specifics of the management system vary with the different ma-terials producers, but it is a feature that virtually eliminates tedious record keeping.

Finally, the advent of computers has brought some other time-saving, work-saving tools for teacher and student alike. Chief among them is the word processor. Probably the most difficult part of writing in a second language is the constant revi-sion that is necessary to perfect a composition. Word processing makes it possible for a student to put thoughts on paper, deal with vocabulary, reorganize the ideas, and polish the product. The composition is then printed and submitted to the teacher. With teacher comments in hand, it is back to the word processor for rewriting. No more does the student have to recopy each composition by hand, risking, with each revision, new mistakes.

Other such tools are data base programs (they facilitate the storage and arrangement of facts for writing or other purposes), programs that allow the teacher to create elaborate crossword puzzles in a half-hour, and authoring shells (prepro-grammed procedures) that allow teachers to create exercises for their students with-out learning a computer language and doing actual programming.

Of course, it is possible to learn a computer language and create original soft-ware to make the computer an efficient part of the teaching team. However, it is far from necessary to be a computer programmer to use computers. Good software is simple to use and can enhance a language program in many ways.

MAKING EFFECTIVE USE OF VIDEO

I am pleased to acknowledge the help I have received from Barry Tomalin, Mike Potter, and David Haines, all presently or at one time with the British Council, who coordinated their talks at the British Council Annual Bologna Conference in April 1984 and gave a comprehensive and honest presentation on the topic of video. There were no holds barred and no mincing of words. They talked of the many advantages of the medium but did not hesitate to point out the abuses that can mar its effectiveness. It is, as always, the teacher who will be the determining factor. They did emphasize that, despite its superiority for teaching language and culture, video use places a heavy burden on the teacher.

What are the advantages of video? It can present a communicative transaction in its totality. The learners can see the people and the situation (the setting where the interaction is occurring). They can see and hear the attitude of the persons involved (the interlocutors). They can hear the linguistic registers and the appropriateness of the language within the situation. They can appreciate cross-cultural relationships by asking themselves if this piece of business would be conducted in the same way in their country. They will become aware of other cultural aspects, such as the gestures used and the distance maintained between the people involved. It is a replica of natural conversation in the real world.

Moreover, there are numerous technical advantages. For example, the pause button permits a frame to be frozen so that questions can be asked about the topic, the people, and the situation in general. The sound can be turned down or turned off, permitting the students to predict what the person speaking is saying or may be about to say. The tape can be moved backward or forward. The teacher can extract a segment of the video program and ask learners to solve a problem similar to the one on the small screen.

What are some of the teacher's responsibilities?

1. To view the video before attempting to use it.

2. To pinpoint the purposes of using the video. Will it be to help the learners repeat the language, imitate the language and gestures, or predict what may happen next?

3. To prepare materials and questions for a discussion of (a) the speakers' roles and personalities, (b) cultural differences, (c) issues raised by the topic of the videotape, and (d) the inferences that it is possible to make about the situation (people, place, time, topic).

The three experts recommended that the video be broken up into four-minute segments. I saw a demonstration of a thirty-second segment, and I cannot begin to tell you how much language was generated by the scene: a train station with people waiting, the train pulling in, people getting out and looking disturbed because no one (they thought) was there to meet them, two men walking uncertainly toward a woman passenger, the hesitant greetings ("Are you Miss Z?" "Yes." "Well, I'm Mr. X, and this is Mr. Y.").

4. *The previewing stage.* The teacher discusses the topic with the learners, puts unfamiliar lexical items on the board, and gives them examples of utterances they may hear. The focus at this stage is the vocabulary and talking about the people.

5. *The viewing stage.* This stage can be handled in several ways depending on the level of the class. In ascending order of complexity, some of the techniques are as follows:

a. Using the pause button and focusing on gestures and the characters' attitudes. There is no sound during this step.

b. Progressing to sound with the use of the pause button.

c. Moving to vision and sound without the use of the pause button.

d. Asking comprehension questions about the segment.

e. Comparing predictions to the actual video with vision and sound.

f. Discussion of issues related to the topic.

6. *The follow-up stage.* This stage includes observation with focus on the language; creating a similar situation and asking, "What would you say?"; writing a letter about the situation; doing a role play; extending the situation. These activities can be done in groups, in pairs, or as homework.

Some final words of wisdom. Play the video a minimum of three times. The first time should be for global comprehension (particularly if you use the four-minute segment). The second time (with the pause button) should be in order to ask many *wh* words or inferential questions. The third time should be to reinforce and consolidate new learning with many "What would you say?" questions applied to similar situations.

Video can be an exciting supplement to your textbook lessons. Let us hope your school can afford to either buy or rent a videocassette recorder. Many firms have rental agreements for equipment. Some even rent the tapes, but most prefer to sell them outright.

MISCELLANEOUS MATERIALS

- A cardboard clock with movable hands.
- A puppet stage (made with an old crate or box).
- Puppets (paper or rag), toy telephones or real telephones supplied by the telephone company, if possible.
- Calendars (large ones showing days of the week and weather signals), maps, bulletin boards.
- A large thermometer with a movable black or red strip to indicate the rise and fall of the mercury.
- Books, magazines, and newspapers.
- Last and most important, the chalkboard and chalk. Use it to make quick sketches or stick figures, charts, diagrams, and so on. If colored chalk is available, you may wish to use it to underline elements in words which will indicate structural relationships and forms.

I could mention many other materials, such as a camera, the opaque projector, the overhead projector, or the slide projector. Any of these machines and others which science will devise are good, but only in the hands of the efficient teacher who uses them judiciously when and where they can be most useful in bringing about the growth of listening, speaking, reading, or writing ability.

Some Teaching Techniques

In the next few pages, I will list some procedures and techniques which will help learners progress toward real control of the language items we are teaching while motivating them to continue their study of English. In our list, I will reinforce some of the pertinent suggestions given in the preceding pages.

1. Use the students and yourself (your clothing, the things you carry, etc.) to teach appropriate vocabulary *before* using pictures or other materials.

2. Start with the *known* environment of your students before fanning out to the wider English-speaking world. Relate your presentations to facets of language or of culture with which you can expect your students to be familiar. For example, if you are going to teach vocabulary related to a beach scene in England, help the students recall a beach scene (or swimming, boating, or fishing) closer to their homes. Use many questions starting with *Do you* or *Have you.*

3. Use dialogues wherever possible. Dialogues duplicate the communication situations in everyday life. Keep building on the same dialogue situation where possible. For example, with classroom objects:

A. Do you (have) a notebook?
Yes, I do.
B. Do you (have) your English notebook?
(No), I (don't).
C. 1. Do you want a notebook with lines?
    2. Yes, please, How much is this one?
    1. Twenty cents.
    2. All right, I'll take it.

The possibilities for expanding the same dialogue situation are infinite. In addition to expanding the dialogue, you may want to give practice in substituting whole utterances in the responses. For example, the response in A above could be, "Yes, Do you want it?" or "Do you want to see it?" or "Do you need it?" The response in B could be "I'm sorry, I forgot it." or "Of course. I always have my English notebook."

Since dialogues appear more and more frequently in textbooks and since they are at the core of situational and functional teaching, let us take a few extra minutes to discuss their use.

A dialogue, as we learned at the beginning of Chapter 3, may be used as the "jumping-off" focal point for one or more lessons—as we present its communicative function, structures, lexicon, or cultural situation. It may be used, however, as a culminating activity to demonstrate the use—in authentic communication—of communicative expressions, structures, and vocabulary items which have been presented in mini situations, in narratives, or through other techniques, for example, the monostructural approach.

To help students *understand* the dialogue or the segment of a longer dialogue you are teaching, you may use any one or a combination of these procedures:

• Give the situation of the entire dialogue simply and briefly in English, pointing to objects or pictures and pointing to each of the figures (stick figures drawn on the chalkboard, drawings, flannel board cutouts, etc.) as you tell what each one is saying. *Students must be helped to relate the utterances to the appropriate speaker.*

- Teach new words and expressions through association with pictures, real objects, pantomime, or gestures before saying the dialogue.
- Give, where feasible, the native language equivalent, not word-for-word translations, of each utterance.
- Explain the situation briefly in the native language if appropriate.

To help students say the dialogue or the portion of that day's dialogue with reasonable fluency, you may wish to follow this procedure:

- Have the students listen to it three or four times. The first two times stand at the board and point to each figure as you speak. After that, particularly if the group is large, you may wish to stand in various parts of the room so that students can see your mouth and your gestures.
- Say each utterance three or four times and engage the entire group in choral repetition.
- Divide the group in half. Help each half of the group take one role in the dialogue.
- Reverse the roles. (Repeat this procedure several times, if time permits.)
- Ask a more able student to come to the front of the room to take one role of the dialogue. You will take the other. (Help the student by standing nearby and whispering the utterance to be produced.
- Follow this procedure with several individual students, depending on the complexity of the dialogue, the interest engendered, and the time available.
- Help two students dramatize the utterances or ask one student to take one role while the rest of the class takes the other.
- Help the students learn the dialogue by writing it on the chalkboard, gradually erasing more and more words from each utterance, and encouraging the students to reconstruct it.

To help make the dialogue a vehicle for teaching and reinforcing communication, you may ask, for example, that:

- The dialogue itself be read, copied, summarized, or adapted (to indicate different speakers, a different time, or a different point of view), preceding and following such activity by dramatization and oral reading.
- Students answer questions about it or they formulate questions which their fellow students will answer. The questions are generally of three kinds:
  a. Those which are based directly on the utterances, people, and situations in the dialogue being studied (often called dialogue variation)
  b. Those in which the dialogue situation is related to the lives and experiences of

the students. If, for example, the dialogue is about listening to records, the questions could elicit the likes and dislikes of the students, their listening habits, and so on (called dialogue personalization)

   c. Those which require the students to make inferences. ("How do we know?" "Why do you think?").

* Students change the dialogues. You can ask more able students at the early levels or all the students at intermediate or advanced levels to suggest alternative whole utterances for a given utterance in the dialogue without changing the situation. For example, a first sentence such as "Let's study together tomorrow" may be changed to "Would you like to study with me tomorrow?"

* Students create a dialogue. As the students build up a repertoire of utterances from dialogues they have learned and as they gain insight into the conversational situations in which the utterances would be appropriate, they should be able to recombine these and create their own dialogues.

* Students should be guided to create dialogues within different sociocultural situations. For example, if they have learned to use the structure *How much* in relation to shopping for food, they should be guided to create dialogues using *How much* in buying a plane ticket or buying clothing. A dialogue about a visit to the doctor should lead to the preparation of another about a visit to the dentist. To illustrate further, a dialogue in which the ending of a business letter is discussed should lead them to write a dialogue about informal letters.

   Activities such as these are particularly important if we wish to avoid the shock that language learners experience in speaking to native speakers when their stimulus sentence is not followed by the response they had been led to expect. This often happens when a dialogue has been memorized without further study or creative recombination.

   You may notice that I have not mentioned memorizing the dialogue. If a dialogue is memorized at all, it should be only by dint of its repetition, dramatization, and adaptation and not because students have been asked to go home and memorize it. More important than memorizing a dialogue is to exploit it by adapting and varying it in ways suggested above.

   Students can write narrative paragraphs from the dialogue. You may wish to do this in two or three steps. For example, sentences (said by each speaker) will first be rewritten with verbs and names as, "No, I can't go," said Jane, and "I'm furious," shouted Donn. Then they can be written as "Jane said that she couldn't go. Donn shouted that he was furious." Later still, the sentences could be rewritten as "When Jane said she couldn't go, Donn became furious."

   4. Plan as many different oral practice activities for each lesson as can be done briskly and with reasonable accuracy. As you write your lesson plan, decide which of the drills outlined above are best suited to the item you are teaching.

   5. Vary the type of student participation for the different parts of your lesson:

- Use chain drills, but break the chain after five or six students and start another chain in another part of the room.
- Call on students in order and then at random.
- Ask a question. Have *one* student answer. (It is unwise to ask for a choral answer to a question unless it has been thoroughly practiced immediately before.) It is also more desirable to ask the question than to call on a student by name.
- Have a student or a group ask you a question. Answer it.
- Have a student ask another student a question.
- Have students manipulate the hands of the clock, the sentences in the pocket chart, or the material on the flannel board.
- Have students shuffle the pictures or the flash cards or touch the desired pictures in the picture series charts and ask questions about them.
- Have pairs of students come to the front of the room often to dramatize a dialogue—even if it is only two lines.
- Use games to reinforce structure and vocabulary.
- Use paired practice. (See Appendix I.)

   6. In drills, *always* give the model sentence or expression two or three times before asking the class or individuals to give it.

   7. Call on your more able students before calling on the weaker ones. In this way, the latter group can practice responses which will be reasonably correct.

   8. Use the students' native language judiciously when it will mean saving time or ensuring comprehension.

   9. Encourage your students to prepare materials (according to their ability, however). Ask them to find pictures, to cut and mount them, to prepare flash cards, to draw pictures, and even to compose or build a dialogue with new words or structures they have learned. At the intermediate or advanced level, ask them to write short conversations and then plays which can later be dramatized.

   10. Simplify and adapt stories which you can tell your students. If you have duplicating facilities, prepare simplified material for reading. I once saw the famous novel *Les Miserables* by Victor Hugo adapted and condensed most effectively into four double-spaced pages. Of course, it did not have the original flavor, but the interest in the story line was very high, and it afforded excellent practice in language.

   11. Create a "cultural island" in your classroom. Do this by having pictures, maps, bulletin boards, proverbs, and labels in English. Use English as much as possible during the hour. (You may want to set aside a few minutes at the end of the hour when students can ask questions or make comments in their native language. This is feasible *only* when all the students speak the same native language and when the language is familiar to you.) Classroom routines (taking attendance, describing materials) and recurring questions, for example, "What does . . . mean?" or "Who sees (hears) an error?" should be *in English*.

12. Utilize community resources and bring the people in the community into your program. This is important not only because it provides additional stimulation for the students but also because it will foster interest in English language learning in the community. There are many ways of doing this:

- Ask English speakers to come to your classroom to speak about their trips, hobbies, interests, or jobs. The preparation for the visit (social amenities, questions to be asked, etc.), listening to the speech, and writing a letter of thanks to the visitor lead naturally to language learning.
- Start an English club to which community members may be invited. Plan topics for discussion, games, songs, and so on, around the interests of the students.
- Ask the local printer (if possible) to help you print an English (or bilingual) newspaper.
- Prepare simple plays to which you can invite parents and other lay people in the community.

13. Utilize the incidental happenings in the school or the immediate community to teach or to review language items. Although I believe firmly in lesson planning, no plan should be so rigid that it cannot include references to unusual occurrences (if these are of interest to your students). The use of special events and incidental happenings not only extends knowledge but also illustrates that the structures or vocabulary practiced within one situation can be used to talk about another one.

14. Give your students the feeling and the assurance that English is a vehicle of communication which serves exactly the same purposes as does their native tongue. What do people all over the world generally talk about? The daily routine of sleeping, eating, shopping, working, and playing; age; births; marriages; illnesses; and so on. Although it is true that we use different words or expressions, there are equivalent expressions for discussing equivalent events in any culture.

15. Provide opportunities for students to act as listeners and as speakers. Students should be able not only to make statements but also to make comments or responses, to ask questions, and to answer questions.

16. Use authentic language at normal speed in the classroom. Often, in the desire to simplify language for our students, we give expressions or words which we consider easier simply because they are shorter. Try to remember that sometimes the longer word may be more similar to a cognate in your students' language. Also, since everything is different for learners, they may just as well learn the expressions or words that native speakers of their age would generally employ in similar circumstances.

17. Spur your students to greater effort by training them to give long responses or multiple responses to a question or to a statement. The ability to sustain a longer conversation which duplicates real speech will give them a feeling of success and achievement.

Use connecting words (*and, but*) and formulas. Let us consider some brief examples of increasingly longer answers:

a. Using a picture series chart of mass nouns, for example, on which you or a student indicates the appropriate pictures, notice the possible progression:

I see milk; I see bread.

I see a bottle of milk.

I see a loaf of bread.

I see a bottle of milk and a loaf of bread.

I see the bottle of milk, but I don't see the loaf of bread.

I don't see the bottle of milk, and I don't see the loaf of bread either.

b. Notice the exchanges possible in talking about an article of clothing:

A. 1—I like your dress.

2—Thank you. I made it myself.

B. 1—I like your dress. Blue is my favorite color.

2—Thank you. It's my favorite color, too.

1—Where did you get it?

2—My mother made it.

1—Is it new?

2—Yes, it is. This is the second time I have worn it.

You tell your students how you want them to respond, that is, tell them that you want them to make a response and then a statement, or that you want them to respond and ask a question. When they have learned the appropriate expressions, you may also encourage them to agree, to disagree, to express surprise, to express pleasure, as creatively as they wish.

18. Summarize what has been done at various times during the lesson. Make sure, through questions, charts, diagrams, and as a last resort through translation, that students understand what they are repeating.

19. Teach—Don't test. This does *not* mean that you should not give quizzes, tests, and examinations. (Testing will be the subject of our next chapter.) In presenting new material, give numerous examples so that students see the word order or new form. Don't try to elicit an original sentence after one or two examples.

Practice activities immediately following the presentation of new material should be confined to repetition after the teacher (class, groups, and individuals) and to simple substitution of one item only. The kind of problem-solving exercises where students have to make four or five changes in a sentence should have no place in a beginning language program.

20. Tailor your course to your students. Their interests, their environment, and their abilities should be kept constantly in mind as you plan the content and activities of your lessons.

Individualizing Instruction

The principles on which the desire for individualized instruction are based are sound and ideal. The diagrams in professional journals which show a classroom with about twenty-five students engaged in about fifteen different (excellent) learning activities embody the dream of every teacher who knows that (1) each learner is a unique human being who has a different pace and rhythm of learning and (2) the learner must be considered the primary person or factor in the learning process.

Individualized instruction must be considered, however, from several vantage points. In situations such as those in the United States, Great Britain, and other countries, where immigrants or migrants enter schools at varying stages of literacy, where fifteen-year-old newcomers may be completely illiterate, or where students register for school at any time during the school semester, individualized instruction is the only feasible means of enabling students to (1) learn the language, and (2) make a personal-social adjustment to the school and community. In this situation, groups of teachers or special bureaus of the school system should prepare individualized worksheets for *every facet* of language at *different maturity* and *learning levels*. (Not enough of this type of material is available, unfortunately.) Paraprofessionals (teacher aides) or student helpers can assist teachers in helping the newcomers.

In teaching situations like those mentioned above, individualized instruction for the greater part of the school day is the only viable, feasible procedure. As described earlier in this chapter, tape recorders, computers, and the language lab can facilitate individualized instruction where equipment is available.

Then my thoughts turn to schools in other countries in which I have worked where (1) the teacher has 70–100 learners in one class (so that he or she might have as many as 400 per day!) and (2) where the ministry of education insists on uniform examinations given at one time. Teachers, although willing, devoted, and dedicated, do not have the physical time nor the resources to prepare materials for individual learners. They *do* individualize by asking different oral questions of their slower and more able pupils, by encouraging supplementary reading, by engaging students in group activities, and by stimulating teaching in pairs. But they would find it unrealistic to give examinations at different times or to prepare varied worksheets for individual learners.

Ideally, individualized instruction is possible and desirable in situations where the entire school and the school system will cooperate in the preparation of different programs—either within the school or within the classroom—which will take into consideration the age of the students, their personal, vocational, or professional interests, and their pace and method of learning. Some concrete suggestions which appear in the literature include

1. Scheduling learning modules in which English learners can be assigned to a teacher for different amounts of time each day and to a resource center where they will find assistants and materials to help them pursue their goals. (Obvi-

ously the cooperation of all the other departments is necessary, and the principal or headmaster must also be committed to the idea.)

2. Preparing a copy of a "contract" for each student (based on grades at previous levels, diagnostic tests, noncompleted work to be covered, individual interests, etc.) which would include a list of resources, a schedule for group work and for tests, the goals he or she is expected to achieve, an answer key, and flexible materials (programmed or textbook).
3. Giving students more responsibility for their own learning.
4. Encouraging them to talk freely to each other about their work and to teach each other (setting up a system of student buddies).

Certainly, the best thinking of educators, psychologists, and linguists should be brought to bear to the fullest degree possible on this challenging question of individualizing instruction. Testing of student progress through sociograms, observation, and questionnaires concerning heightened or lessened student motivation should be included in any survey.

A Potpourri of Usable Ideas

READING

Arrange sense groups (meaningful chunks of language) within sentences in vertical columns. Learners will then write out the sentences.

Pick out the topic sentences, indicating the subject and the main verb.

Skim a passage—within an established time limit—and give the gist of the passage.

Scan a passage—within a set time limit—to find details (of people, place, attitude, etc.).

Take a cloze test where every fifth to seventh word is omitted.

Transfer written information in a text to a grid or to an outline.

WRITING

Put ideas found in a grid into connected discourse.

Expand items in a diary. Give the diary to the teacher from time to time for a response or reaction.

Write an original dialogue (on a specific topic).

Change a dialogue to reported speech (indirect discourse).

MISCELLANEOUS

Give instructions for drawing a picture or describing a process.

Take the role of job seeker (this will depend on the age of the learner) in an interview.

Discuss the merits of a book or article with a group of three other students. (Social amenities, attitude, and many other personal traits will become apparent as well as language ability.)

For Review and Discussion

1. What categories would you use in a picture file?
2. In groups, prepare sentences that include a communicative function for a count nouns chart.
3. With a partner, prepare exponents for a mass noun chart. [Use *some, any* (in questions) and then quantity words.]
4. Devise questions and statements for the work activities chart.
5. Make a series chart and use it with at least five tenses or verb aspects.
6. Use the verb chart on p. 142 to present a use of the present perfect.
7. How would you use a pocket chart?
8. How would you use a flannel board?
9. What are your feelings about the use of a computer as a help to you? What programs would you like to see on it?
10. What would you like to see on video? Why? How would you motivate your students with it?
11. What are your favorite language games? Would you share them with your colleagues?
12. Are there songs in the learners' native language whose melodies you can use in English songs? (Work in groups of four.)
13. How do you individualize instruction? Do learners enjoy such activities? If not, what are the problems?
14. Try to think—with a partner—of two effective teaching techniques.
15. What five facts or language activities did you learn from this chapter?

5

Testing and Evaluation

Provision for evaluation should be an integral part of the English curriculum. Indeed, criteria and measures for judging its efficacy should be built into the program from the very outset. The curriculum, in turn, should be revised and revitalized continuously in light of the findings of a valid, reliable, comprehensive testing program.

The term *evaluation* in the title of this chapter is broader than the traditional term *testing*. Evaluation includes assessing the students' progress toward the linguistic objectives of the course, determining their attitude not only toward English language learning but also toward native English speakers, judging the results of the methodology and the materials in use, and appraising the effectiveness of the total English program in serving the needs of the learners for whom it is intended.

In this section, we will consider four major questions in relation to testing. In as succinct a fashion as possible, we will discuss the following questions: (1) Why do we test? (2) When do we test? (3) How do we test? (4) What do we test? These are the questions of primary interest to teachers.

Before proceeding to a statement of some basic premises under each of these questions, I would like to make a few comments about two tests which are often mentioned in relation to language study. The use of written ''attitude'' tests to judge cultural appreciation and understanding (and here we are using *cultural* in the broad anthropological sense) is still in the experimental stage. At the present time, therefore, the more satisfactory way to judge attitude is through observation of students' reactions to reading material, to native English visitors, and to questions about English-speaking countries. Their interest in language is easily judged through their participation in class. Do they volunteer? Do they give sustained answers? (Of course, lack of response may indicate timidity rather than apathy!) Do they prepare their work? A perceptive teacher is usually the best judge of desirable attitudes.

The other type of test to which I referred is the so-called prognostic test. In many school systems, students are tested *before* being admitted to a language program in order to determine whether they have the capacity to learn a language successfully. In the considered judgment of many teachers, results of the prognostic tests available at this time are not reliable or conclusive. The test score would have to be studied with additional extensive data about each student before an accurate determination of future success could be made. Experiments have demonstrated clearly that motivation and perseverance on the part of the normal student and good planning on the part of a competent and sympathetic teacher are more reliable criteria of success in language learning than a score on a prognostic test.

We will confine our discussion, therefore, to diagnostic and achievement testing or, to put it in another way, to testing in order to discover our students' problems, weaknesses, or strengths and to ascertain their progress toward the goals of the English program.

Why Do We Test?

There are several reasons—some of which have broad implications, as you will see:

1. The obvious reason is that we have to grade students so that we can move them forward to the next higher class or retain them at their present level. They can derive the greatest benefit only from classes working at their level.

2. Another reason is that through appropriate tests we can set realistic standards of achievement for groups or individuals. By comparing our test results with results in similar classes or communities under similar conditions, we can judge whether we are setting our standards too high or too low.

3. Tests can also help us assess the effects of experimentation. For example, through a carefully controlled experiment, we may wish to determine whether the use of the students' native language in the classroom retards or increases their progress. Only a reliable and valid testing instrument will provide the answer.

4. The three most important reasons for testing as far as classroom teachers are concerned are: (a) to diagnose the specific features of the language in which individual students or groups are having difficulty, (b) to help us gauge our ability as teachers, (c) to find out how much our students have learned or achieved.

A few parenthetical remarks, particularly in relation to Item b may be pertinent at this point. Failure on the part of a few students does not necessarily mean that we have not planned or taught well. We are all aware that many factors (intellectual, physical, emotional, social) within an individual student may be at the root of the failure.

On the other hand, if the majority of the students fail a test, it would be desirable for us to review critically our presentation and the practice activities we used in teaching the language item we are testing. It is only to the extent that the classroom teacher *translates the results of tests into more effective teaching procedures* that students will derive any benefit from a testing program. It goes without saying that poor grades by the majority should signal reteaching and retesting of the item or items involved.

When Do We Test?

In any school system, there are usually midterm and end-term examinations in which the proficiency of pupils is tested. These examinations are very often schoolwide or communitywide tests which include the language items covered in a prescribed number of units of work.

In addition to these tests, you will find it desirable to give a long comprehensive examination at the end of each unit of work and, at the beginning levels of language learning, a brief quiz daily or as many times as is feasible each week.

The brief quiz is an excellent teaching device and can serve many purposes:

1. If the correct answers are given immediately after the test (as should be done), the knowledge of the correctness or lack of correctness of their responses will reinforce the students' learning of the response.
2. It gives the students a sense of achievement if they've done well. (Below we will indicate some techniques for ensuring success.)
3. It gives you insight into students' difficulties and into segments of the unit which may have to be retaught *before* you proceed to new material.
4. It may be used as the springboard for the new lesson to be presented that day.
5. It gives you and the students a frequent "barometer reading" of progress.
6. An average of the many grades accumulated through this process does away with the unfortunate practice of giving a student a final grade based primarily on one or at most two examinations. An able student, prevented by illness or some other cause from doing well on one examination, may be saved from end-term or end-year failure by a consideration of the grades obtained on the daily quizzes.

In schools or classes where students work individually under contracts which list performance objectives, tests are generally given when learners feel they have fulfilled their contracts to their satisfaction and are thus ready to take the test.

In stating performance objectives, several criteria are generally noted: (1) the structure or category to be studied, for example, the simple past tense of regular verbs; (2) the number of practice sentences the learner is to do; (3) the time he or she should take to do them in; and (4) the degree of mastery (e.g. twenty-four out of twenty-five must be grammatically correct, said without false starts and unnecessary pauses, etc.).

I should add that some educators are beginning to question the advisability of using performance objectives in many situations. While it is true that students should know what is expected of them, factors such as strict attention to time, degree of mastery expected, and other motivational problems have made psychologists and others pause in their advocacy of performance objectives. They feel that many learners would suffer under such pressure.

How Do We Test?

Today's accepted principles of language teaching demand that we emphasize oral tests as well as written tests. Let us consider written tests first.*

These, as we know, are of two types—short-answer tests and integrative essay tests. Short-answer tests may duplicate the practice activities outlined above. They may be of the multiple-choice, completion, substitution, or transformation type. They have several advantages: They are objective; they can be scored easily and quickly; they permit the testing of a wider area of knowledge.

Essay tests have no part in a *beginning* language program. They are useful and desirable at the more advanced levels, however. Only through essay tests can we judge the students' use of varied structures, the richness of their vocabulary, and their ability to express ideas with clarity and precision. In other words, the longer essay tests permit us to judge the ability of the students to use language as a tool for written communication.

From the teacher's point of view, essay tests are difficult to grade. (A scheme such as the one given for grading compositions will be found useful.) From the student's point of view, the subjective elements in the essay test may cause apprehension.

Oral tests are indispensable for judging oral production of sounds, stress, rhythm, and intonation patterns; fluency; and automatic responses to oral or written stimuli. Oral tests may be time-consuming, however. Several time-saving techniques you may wish to consider follow:

1. Make a chart of five or six points you wish to grade. Each day, for a week or two, call several students to your desk individually. Ask each to repeat, read, follow directions, and so on, as indicated below. (Give only as much material as is needed to ascertain their knowledge of the language items you are testing.) Grade them only on the key points on which you have decided to grade them. Ignore (although it will be painful for you to do so in many cases) all other incorrect features.

2. If you have one, use a tape recorder on which directions or stimuli are given. Have the students record their responses on a tape. (Each student will be asked to start at a different number on the counter and give his or her name at the end of the test.)

3. Use the tape recorder to give directions and cues. Have the students write their responses (making a cross or check) on an answer sheet. (This would test aural comprehension only.)

---

*It goes without saying that written tests can be used to test understanding (recognition) and oral production.

Combinations of aural and written tests would include those in which students take dictation (full or spot as explained above) or perform a comprehensive exercise in which they answer, in writing, questions (given orally or in writing) on a dialogue or narrative paragraph they have heard.

What Do We Test?

Simply stated, we should test everything we consider important enough to teach in language learning. That means we should test the students' knowledge of the phonemic, communicative, structural, and lexical systems, as well as their insight into any cultural aspects we have given them.

We should test the students' ability to understand, to speak, and—as soon as feasible—to read and to write. Within these listening and speaking skills, we should judge their ability to understand the formulas of the language, to ask and to answer questions, to make the normal responses which a situation demands, to start a conversation, or to narrate an event.

Integrative tests evaluate the students' ability to use discrete items of the subsystems of language appropriately in communicative and interactive activities, both oral and written.

The construction and content of the test must be in harmony with the aspirations and goals of the community or society, as well as with the current, most modern learning approaches—if these have been accepted.

Of importance to teachers and curriculum writers are John Carrol's criteria for the construction of a valid, reliable test: relevance, acceptability, comparability, and economy. Very briefly stated, by *relevance*, Carrol refers to the congruence of test content and course goals; by *acceptability*, he questions whether the students are willing to take the test; by *comparability*, he discusses the necessity for comparing students' scores with those of others; by *economy*, he reminds us that a lot of information about our students and ourselves should be revealed by a short test.

As noted above, there is bound to be overlapping in many tests. For example, taking dictation tests listening and writing skills and enables us to consider the students' grasp of the sound, structure, and vocabulary features contained in the passage.

The test stimuli or cues should be varied just as they are in the classroom practice activities. The stimuli might therefore include (1) hearing spoken words or utterances (live or on tape); (2) looking at a picture or several pictures; (3) looking at real objects; (4) reading a word, an utterance, or a passage.

Let us consider some simple tests which can be given in the classroom. Whether some of these are done orally or in writing (or by placing a correct symbol or letter on an answer sheet) will depend not only on the nature of the test but also on the age of your students. For these reasons, test suggestions are listed in no particular order.

Testing the Features of Language

To test their knowledge of the sound system, have students:

1. Indicate whether two sounds—given orally or in writing, isolated or in words—are the same or different.
2. Indicate which pairs of words rhyme (e.g., *send/lend, friend/fiend, enough/ through*).
3. Mark the syllable having the loudest stress (e.g., *again, never, turn on, apple tree*).
4. Indicate (by prearranged code) rising or falling intonation (e.g., Did you go to school? Where did you go?).
5. Indicate from which column of words or pictures you (or a tape) are pronouncing a word or an entire utterance (e.g., *think/thing*; I saw the ship/I saw the sheep.).
6. Imitate sentences of varying lengths (e.g., I want a dress. I want a pretty red dress. I want that pretty red dress.).
7. Indicate stress and juncture in pairs of sentences (e.g., I saw him by the tree. I saw him buy the tree.).

To test their grasp of grammatical items, have students:

1. Select the appropriate word from two or three words by underlining, numbering, or filling in a blank on an answer sheet [e.g., The (*boy, boys*) usually walk to the door slowly.].
2. Perform any of the transformation exercises indicated in Chapter 3 (e.g., Make this a question: He went to the door. Say you have *two*: I have a box. Ask a question with *Who*: Mr. X is a mailman.).
3. Use the words *get up* (for example) in these sentences (e.g., It's seven o'clock in the morning. I'm _____ now. Yesterday I _____ at seven o'clock too. I usually _____ at seven every day.).
4. Answer questions in the negative using a full sentence (e.g., Do you have some bread? Did you find someone there?).
5. Ask direct questions based on indirect questions (e.g., Ask X how old he is. Ask someone whether he knows Mr. . . . .).
6. Give the paired sentence (e.g., Mary is going to read later. The boys are going to study later. Mary reads every day. The boys _____).
7. Make all changes required by a cue [e.g., (These) This boy is tall.].
8. Indicate which pictures you are mentioning (e.g., This is a foot long. This is a long foot. This is a station wagon. This is a wagon station.).
9. Complete sentences [e.g., I _____ thirsty (*am, 's, have*). I'd go if I _____ time (*have, were, had*).].

10. Answer questions of various types (cf. Chapter 3). Indicate whether you want a yes-no answer; whether you want a short answer or a long answer; whether you want a combination short and long answer; whether you want them to agree, disagree, express surprise, sympathy, anger.

11. Choose the correct form [e.g., The woman's name is _____ (*Peter, Mrs. Jones, Miss*)].

12. Combine sentences (e.g., She's a student. She's very good. That man is my father. He's talking to Mr. Brown.).

13. Match the stimuli and responses. Have one additional response so that guessing will be minimized.

I	II
1) Thank you.	a) Better.
2) How old is he?	b) He's twelve.
3) When are you leaving?	c) Of course.
4) How are you feeling?	d) You're welcome.
5) May I go out?	e) Tomorrow.
	f) In school.

14. Rewrite the sentence placing the adjectives in the correct position [e.g., (*small, four*) I have puppies.].

15. Indicate where a word belongs (e.g., *usually*, in the sentence: He *A* goes *B* to the park *C*.).

16. Select the appropriate coordinating conjunction when two are given [e.g., (*and, but*) I'd go _____ I'm tired.].

17. Select the appropriate subordinating conjunction when two are given [e.g., (*while, unless*) She went to work _____ he took care of the house.].

18. Select the appropriate connector [e.g., It was freezing (*However, Otherwise*) we went out.].

To test their knowledge of vocabulary, have students:

1. Indicate whether a statement is true or false (e.g., Spring comes before summer.).

2. Complete a sentence [e.g., The cow _____ (*barks, moos, shrieks*).].

3. Select an unrelated word from a group of words (e.g., *meat, soup, eraser, peas*).

4. Give a synonym or choose one from a list [e.g., *start* (*begin*)].

5. Give an antonym or choose one from a list [e.g., *finish* (*start*)].

6. Give two other words from the same family [e.g., *jewel* (*jewelry, jeweler*)].

7. Make nouns from the following verbs (e.g., *arrive, deny, permit*).

8. Make adjectives from the following nouns (e.g., *man, child*).

9. Use the prefix meaning "not" in these words (e.g., *ability, able, rational*).

10. Use the suffix meaning "pertaining to" in words such as *region, nature*.

11. Select the appropriate word [e.g., *(in, on)* The picture is _____ the wall.].

12. Select the appropriate word [e.g., *(too, very)* I can't drink the tea. It's _____ hot.].

13. Choose the word(s) with the same meaning as the underlined word(s) [e.g., *(must, should)* I have to leave now.].

14. Choose the appropriate word [e.g., *(breakfast, lunch, dinner, supper)* We always have _____ at seven in the morning.].

15. Paraphrase a sentence using the same structure but different vocabulary.

16. Write three or more sentences using different meanings of a word (e.g., He *got* an A. He *got* the book. He *got* worried.).

Testing Communication Abilities

To test their listening comprehension, have students:

1. Carry out a request. Use one utterance with beginners and more than one with more advanced students, e.g., Go to the board. Go to the board and write your name. Go to the board, write your name, and then erase it.

2. Take a spot dictation.* Distribute a test sheet with a passage containing some missing words. As you dictate, students will write the missing words on an answer sheet.

3. Perform an aural comprehension exercise.

4. Complete the sentence when a choice is given [e.g., It's raining. I'll have to take an _____ (*examination, umbrella, envelope*).].

5. Tell whether the items they hear are singular or plural, present or past, present or future.

6. Answer questions according to the cue or direction [e.g., *(movies)* Where did you go last evening?].

7. Select an appropriate rejoinder (when several choices are given) to a statement or request [e.g., May I smoke? (You may of course.)].

8. Identify the central theme or the nature of a talk when listening to a news broadcast (e.g., social, political, artistic, educational).

9. Tell which statement (given orally or in writing) embodies the main idea of a passage they hear.

10. Give a summary of a talk they have listened to—live or on tape.

11. Take the role of listener or speaker in a dialogue.

12. Engage in role-playing exercises.

*For procedures see Chapter 3.

To test their speaking ability, have students:

1. Repeat sentences of varying lengths.
2. Say a passage, poem, or dialogue they have learned.
3. Take one of the roles in a dialogue.
4. Answer questions either when specific instructions are given or without a cue.
5. Make a rejoinder to a statement or request.
6. Read aloud a passage of familiar material.
7. Read aloud a passage containing new material.
8. Ask direct questions when an indirect statement is given (e.g., Ask me how I got to school this morning.).
9. Transform sentences according to the directions given.
10. Give the equivalent of a short native language utterance. (Exercise caution.)
11. Formulate questions about a passage.
12. Tell what they would say (or do) in a certain situation. They would hear (or read) one or more sentences describing a situation, and they would tell what they would respond [e.g., You know it's a friend's birthday. You meet her (him) on the street. What would you say? Someone tells you his mother is ill. What would you say?].
13. Describe what they see in a picture.
14. Tell about something they did at some particular time (before coming to school, perhaps), something that happened, or something that is going to happen.
15. Give a summary of something they are asked to read at the examination or that they have read at some time before.

*To test their reading ability,** have students:

1. Complete sentences based on a passage read when a choice is given.
2. Complete sentences when a choice is not given.
3. Complete a logical inference [e.g., He had worked eighteen hours without stopping. He was _____ (*rich, tired, stupid*).].
4. Read an unfamiliar passage aloud and answer questions about it.
5. Formulate questions about a passage.
6. Answer several questions about a passage read silently.
7. Give definitions of selected words in a passage. (The ability to use contextual clues would be apparent.)
8. Outline a paragraph.

---

*Since the ability to read requires a knowledge of structure and vocabulary, many of the tests already suggested will also serve to judge reading power.

9. Summarize a passage.
10. Indicate a possible rejoinder or sequence utterance to a statement or a series of statements.
11. Say whether a statement is true or false.
12. Indicate the characters in a story who have expressed a point of view or performed some action.
13. Read a passage crossing out irrelevant words.
14. Read a passage silently within a limited time and answer questions about it. (This would enable you to test fluency and speed as well as comprehension.)
15. Discuss the cultural allusions in a poem or passage.
16. Give synonyms, antonyms, or paraphrases of certain words or expressions.

To test their writing ability, have students*:

1. Insert punctuation marks and capital letters in a paragraph.
2. Write out in full the words for symbols or abbreviations (e.g., +, %, Mr., Inc., etc.).
3. Reconstruct a sentence from several words (e.g., *boys/movies/yesterday*).
4. Complete a sentence using the same verb in both spaces [e.g., (eat) He _____ as he had never _____ before.].
5. Expand several sentences into a letter, dialogue, or story.
6. Add details to a topic sentence.
7. Answer questions about themselves or some material they have studied.
8. Answer questions substituting pronouns for all nouns.
9. Take dictation—spot or regular—or do a dicto-comp.
10. Perform an aural comprehension exercise.
11. Rewrite a passage or story from their point of view, or in the past or future.
12. Write what they would say or do in a situation.
13. Write what they see in a scene.
14. Summarize a passage.
15. Formulate questions about a passage.
16. Write an essay on one of three topics you indicate (based on their interests, their reading, a cultural topic, a news item, etc.). You may wish, at times, to include some of the ideas they are to treat.
17. Rewrite a paragraph using a more casual (or a more formal) style.
18. Complete a dialogue when words are omitted from each utterance or when entire utterances are omitted (or write an original dialogue).
19. Give the English equivalent of a passage in the native language, or vice versa.

*Systematic sound-spelling correspondences should be tested, of course. In addition, any of the oral drills in Chapter 3 can be written.

20. Write a story based on a series of related pictures.

21. Write a letter—business or personal.

Testing Cultural Understanding

Objective tests and essay tests may be used to test knowledge of facts and insight into cultural behavior. Following are some examples. Students may be asked to:

1. Complete a sentence [e.g., In . . . there is no school on _____ and _____. The _____ is the center of social life.].

2. State which is true or false [e.g., Most (Americans) have lunch at noon. X was written by Y.].

3. Choose (by circling, underlining, or writing on a separate sheet) the correct answer [e.g., Americans belong to unions (some, all, none).].

4. Identify people or places (e.g., All of the following are poets except: Keats, Browning, Eliot, Damrosch.).

5. Define or identify by completing a sentence (e.g., Mardi Gras celebrates _____ .).

6. Explain a situation in a brief statement (e.g., The shop will be closed on Boxing Day.).

7. Indicate which behavior may be considered typical, A or B [e.g., In _____ (A) people go to the theater at 2 P.M. (B) people go to the theater at 9:30 P.M.].

8. Write a brief paragraph when a topic sentence is given (e.g., Children and adults always look forward to New Year's Day.).

9. Write an essay on any pertinent topic.

Testing Literary Appreciation

Both objective tests and essays are useful. The objective tests can be of the types indicated above under "Cultural Understanding." Students may be asked to complete sentences when a choice is given or, when no choice is given, to identify, to match, to define, or to give an explanation.

The knowledge tested will depend on the material taught. It may be related, for example, to:

1. Authors and the names of their works.

2. Literary movements—time and milieu (e.g., The Romantic movement flourished in _____ during the _____ part of the _____ century.).

3. Story line or plot.

4. Works in which certain characters appeared (e.g., Portia and Shylock are characters in _____ .).

5. The main theme of a poem, play, or novel (e.g., _____ is at the root of the tragedy of *Othello*.).
6. Cultural allusions in a poem, play, or novel.
7. The use and meaning of certain words or expressions in a literary work.
8. The form of a poem [e.g., _____ is a(n) sonnet, ode.]

Essay tests should be required at advanced levels. If we feel that the student has the necessary ability to read a literary work in the original, we must also assume that his or her writing ability has kept pace. Only through an essay can we judge the students' ability to analyze a literary work—to discuss the differences between the techniques of Shaw and O'Neill, for example, or the differences or similarities between the philosophical theories of Dewey and Russell. In the majority of secondary schools, however, such abilities cannot be assumed even if the study of English was started in the elementary school. Again, each school will have to decide whether such tests are possible with its particular student population and resources.

Further Comments on Testing

In order to eliminate the fear of testing from the minds of your students and in order to make sure the results have validity, it is desirable to follow several elementary principles of test construction and procedure:

1. Announce your tests in advance.
2. Tell students exactly what you will hold them responsible for. (Students will study for the kind of test they know they will be given.)
3. Test only what you have taught thoroughly.
4. Make sure the directions are clear and familiar to the students. Use their native language if necessary. (You should use the native language when feasible when you are giving an unfamiliar type of question or test.)
5. Give an example, if possible, of the response you are seeking.
6. Start with the simplest items first.
7. Test their knowledge of English and not their memory of facts (unless it is a test of cultural understanding). A question such as "Marconi invented the _____ " is *not* a test of English.
8. Make aural comprehension exercises short and relatively simple—at the beginning stages particularly—so that again responses do not become solely a test of memory.

As our knowledge about language and the learning process increases, changes in classroom organization, in methods, and in testing are bound to emerge. Two trends in the field of testing bear further study and examination:

1. Rather than *norm-referenced* tests in which a student's performance is

compared with that of other students, some scholars recommend the use of *criterion-referenced* tests which report the student's performance in *absolute* terms. For example, the student reads well enough to read recombined passages with familiar vocabulary.

    2. Mastery of clearly specified performance objectives should be promoted for all students, and *formative evaluation* tests should be given to judge the degree of mastery attained. Such tests cover a unit of instruction and are graded on a mastery-nonmastery basis. Students are given as many chances as they need to attain the mastery level. Since these tests are also designed to diagnose a student's weaknesses, the student is told what he or she should do to remedy the problems revealed by the testing instrument before being encouraged to take the test again.

    The measurement of students' progress toward the goal of creative communication is a vitally important facet of the language program. Testing should be a continuous process which will help reinforce our students' interests. Knowledge of one's progress and success, as we all know, acts as a powerful stimulant to learning. The cliché "Nothing succeeds like success" is never truer than in a language classroom.

    In addition, test results which point up a serious difficulty in some aspect of the curriculum will enable us to apply remedial measures quickly. Since language is a cumulative subject, it would be unwise to attempt to build a second or third story when the building blocks of our foundation are not well cemented.

    In judging achievement, we should use our observation of students' performances as well as scores on more formal instruments of evaluation. For example, the preparation of assignments, participation in classroom activities, and the "carryover" of language in clubs or afterschool experiences also demonstrate interest and growth.

    While good testing is essential, good teaching is infinitely more so. As a colleague remarked not long ago, "Let's stop weighing the baby all the time. Let's feed it instead."

For Review and Discussion

1. In groups, discuss the advantages (or the disadvantages) of giving brief quizzes.
2. Do you feel you should change some of your techniques when test results are poor? How?
3. Have you found immediate feedback to your students about the correctness of their responses desirable or undesirable?
4. Explain in your own words what is meant by a formative test.
5. What should be tested and why?
6. Why do we test? Give three reasons.

7. When do we test? In a small group, give three points at which tests should be administered.

8. Do you allow pairs of students to grade each other's tests?

9. Name four kinds of tests you can give, for example, a cloze test.

10. What are some cautions or reminders in giving a cloze test?

11. How do you usually test the discrete features of language?

12. In addition to the recommendations made in this chapter, how would you test the integrative abilities of your students?

13. In a foreign language situation, how do you feel about giving passages to be translated from English to the native language, and vice versa?

14. What other suggestions do you have for testing cultural understanding?

15. Do you have special criteria in your school community or in your country for the construction of tests? What are they?

6
What if . . . ? Some Do's and Don'ts

Although I hope you will agree that the material on the preceding pages is practical and generally applicable to a variety of teaching situations, it would be presumptuous to assume that all questions related to the teaching of English have been answered. Many others sometimes arise in the minds of teachers, particularly of new teachers, who find themselves in what they consider unusual teaching situations.

Before attempting to deal with the situations which some teachers deem unusual, let me state for whatever solace it may offer that teaching situations are surprisingly similar in most corners of the globe. This can be deduced from the fact that the same questions recur wherever I have lectured or worked. The conscientious teachers usually start with, "Yes, but, what if . . . ?" I have thought, therefore, that it might be worthwhile to list some of the most frequent questions and to answer them briefly by giving some dos and don'ts where they are pertinent. This procedure will serve also to summarize or recapitulate what has been said in preceding chapters.

For the sake of convenience, the questions will be listed under several categories: the students, teaching colleagues, the school, materials, and methods.

Each of the following statements should be prefaced by "What if . . . ?"

The Students

1. There are over 65 students in each class.

   a. Devise a set of hand signals and gestures to elicit various types of student participation (chorus, half-class, groups, rows, individuals).

   b. Divide the class into four groups for the purposes of choral repetition. You may want to give each group a name for easy reference.

   c. Use choral repetition and group repetition techniques.

   d. Train student leaders to help check homework and correct short quizzes.

e. Establish routines of classroom procedure from the first day (e.g., for taking attendance, distributing and collecting materials).

f. Seat students in alphabetical order or in an order which they will maintain each day.

g. Prepare a seating plan which you will keep in front of you at all times.

h. Walk to various parts of the room as you model sentences and as you conduct various portions of the lesson so that all of the students can see you.

i. Change the students' seats in the middle of the semester so that those who had been sitting in the back will move forward. (Make a new seating plan.)

j. Engage in many chain drills but break them after six to eight people have recited. Start a new chain in another part of the room.

k. Call on individual students from various parts of the room to ensure attention.

2. Some students are very able; others are quite slow.

a. Make use of the abilities of your students. For example, have the more able students go to the chalkboard to write dictation and the answers to aural comprehensions. Have them recite first after you give the model so that other students will be exposed to reasonably correct answers. If you also provide activities in which the less able students can achieve success (doing the simpler pattern practice exercises on the board, coming to the front of the room, indicating pictures or objects and calling on a classmate, helping to grade papers based on a model), there will be no question of lowered morale on their part.

b. Ask the more able students to help the less able students in such activities as preparing assignments or writing compositions.

c. Seat able students next to weaker ones so that the latter will be sure to hear more reasonably accurate pronunciation.

d. Gear your lessons to the average students. Move forward to another unit of work as soon as the majority of students have grasped the content of the one you are teaching. Do not slow down for the less able students but make provision for giving them help at their stage of language learning in order that they may catch up to their classmates.

Since language learning is cumulative and since the reintroduction of learned material is a basic principle of current teaching practice, the less able students will have many opportunities to learn—with ever-increasing thoroughness—some language item they may not have grasped fully the first time.

e. Differentiate your assignments. The slower students should write out many pattern practice exercises; the more able students can answer questions, formulate questions to be asked of their classmates, write summaries, prepare dialogues, or write creative essays.

f. Don't expect all students to reach the same level of comprehension and of oral production in the same length of time. Some will have to stay at the repetition and pattern practice stages longer than will others.

3. The students do not appear interested.

a. Plan lessons in which there is a great deal of variety. Devote the longest time span in each lesson to oral practice activities. Subdivide these activities into four or five different types to avoid boredom.

b. Ensure wide student participation. Let students formulate questions, prepare pictures or other instructional materials, give cues for oral activities, lead games and songs, dramatize conversations, or help prepare a student publication.

c. Keep the pace of the lesson very brisk. Give the students the feeling that they're moving ahead all the time. When a student cannot answer a question, give the correct answer quickly or ask a more able student to give it. (Give a student reasonable time to answer; then move on to someone else and come back to the first student a little later in the lesson.)

d. Don't correct every mistake the students make. During the warm-up and motivation segments of the lesson especially, correct only those errors which impede understanding. Make a mental note of minor errors and give practice in their correction later in the hour or in a future lesson.

e. Don't strive for immediate mastery. Accept reasonable fluency and reasonable accuracy (particularly of difficult sounds) since you will reintroduce all language items many times during the course.

f. Encourage your students by making it possible for them to enjoy many small successes frequently. Do this by announcing tests, differentiating assignments, and creating an audience situation when they have done supplementary outside reading or when they have learned the lines of a poem or a play.

g. Praise them—judiciously of course—but don't wait for them to give a perfect response before you do so. If their response today (although still poor) is better than yesterday's, it is reason enough for praise.

h. Make it possible for them to talk, as quickly as feasible, about the things they would talk about in their native tongue. Demonstrate that English is another mode of communication which permits them to say anything they can say in their language.

i. Utilize the people or places in the community to reinforce the students knowledge of English while lending interest and variety to your lessons.

j. Plan a little more than you think you can cover in an hour. Plan for the slow and for the gifted.

k. Be flexible in your planning. If something of interest happens in your school or community and if you can use the happening to reinforce or to teach language items or an aspect of the culture—or, just as important, to strengthen your rapport with your students—put aside the lesson you had planned and discuss the interesting occurrence.

4. Their native language is completely different from English.

a. Give many examples of new structures. Engage in extensive choral repetition and in intensive practice activities.

b. Point out the contrasts and help students arrive at workable descriptions of the function and use of language items they are learning.

c. Introduce difficult items early in the program and reintroduce them as often as possible—in different situations and with other language items.

d. Teach vocabulary items around a center of interest (buying food or clothing or transportation) so that students can learn to remember words and concepts through association.

e. Teach word families, prefixes, suffixes, roots.

f. Show students how to find the meaning of long English words from the smaller words they contain (provided the root meanings are the same).

g. Grade the material you teach very carefully, building always on known language items *in English*. For example, teach "What do you eat at noon?" *after* you have taught "Do you eat at noon?"

h. Teach and, in the initial stages, practice words or structures with other words which serve as clues. For example, use *now* with the *ing* present; *yesterday* with the simple past.

i. Use many devices (chalkboard, charts, diagrams, pictures) to ensure understanding.

j. Again, don't expect mastery or complete accuracy too soon. Practice the same material at ever-increasing intervals. Teach something on Monday, for example, review it on Tuesday, practice it again on Wednesday, then on Friday, and then on the following Friday. Keep all the language items worth knowing "alive" by reintroducing them constantly with newly acquired items in new cultural contexts.

5. There is a wide age span in my class. Some of my students are children; others are adults.

a. All students will require the same kind of initial presentation. All will need to (1) understand what they are going to repeat, (2) repeat an utterance many times based on your model, (3) practice language items in a variety of drill types.

b. Divide your class into two groups *after* these three steps. Children will continue practicing by means of games, puppets, and dramatizations. Adults will gain insight into the description of the grammatical phenomenon, will read and write, perhaps, and will engage in more complex drills.

c. Train group leaders for each group. For example, a very able adult can help you with the younger students a few minutes during each lesson.

6. Students have different native language backgrounds.

a. Prepare a brief chart of the English phonemes and structures you plan to teach in the early stages of your beginning-level course.

b. Ask teachers or bilingual members of the community to indicate which of the phonemes and structures exist in the language backgrounds of your pupils. List these on your chart. Plan more repetition drills for those which do *not* exist in one or more native languages. All students will profit from the additional drills if you present them briskly and in an interesting manner. Those for whom the drills present no serious conflict will learn to say them more accurately and with more fluency.

c. Give very simple directions in English which you will illustrate and practice many times. At the beginning you will need only a few: *Listen* (place your hand behind your ear). *Repeat* (indicate through gestures that you will say something and they will say it after you). *Say. Ask. Answer.*

d. Start teaching those structures and words which you can easily demonstrate.

e. Use numerous pictures and real objects.

f. All students will have to learn the same sounds and structural features of English, the common core of the language. You will teach these through the techniques indicated above and any other that works for you. You will be able to note, after the very first repetition, problems caused by conflicts with a particular native language. If you feel that your normal plans for teaching particular items to the entire class need to be supplemented for students of a special native language background, assign some meaningful work to the group that does not need the practice (using pattern practice with a student leader, listening to a tape or record, preparing picture cards, etc.) and work intensively on elimination of the problem(s) with the students who are experiencing difficulties.

g. It is desirable not to use *any* native language in the class (even if you are familiar with one) so that all students will have the feeling that they are members of a group and that no one group has special advantages over the other.

7. Some students are discipline problems.

a. Attention to some of the points made up to now will minimize discipline problems.

b. Keep the students busy with interesting work in which all participate. Establish routines. Change seats where necessary to separate the problem students.

c. Make few and very reasonable demands but insist that they be carried out when you *do* make them.

d. Accept reasonable excuses for nonpreparedness.

e. Excuse them from examinations when they have been absent.

f. Praise them!

g. Keep your expectations for them within their ability levels. Challenge the brighter ones, for example, by giving them more difficult assignments or by asking them to help their less able friends.

h. Make sure they understand exactly what you expect of them. Give directions in their native tongue if necessary. Give several illustrations of the response you desire.

i. Don't ask for a choral response to a question unless you are specifically practicing that question and answer. In that way, you will model the answer just prior to their giving it, avoiding the confusion caused by students calling out different responses.

j. Train students, patiently, to keep together in choral repetition.

k. Don't raise your voice or continue to work when students are talking. Just stop and stand quietly. They will soon become attentive.

l. Don't penalize the wrongdoers! Reward, with praise, those who are attentive. The other group will soon be seeking your praise too.

8. Adult students have varied interests and specializations.

a. All students at the beginning level need to learn the same sounds, the same structures, and much of the common vocabulary which underlies our language.

b. At intermediate and advanced levels, suggest magazines for them in their specialties. Help them read the articles. Give them the specialized vocabulary in their field and show them where and how to insert it in the language pattern you are teaching.

c. Have them prepare brief talks about their interests for other class members.

d. Encourage students to ask each other questions about their interests.

e. At the advanced level, give individual reading assignments based on their interests.

Our Colleagues

1. Each person in the school (or department) teaches another facet of the English course.

a. Arrange for frequent meetings so that you can correlate your work. The person in charge of teaching pronunciation and intonation, for example, should give practice in the patterns which have been learned in the structure class. The teacher of reading should be aware of the vocabulary and the structure patterns which have been taught.

b. Plan jointly sponsored activities in which students see and appreciate the fact that any utterance or any conversational exchange includes features of the sound, structure, and vocabulary systems as well as aspects of culture.

2. The other teachers haven't used my methods and materials. Students have never. . . .

a. Spend the first few days training your students to respond to your hand signals or gestures, to engage in chain drills, to ask and answer questions, to dramatize dialogues, to keep together in choral work. Establish types of standards for student participation.

b. Find out how much your students know by asking many questions in English the first few days. Don't ask them what they have learned, but elicit the information by asking questions which incorporate the structures and vocabulary you might assume they have learned. Start teaching them from that point.

The School

1. We must use the syllabus supplied by the school.

Use it, by all means. Within the items or skills listed in the syllabus, prepare a variety of activities, engage in oral work, follow the six steps in language learning, and change the order of presentation of material if the order in the syllabus is not in harmony with some of the principles we have discussed and with which you may agree. You will find it possible to cover the same amount of material prescribed for you but in a manner which may be more interesting to you and to your students.

2. The school (or the ministry or the education department) prepares the examinations.

Everything that has been mentioned above can be repeated in answer to this question. One word must be added, however. If the examination also includes translation of unrelated sentences (as may be the case), help your students prepare for such translations. Do so by taking typical sentences from translations and by giving pattern practice of each type as explained in Chapter 3.

The Materials of Instruction

1. The textbooks are traditional.

a. Examine each unit carefully. Regroup the structure points for presentation; prepare interesting oral practice drills; practice only the logical and authentic sentences in the text; prepare question-answer drills and dialogues; present and practice everything orally in mini situations before assigning writing exercises.

b. Don't use the textbook entirely as it is. For example, do not emphasize words and sentences which are not of high frequency. Formulate (or have the students formulate) interesting questions about the reading material.

c. Choose a limited amount of material for each lesson and build interesting exercises around that limited material.

d. Prepare or help your able students prepare two or three dialogues using the structural items and vocabulary found in the textbooks. Help the students understand, dramatize, and perhaps read and write the dialogues.

2. The school has no money or limited money for equipment.

a. Chalkboards and chalk are found in nearly every school. Things like pictures can be made on any paper, with pencil, pen, or crayon.

b. No one would deny that record players and tape recorders could enrich a teaching presentation, but electronic equipment should always be considered supplementary equipment. You alone can create a pleasant and productive language class by your enthusiasm, your attitude toward your students, and your careful attention to lesson planning.

Methods

1. The students cannot understand a dialogue or a reading passage.

Help them to understand by showing pictures, dramatizing the material, giving cognates, and even by giving the native language equivalent (if all speak the same native language and you are familiar with it).

2. The students have trouble making the . . . sound even after I have taught it.

a. Reteach it and practice it whenever you can. Use diagrams, descriptions of vocal organs, phonetic symbols, and reminders of other sounds they know in their native tongue or in English to help them hear and produce the sound.

b. Reintroduce it whenever possible. Don't expect mastery too soon!

c. Make sure it appears frequently in some of the pattern practice exercises and conversations.

3. The students get bored with (forty) repetitions.

a. No one says that everything should be repeated (forty) times! If ten repetitions are enough to ensure reasonably good pronunciation and accuracy, go on to the next phase of learning.

b. Strike a happy medium between giving enough repetitions to form the correct habit and avoiding boredom. As soon as you note a slackening of interest, proceed to something else but make a note to reintroduce the material which may not have been learned to your complete satisfaction.

4. Students are afraid to speak in class.

a. Start with choral repetition, followed by group repetition.

b. Call on the more able or less timid students first.

c. Be patient with really timid individuals. In the beginning stage, have them come to your desk and repeat things after you. (The other students can be busily engaged in another type of language work.)

d. Praise them for any effort, no matter how slight.

e. If they are young, use puppets to give them the feeling they are not seen as they speak.

f. Use paired activities. (See Appendix I.)

5. Students want to know why things are said the way they are.

a. Help them answer their own questions about grammar by saying and showing numerous examples of any structural item.

b. Prove to them that a knowledge of the rule will not help them to create sentences or to communicate. Demonstrate the value of a statement which describes what actually happens in saying an utterance.

c. If they are adults and if you know their native language, show them that there may be no reason or logic behind a word or utterance in their language.

d. Discuss with them the nature and function of language.

6. Students want to keep their books open when you are reading to them.

a. Although some educators consider it desirable for students to keep their books closed during the teacher's initial oral reading, this need not be a hard and fast rule. If you have an English I course, you should be able to train students from the outset to keep their books closed and to listen to you with understanding (if your principal or supervisor insists on this).

b. If they have not received training in listening with their books closed, you may prepare them for closed book reading by using very simple material, by reading very short segments at a time, and by asking simple questions.

c. Encourage them to try to understand with their books closed. Read the same sentence several times, if necessary, until they develop confidence.

d. Vary your procedures. Have open book reading sometimes and closed book reading other times.

e. Remember that reading means looking at written words.

7. The school wants us to start reading very soon in our program.

a. Introduce reading if your syllabus requires it but make sure your students can say with reasonable fluency the words and sentences they are going to see.

b. Clear all difficulties *first*—of pronunciation, of structure, of vocabulary—before reading.

c. Read the passage orally for them several times.

In Conclusion

Other questions and problems will undoubtedly arise as you teach various groups of students or as you move from one school or community to another. No two individual students, no two schools, no two communities, and no two teachers are exactly alike.

All any book can do or should do is set down the principles and practices which have been found effective by a representative group of teachers in representative communities throughout the world.

A grave injustice would have been done you if I had led you to believe that there exists only one acceptable method or only one set of materials or techniques. While it is true that our current knowledge of the nature of language and of language learning makes certain principles of teaching more desirable and effective than others adhered to in the past, it is also true that within those principles there is ample opportunity for teacher creativity and for flexibility of procedure and activities. While it is also true that we are teaching English as a second or foreign language, we cannot lose sight of the fact that we are teaching it to human beings. As teachers we are, in effect, attempting to graft new habits and new behavior patterns on individuals who come to our classroom with highly diverse backgrounds of ability and of experience.

Moreover, advances in many branches of science may require you to modify or add to your store of knowledge or skills of teaching English at any time in the future. It is my hope that some of the guidelines I have indicated will prepare you to adapt your teaching to any situation in which you may find yourselves and to accept new ideas in the context in which you know they will be most helpful to you and to your students.

The suggestions in this book have been so briefly stated, constituting as they do a synthesis of observation, interviews, and workshop experiences, that a concluding statement becomes exceedingly difficult to write. Nevertheless, it may be desirable to reaffirm several comments and principles which have been scattered throughout this text:

1. You, the teacher, are more important than any method or material. It is what you do with any method or with any piece of material which will determine its effectiveness in helping your students learn. Student growth should be judged not only in terms of number of language items acquired or increased fluency but also in terms of attitude toward English-speaking peoples and toward the continued study of English.

2. Student growth depends to a large extent upon your own professional growth. In a dynamic field such as ours, no teacher can afford to remain at a standstill. We should keep up with new findings, with new materials, and with the reports of teaching and learning experiences of our colleagues. This is possible by subscribing to journals in the field, attending conferences where possible, becoming members of professional organizations, and doing extensive reading. You should conduct experiments of your own. Many facets of theory and practice are still in need of further research. Your contribution, added to that of others, cannot help but be of value to many persons engaged in the field.

If English is not your native language, you may want to increase your competence in the language (or maintain it if you are not working in an English-speaking country) by taking advantage of the numerous seminars which are organized for teachers of English. If possible, you should arrange visits to English-speaking countries.

3. Under professional growth should be included a knowledge of many other areas of learning. Interested and interesting teachers constantly enrich their personalities and hence their teaching through the study of aspects of method or knowledge culled from other subjects in the school curriculum and from other sciences.

4. You should learn to blend many ingredients together in order to give students the kind of learning experiences which contribute to the development of correct habits, broad interests and knowledge, basic skills, and desirable attitudes. Every learning experience should be carefully planned. It should have well-defined, carefully circumscribed objectives; it should be made interesting to the students because it uses *them, their* interests and ability, and *their* environment as a starting point; it should ensure the active participation of all the students; it should utilize varied materials and activities; it should look back on what has been learned and lead to further language growth. Every segment of newly acquired language should be skillfully woven into the existing fabric of communication.

5. In addition, participation in each class hour should give the students the conviction that they are moving ahead. This does not mean that they have to learn a new large body of material each time or that they have to begin a completely new unit. It may mean that they acquire a little more accuracy in producing a sound, a little more fluency in saying a familiar sentence or a new word, a new way of doing a drill through a different use of material or a different type of student participation. Our goal should be continuous and gradual progress rather than immediate mastery.

6. In the philosophy underlying some language learning programs, great emphasis is placed on the ability of the teacher to detect errors in pronunciation (even in choral recitation), to identify and diagnose speech problems of students, and to model new structures. In short, it is considered important that the teacher develop what is generally called a "listening ear." I would like to suggest that a "listening heart" is of equal importance.

The teacher who can give students the feeling that they are an important part of a group, that they are capable of learning, and that they can achieve success; the teacher who can demonstrate an understanding of conflict—both environmental and linguistic; the teacher who, through enthusiasm, art, and skill, makes language learning a subject to be looked forward to—will in the final analysis be the one who will forge ahead of less perceptive colleagues in promoting the desirable habits and attitudes needed for language learning. Teachers who embody the personal and professional characteristics outlined here cannot help but push aside the language barriers which impede communication among peoples.

Appendix I

Practice in Pairs

This article by Geoffrey Broughton*, written for the Brazilian journal *English Teaching* and reproduced in the Italian journal *LEND* in cooperation with the British Council of Italy, is so valuable that I have decided—with Professor Broughton's permission—to use it exactly as I found it. I am sure you will find the suggestions as practical and realistic as I have found them.

Practice in Pairs

by Geoffrey Broughton

The teacher of English is often faced with the conflicting problems of teaching large classes and the need to give them massive practice in the structures of the language. What is more, few course books, if any, give sufficient practice material to ensure controlled oral drill to the point of saturation in the patterns that have been taught. Understandably many teachers take the line of least resistance to these difficulties, and limit their oral work to a minimum of class repetition and a few scattered questions.

Yet massive oral practice is possible with large numbers of learners and one device open to the teacher in such a situation is to set the students working orally in pairs. This article is an attempt to suggest how it may best be done.

After all, the essence of language is communication, at its simplest meaningful verbal intercourse between two people. Common patterns are found in seeking information (by question and answer), seeking confirmation (by affirmation and agreement), eliciting disagreement (by affirmation or negation), or eliciting verbal action (by command and obeying). And these are some of the modes that the teacher

---

*I am very grateful to Professor Broughton for permitting me to use this article in the fourth edition.

can readily harness to paired language practice. This, at the reinforcement stage of language learning, gives a communication situation in its simplest form, yet with an optimum control over the resulting dialogue.

Perhaps an example will best illustrate the advantages and potential of oral practice in pairs. Imagine the situation where the teacher has introduced defining relative clauses—with *who* and *whose* (e.g., The man who brings the milk; The man whose car is outside; etc.). The learners have met and understood examples and see how they work in context. Now is the time for practicing them and the "line-of-least-resistance" teacher sets a written exercise from the book. But this can hardly be called massive practice, and the ten or fifteen sentences each student writes (even if correct) can hardly be sufficient to drive home the new patterns to the point where they are integrated with the general body of his language mastery. The written exercise certainly has its place as a slightly different kind of reinforcement, but it should be preceded by oral drill.

The paired practice is introduced by the teacher putting on the blackboard:

a nurse

a librarian

and asking: "*Where does a nurse work?*" ("A nurse works in a hospital.") and "*Where does a librarian work?*" ("A librarian works in a library.") Then comes the new pattern in the questions: "*Which one is the person who works in a hospital?*" ("A nurse.") and "*Which one is the person who works in a library*" ("A librarian.")

Now the teacher adds to the blackboard list familiar nouns which fit the pattern: a waiter, a secretary, a cashier, a shop assistant, a bus driver, a teacher, an actor, a hairdresser. Then he asks the class, "*Which one is the person who works in a _____?*" He asks five or six questions, if necessary writing up the place of work opposite each noun:

a nurse	*a hospital*
a librarian	*a library*
a waiter	*a restaurant (a café)*
a secretary	*an office*
a cashier	*a bank*
a shop assistant	*a shop*
a bus driver	*a bus*
a teacher	*a school (a college)*
an actor	*a theater*
a hairdresser	*a hairdresser's*

Now the class is able to do its first piece of work in pairs. "Practice in pairs," the teacher says, "the person on the left asks the questions; the person on the right answers." Notice that there is no problem for the learners as to what to ask and what to answer. Notice also that the teacher has made things easy for the weaker and less enterprising students who will ask the questions they have heard the teacher ask; but the more enterprising will want to start with the questions the teacher deliberately left out.

Watching and listening carefully, the teacher decides when to change the questioners and, when he judges that the material has nearly been used up, instructs the persons on the right to ask the questions and those on the left to answer.

After a suitable time for this practice, the teacher stops the activity and prepares the class for the development of the activity. So far, all the questions have started, "*Which is the person who works in a _____?*" But we can make the question more general by adding more nouns to the blackboard and giving more choice in the question, though still practicing the same pattern.

So a new blackboard list is begun alongside the first, starting with:

a postman

a pilot

As before, the teacher puts the first questions to the class: "*Which one is the person who brings our letters?*" "*Which one is the person who flies planes?*" Now this second list is developed on the blackboard by the addition of familiar nouns, and these are used to frame questions. Again, if necessary, a brief help towards the answer may be added:

a postman	*brings letters*
a pilot	*flies planes*
a farmer	*grows food*
an author	*writes books*
a musician	*makes music*
a window cleaner	*cleans windows*
a dentist	*looks after teeth*
a florist	*sells flowers*
a tennis player	*plays tennis*
an architect	*designs houses (buildings)*

After five or six questions to the class, they are told for the second time, "Practice in pairs," with one member of each pair being the questioner to start with, and later the other. This practice continues for a suitable period—up to two minutes—before the teacher brings it to a stop and introduces a related pattern. As a reminder, he puts part of the familiar pattern on the board—"The person who works in a hospital." Now he asks: "*What's a librarian?*", eliciting the answer "A person who works in a library" and "*What's a postman?*" ("A person who brings letters.") Two or three other examples show the class the new, related pattern of question and answer. ("*What's a _____?*" "A person who _____.")

And the learners are ready for the third short session of work in pairs.

This particular set of twenty nouns has been selected to be used with other related patterns, using *whose*. So, after the third paired practice, the teacher reminds the class of one of the *whose* patterns. *"Which one is the person whose work is in a hospital?"* (A nurse.) *"Which one is the person whose work is bringing letters?"* (A postman.) A fourth paired practice follows, and the fifth, using the same lists and a *whose* answer, is started by sample questions and answers like: *"What's a waiter?"* (*"A man whose work is in a restaurant."*) *"What's a farmer?"* (A man whose work is growing food.")

Set out like this, such an activity appears to be more tedious than it is. Notice that all the sentences are meaningful to the learners, that they are being drilled in making correct sentences, and that the periods of paired practice are broken up by the teacher's exposition and questions. So that, in fact, the learners here have done a total of some eight or ten minutes of very solid practice in two kinds of defining relative clauses and during that time have personally either asked or answered up to a hundred questions using the relevant patterns. This is the kind of massive practice which reinforces the active handling of structures in preparation for the written exercise.

The experienced teacher will soon recognize what a wide range of patterns can be practiced in this way. There is the obvious range of structures which involve direct questions—What's that? Is that a NOUN? Is that an ADJECTIVE? Where is the NOUN? and many others. Question tags, using the anomalous finites (*can, must, may, will*, etc.) are a very profitable area—You can swim/run/drive/dance/, etc., can't you? You can't fly/walk on your hands/see an elephant, etc., can you?

Rather less obvious, however, is a range of traditional exercises, which may easily be converted to oral practice in pairs. For example, one coursebook, practicing *used to*, gives an old school timetable, followed by this substitution table:

How many sentences can you make?

The class
The boys
used to

do
have
study
learn

play football

French, German, English,
History, Geography,
Math, Science, Music

on

Monday.
Tuesday.
Wednesday.
Thursday.
Friday.

For practice in pairs, the teacher need only start asking, "*When did the boys use to have French?*" and so on. Then, with the school timetable on the blackboard, the learners can continue in pairs asking each other similar questions. The related pattern "*What did they use to do on* _____?" follows naturally.

Some traditional exercises are more difficult to turn into question and answer, but can be rephrased to give a challenge and its reply. The familiar conversion exercise where direct speech is to be reported can be handled in this way. For example, the following sentences might be set for reporting:

She said, "I want to see that film."
She said, "I'll go tonight."
She told him, "I think I'll get the best seats."

A way of working these in pairs would be like this:

A. She said, "I want to see that film."
B. Yes, I know. She said she wanted to see that film.
A. She said, "I'll go tonight."
B. Yes, I know. She said she would go tonight.
A. She told him, "I think I'll get the best seats."
B. Yes, I know. She told him she thought she would get the best seats.

These short periods of oral work, of course, are intended to give maximum practice for the class and are certainly more demanding on the teacher. Not only must he plan the sequence of the drills with great care, but while the pairs are working, he should move around the class to make sure that mistakes are not being made, and generally keeping his finger on the pulse of the class. In this way he knows when to stop the activity as the students are reaching the last examples, or in the rare cases where individuals have not properly understood the procedures. Another advantage of the teacher moving about is that he can control the noise level. Though if he is firmly in control of the learners he can usually make sure that the general noise level does not rise above an acceptable hum of interested conversation.

Perhaps these considerations suggest the fundamental secret of the success of this kind of oral activity. It depends completely on the willingness of the class to participate (a matter of discipline) and their understanding of what they are expected to do (a matter of organization). The young or inexperienced teacher may be chary of letting control go out of his own hands and may even encounter difficulties when he tries paired practice for the first time. But its advantages repay the organizational efforts involved. It is worth spending extra time in getting the pairs working well on the first occasion. The earliest drills should be straight repetitions of class practice. It helps when learners always work with the same partner, so that a routine is established for the activity.

Notice too, how the use of the blackboard as a focal point gives each pair something external to themselves to concentrate on. Not only does it keep them working, but it also discourages them from drifting into a non-English private conversation. But perhaps most important is the challenge of running correctly through an interesting and meaningful exercise: once it becomes meaningless or tedious it loses interest.

Here, then, is an activity method which the teacher of the largest class can use, one in which no learner need leave his seat, one in which the maximum use is made of the learners' time, and if it is devised with a little imagination from the teacher, one which the learners will enjoy whenever the teacher says—"Practice in pairs."

Appendix II

Picture Compositions

This stimulating article by Donn Byrne*, English Language Officer of the British Council in various countries, will undoubtedly open up new vistas to many readers. I had the privilege of seeing Mr. Byrne demonstrate the use of the pictures with a large group of learners. The language he elicited—at various levels and in different varieties—was indeed amazing and the interest engendered, even more so.

Visual Sequences
for the Production
of Dialogue

by Donn Byrne

Visual sequences of the kind depicted below, where the dialogue is implicit in the situations, have to be interpreted rather than described. There are two main ways in which the dialogue element may be 'extracted':

(1) The students may first be asked to say what they think the pictures are about. For example, in Picture A, Mrs. (Ball) wants some sugar. She asks her husband to go and get it. Perhaps at the start her husband is reluctant to go (Why?). So she has to persuade him (How?). In Picture B she offers him a list because there are other things which she needs (What are they?), but he refuses to take it. The students are then asked to devise appropriate dialogue to fit these statements. All this may be done as a group activity.

(2) Alternatively, the dialogue may be cued directly by providing the first line of the exchange. For example:

*My gratitude to Professor Byrne is boundless for granting me permission to use this article in the fourth edition.

T (= Mrs. B): Will you go to the grocer's and get some sugar, please?

S (= Jack): . . .

T: If you don't go, I can't make you a (pudding).

S: . . .

T: I want sugar, salt, coffee. . . . Here's a list.

S: . . .

Several students may be asked to suggest possible replies. Alternative questions may also be proposed. After all suggestions have been given, the students may be asked to repeat—in pairs—the dialogue implicit in *both* pictures, giving appropriate variations.

The next three pictures may be similarly exploited to produce, for example, a short conversation about the weather and gardening (C), Jack ordering the things he wants from the grocer—but forgetting the sugar! (D), and a conversation about the news (E). F involves giving directions and is therefore an important picture which can be developed in detail. (This is done in the next paragraph.) Since it is obviously 'open-ended,' there are many possibilities. Finally, in G and H, we have the conversation between Mrs. Ball, who is angry because her husband has taken such a long time, and Jack, who tries to make excuses—only to find that he has forgotten the sugar!

The picture which lends itself to the most exploitation is F, from which dialogues with a number of exchanges can be developed. One or two model dialogues may be produced first with the help of the class. For example:

(1) Man: Excuse me, can you tell me the way to the station?

   Jack: Certainly. Cross over the road, go as far as the newsagent's* and then turn left.

   Man: Is it a long way?

   Jack: About half a mile.

(2) Man: Could you tell me the way to the museum, please?

   Jack: Which one? There are two.

   Man: The Natural History Museum.

   Jack: Ah, yes. Look, go down this street, take the second turning on your right, and then turn right again at the post office. It's next to the library.

   Man: Did you say the *second* turning on the right?

   Jack: Yes. There's a butcher's on the corner.

   Man: Thanks very much. How long will it take?

   Jack: Oh, about fifteen minutes.

The class can then be divided into groups to produce other dialogues, which can be acted out in front of the class.

Further work can also be done. For example, a set of questions which might be asked about Picture A could run as follows:

(A) Where was Mrs. Ball? What was she doing? Why did she call her husband? What did she want him to buy? Did he want to go to the grocer's? What did she say to him?

Newsstand in American English.

Similarly a true/false drill can be carried out. For example:

Ask the students to say whether the following statements are true. If they are false, get them to give the correct ones.

(1) Mrs. Ball was reading the paper in the kitchen.
(2) Mrs. Ball asked her husband to go to the grocer's.
(3) Jack wanted to go to the grocer's.
(4) Jack took the list which his wife offered him.

Finally, the students may be asked to reconstruct the entire story, using suitable dialogue, with minimum cues from the teacher. At this stage it should be sufficient to say: *Picture A—Mrs. Ball* to elicit a whole series of statements:

Mrs. Ball was in the kitchen.

She was cooking.

She found that she did not have any sugar, so she called her husband.

"Jack!" she said . . . , etc.

Similarly the callword *Jack* should elicit:

Jack was (watching TV).

He came into the kitchen . . . , etc.

Numerous composition exercises can be based on this oral preparatory stage, including of course the writing up of dialogues. An interesting group project would be to ask the students to write in the form of a short play, divided into scenes and with appropriate stage directions, an account of what the various people in the story did and said. For example:

Scene 1—Mrs. Ball is cooking in the kitchen. She finds that she does not have any sugar.

Mrs. Ball (calling her husband): Jack!

There is no answer.

Mrs. Ball: JACK!

Jack (coming into the kitchen): Yes, dear! What is it?

Mrs. Ball: I've run out of sugar. Run along to the grocer's and get me some, please.

Jack: But I wanted to watch TV . . . , etc.

Appendix III

Situational Topics

The list below will be useful to you in planning numerous types of language activities. It may suggest (1) possible themes for a dialogue, dictation, a listening comprehension exercise, a reading passage, some directed dialogue, a discussion, a written composition, (2) topics for cross-cultural research, or (3) situations around which to present and practice language items and structures.

Addresses
Addressing people
Age
Appointments, making
Art
Banking services
Barber shop, going to a
Beauty shop, going to a
Clothing (see also Shopping):
      altering
      buying
      cleaning
      describing
      making
      taking care of
      wearing
Dancing
Dates
Days of the week

Hotels:
>   making reservations
>   staying in

Housing (see also Homes, Hotels)

Introductions, acknowledging and making

Lending library

Letter writing

Mail, receiving and sending

Materials (See also Clothing, Shopping)

Measures:
>   distance
>   quantity
>   size

Months

Movies

Museums

Names of persons

Newspapers:
>   buying
>   printing
>   reading

Numbers (See also Addresses, Telephoning):
>   cardinal
>   ordinal

Opera

Ordinal numbers

Parties:
>   enjoying
>   going to
>   planning

Pets:
>   care of
>   kinds

Places in the community

Places to live (See also Home)

Place names:
>   cities
>   countries

Post office, services in
Public library
Quantity, expressions related to
Radio, listening to
Recreational activities
Relations, family
Repairing things
Responsibilities:
     home
     school
Restaurants (See also Eating, Food, Meals):
     ordering food in
School activities:
     examinations
     homework
     materials and objects used in
     subjects studied
     teachers
     transportation to
Seasons
Shopping for:
     clothing
     food
     household supplies
     medicines
     toilet articles
Sizes (See also Clothing, Shopping)
Sports (See also Recreation)
Telephoning:
     getting information
     leaving messages
     long distance
     public booths
     saying phone numbers
Television
Telling time
Theater
Time, expressions of

Transportation:
    buying tickets
    means of
    schedules
    terminals
    timetables
    using a car
Visiting, people and places
Weather
Work:
    aspiring to certain kinds of
    hours of
    laws related to
    looking for
    payment received for
    preparing for
Worshipping

Appendix IV

Definitions of Useful Terms

On the pages which follow, you will find, in alphabetical order, brief, simple definitions of terms as I have used them in this book and other terms you will find in your reading.

Accent. (1) A synonym for *stress* (See **Stress**.) (2) Marks indicating the four word, phrase, or sentence stresses: ´ (primary), ˆ (secondary), ` (tertiary), ˘ (weak). (3) A written mark over certain vowels of a word to differentiate it from another word spelled in the same way—Italian: e (and), è (is). (4) A written mark indicating syllabic stress—Spanish: está (he is), ésta (this one). (5) A written mark indicating vowel quality—French: père (father), allé (gone). (6) A foreign accent—a pronunciation deviation in the target language which identifies or marks the speaker as nonnative. (7) Regional or dialectal accents.

Achievement Test. One which measures how much of a body of language material taught has actually been learned by the student.

Action Series. (also called the Gouin series from the name of its originator): Utterances which verbalize a series of sequential actions being performed, e.g., I'm getting up, I'm going to the board, I'm writing my name, etc.

Activated Headphones. Those which amplify a speaker's voice and permit the speaker to hear him or herself while speaking.

Active Vocabulary. The content and function words of a language which are learned so thoroughly that they can be used in the performance of any communication act; the vocabulary which can be easily recalled for production. (See **Passive Knowledge**.)

Affective. Referring to the feelings and needs—emotional or psychological—of a person which should be satisfied in order to ensure learning.

Affective Filter. A mechanism in the human mind which will reject knowledge when emotional or psychological stress is too high. (The affective filter should be kept low, as in a relaxed learning atmosphere, to permit acceptance of the new material.

Allophone. One of the variant sounds of a phoneme. For example, the different *p* sounds in *pill, spill, cup* are all variants, or *allophones*, of the phoneme /p/. Allophones do not differentiate meaning.

Analogy. The ability to form a word or pattern on the basis of knowledge of similar words or patterns. For example, if your students know the forms *boy/boys, girl/girls, ruler/rulers*, they should by analogy be able to give the form *pencils* when you give the stimulus word *pencil*.

Anomic. A traumatic feeling experienced by learners who no longer identify with the native language community but who are not yet ready to "belong" to the English-speaking community.

Anthropology. One of the social sciences which studies all the features of the culture (including language) of a society.

Articulation. (1) The smooth, continuous development from one level of language learning to the next. (2) The production of distinct sounds by the vocal organs—e.g., tongue between the teeth or tip of tongue against the tooth ridge.

Audio-lingual. (1) A term used to indicate an approach to language learning—first by hearing, then by repeating. (2) Listening and speaking. (Another term for audio-lingual is aural-oral.)

Backward Build-up. The teaching technique whereby long sentences are divided and reconstructed from the end into small meaningful segments for ease in repetition.

Behavior. (1) A way of doing something habitually as a result of the assimilated acquisition of a skill or a body of information or knowledge. (2) The visible activity displayed by a learner which can be observed and evaluated.

Biculturalism. The state of being able to operate comfortably and appropriately in two cultural settings.

Bidialectalism. The state of being able to use two dialects (e.g., local, regional, standard). The level of competence will depend on such factors as environment, age, and use.

Bilingualism. The state of being able to use two languages with almost equal facility.

Bottom-up Processing. In reading, comprehension based on details and comments in the text. (Also called **Data-driven** processing.) (See **Top-down processing**.)

British Terminology (primarily).

class: sets of language elements, e.g., verbal, noun.

form: grammar and lexis.

structure: the systematic relationship between classes.

substance: form and content.

system: a restricted group of items which provides a choice of possibilities for a particular function, e.g., person, number, demonstratives (this, that).

unit: any stretch of speech carrying grammatical pattern (morph, word, group, clause, sentence).

Catenation. Combinations of sounds permitted in the language system.

Chain. The type of pupil activity in a classroom in which a student makes a statement, asks a question, or responds, and then the student next to or behind him or her makes a statement, responds, or asks a question.

Choral Repetition. The imitation of spoken material by an entire class or by a group speaking together.

Cloze Test. One in which students are to restore words which have been systematically omitted.

Cluster. (1) The sequence or bunching together of consonants, e.g., wo*rks*, sp*ring*. (2) The sequence or bunching together of other language elements (vowels, nouns, verbs, etc.).

Code. The total shared language system of a community. (See **Parole** and **Language Variety**.)

Code Switching. The human being's ability to change the register (or variety) of the language he or she uses, depending on the social situation.

Cognate. A word in one language which looks similar to and has a meaning equivalent to a word in another language, e.g., (Spanish/English) *nacional/national*. Beware of false cognates, i.e., words which look the same but have different meanings, e.g., (Italian) *attualmente* = at the present time, (English) *actually* = really.

Cognitive. Pertaining to the acquisition of knowledge or learning through mental processing.

Cognitive Code Theory. One which holds that (a) the learner perceives (or is guided to discover) the rule or generalization underlying a feature of language from several examples of it, and (b) language is rule-governed behavior.

Cohesive Devices. Linking words like *however, nevertheless*, etc., which hold the thoughts in a passage together.

Collocation. The co-occurrences (of sounds, structures, or lexical items) permitted by the language system. (See **co-occurrence**.)

Communicative Competence. The ability to recognize and to produce authentic and appropriate language correctly and fluently in any social situation.

Competence. (1) In a psycholinguistic sense, the achieved ability of the speaker or listener to understand and produce language utterances. (2) In transformational theory, the ability to recognize well-formed sentences, deviant (nongrammatical) sentences, "look-alike" sentences which come from different deep structures, and synonymous sentences having different surface structures. (See **Performance**.)

Compound System. One in which the foreign language is learned and used in relation to the native language. (See **Coordinate System**.)

Computer. An electronic machine which can assist learning through software programs, interaction with learners, and immediate feedback. The "heart" of the computer is the *central processing unit* which stores the programs and permits instant retrieval.

Confirmation. Knowledge given a learner—orally or through some other technique—that his or her response is correct.

Conflict. Interference or problem in learning a second or foreign language caused by the ingrained habit of saying something in a certain way in one's native tongue.

Connotative. The personal meaning a word may have for individuals depending on their experiences with the word or its referent.

Conscious Selection. The step in the learning process in which students choose between two language items which are in contrast.

Console. The teacher's control center in a language laboratory.

Constituent. Any one of the smaller structural units linked together in a larger construction. For example, in "The boys bought balls," *the boys* (the NP or noun phrase) and *bought balls* (the VP or verb phrase) are the *immediate constituents* of the sentence. The *ultimate constituents* would be *boy/s* and *ball/s* which cannot be divided further.

Constituent Theory. The binary division of an utterance into smaller and smaller constituents until ultimate constituents are identified. (These may be segments of words.)

Content Words. Vocabulary items that refer to things, actions, or qualities. (See Notions.)

Context. The forms or words within any connected stretch of speech which surround other words and thus help to give them their particular meaning. (Often *context* and *situation* are used interchangeably, but they should not be.) Context is *intralingual*, whereas situation is *extralingual*. (See Situation.)

Continuant. A sound which can be prolonged indefinitely like *m* or *f*.

Continuum. An uninterrupted sequence of steps or phases in a process. In language learning, we speak of the stages in acquiring full listening comprehension, for example, as points or steps on a continuum.

Contrastive Analysis. A comparison of all the features of the native language of a learner which differ from those of the target language.

Co-occurrence. (1) The normal, permitted combination of words in an utterance; e.g., we can say, "I watched a film," but not "I watched a book." (The British term for this is *collocation*. (2) The environment (the surrounding words) of a word or structure, e.g., The Queen *of* (England).

Coordinate System. One in which the target language is learned as a parallel, completely independent system without relation to the native language. (See **Compound System**.)

Correlation. (1) The act of bringing together learnings from more than one subject area for mutual enrichment. (2) A positive or negative relationship between two tests or two abilities or factors; e.g., there is not necessarily a high (or positive) correlation between intelligence and the ability to learn the elementary mechanisms of a foreign language.

Count Noun. One that can be modified by a numeral, e.g., four *apples*. *Ink* on the other hand is called a *mass noun* since it cannot easily be modified by a numeral.

Coverage. In semantic theory includes definition (does the replacing word define the other?), inclusion as in synonyms, extension of a meaning to cover another, power of combination to form other words.

Cross-sectional Studies. In second language acquisition research, studies based on the performance (the output) a language learner can produce at the present time. (See **Longitudinal Studies**.)

Cue. A stimulus which is given to elicit a response. The cue may be a gesture, a picture, a word, a sentence, etc., which is used to call forth a desired response.

Cultural Island. The total immersion of the foreign language learners into the foreign culture through the continuous use of the foreign language in class, the display of its authentic materials, the listening to its speakers, etc.

Cultural Pluralism. A condition in which various ethnic communities coexist in one nation. An appreciation and understanding of the similarities and differences of various groups are essential in a multiethnic society.

Culture. The language, customs, values, beliefs, art forms, and achievements of a society.

Curriculum. The knowledge, information, skills, abilities, activities, materials, etc., which are included in the teaching of any subject.

Decode. The process by which a hearer derives the total meaning (linguistic and cultural) of a verbal message. (See **Encode**.)

Deductive Process. One in which a rule is formulated first and then followed by examples which conform to it. (See **Inductive Process**.)

Deictive Features. The relationships existing between nominals and their pronominal referents; e.g., *My car* is old but *it* still runs.

Denotative. The dictionary meaning of a word. (See **Connotative**.)

Derived. An utterance, word, or expression produced by the application of a transformation rule to a basic word or utterance; e.g., *kindness* is derived from *kind*; *Hamlet was written by Shakespeare* is derived from *Shakespeare wrote Hamlet*.

Determiner. A word such as an article, a possessive adjective, or a partitive, which marks a noun, e.g., *the, a, some, each, any*.

Diagnostic Test. One which permits the examiner to judge the student's strengths or weaknesses, problems or difficulties.

Dialect. A variety of the national language used by members of a speech community living in a given geographical area.

Diphthong. A sound which combines two vowel sounds, e.g., /ɔɪ/, /aʊ/.

Distractor. An incorrect item given purposely by the examiner in a test.

Encode. The process through which a speaker conveys his or her thought by means of a verbal message; to put thought into linguistic form. (See **Decode**.)

Environment. (1) The surrounding sounds, syllables, or words of any element of language. (2) The surrounding community.

Equivalent. A word, expression, utterance, or sentence in one language which is not a word-for-word translation of a word, etc., in another language but which conveys the same meaning.

Errors. (1) *Global-syntactic*: Mistakes in overall sentence organization impeding listener or reader comprehension. (2) *Local*: Single, minor morphological errors which may irritate the listener or reader but will not prevent comprehension of a message.

Evaluation. Tests (oral, written, short-answer, essay, etc.) and other measures such as observation and questionnaires for ascertaining results being achieved and progress being made toward objectives of language learning.

Exponent. In communication theory, an utterance which contains the *communicative function*, the relevant elements of the *situation*, the *grammatical structure*, the *specific notions*, and the *surface realization* (what we hear or read) of a message.

Fade. (1) In teaching, the gradual withdrawal of cues so that the student is required to produce utterances on his or her own. (2) In speech, the lowered volume at the end of an utterance.

Feedback. (1) The control of one's performance derived from the awareness of its effect; e.g., the speaker controls his or her flow of speech by hearing his or her own words or by listening to or noting the reaction of others. (2) Error correction by a teacher or by a computer or other device.

Fit. The relationship between the sounds of the oral language and the writing systems which represent it.

Formal. Pertaining to the arrangement of sounds, letters, or words in an utterance.

Formula. A fixed expression of greeting, thanks, agreement, etc., such as Thank you, How do you do which native speakers use habitually in communication.

Formulaic Speech. Speech which is learned as a *whole* in greeting, leave taking, or other social transactions. (Also **Prefabricated Routines**.)

Formulate. Verbalize; put into words.

Frame. (1) In programmed instruction, a minimal unit of instruction. (2) A syntactic pattern, each slot of which always contains words of the same class (determiner, noun, verb, etc.). (3) A scene (or image) on film or video held for some time, reinforcing perception or knowledge. (4) A structure or network of known material in the mind which permits intake (the appropriate combination) with incoming knowledge (heard or read).

Function. (1) The grammatical role of an item of structure, e.g., subject, object. (2) The purpose or intention of the speaker.

Functional. Pertaining to real use; communicative.

Functional Categories. A system for grouping language functions, such as personal, interpersonal, directive, referential, metalinguistic, creative.

Function Words. Words which have little or no meaning by themselves but which are used in utterances to signal grammatical relationships (e.g., auxiliaries and prepositions). With *content words*, they constitute the vocabulary or lexicon of a language.

Generalization. The verbalized rule or description of a language item which results from the learner's perception of its recurring, consistent sound, form, position, grammatical function, and meaning.

Generate. (1) In generative-transformational grammar, to list the rules which account for the existence of all the acceptable (well-formed) sentences in the language. (2) To create or produce.

Gist. The main ideas extracted from a piece of material that has been heard or read.

Habit. A permanent ability to act in a particular manner.

Here and Now Material. What learners can sense (see, touch, hear, taste) in the classroom or in the immediate environment (their home or community).

i + 1. A second language acquisition hypothesis stated by Krashen and Terrell. The *i* refers to the present level of the learners' competence; the "one" refers to a word or expression the teacher will include (in a presentation of material) which should ideally follow the natural order of language acquisition. (Author's note: Any word needed in your community which fits in the context would be appropriate.)

Idiolect. The way the individual uses the language of the community; his *parole*.

Idiom. An expression whose total meaning cannot be derived from the meaning of each individual word within it; e.g., I can't do without you.

Immediate Constituents. Two or more units on one level of structure which form a single unit on the next higher level; e.g., the subject and predicate are *ICs* of the sentence; the verb phrase and complement are *ICs* of the predicate.

Incremental Learning. Learning in small steps.

Inductive Process. One in which a series of examples or model sentences is given in order to enable the learner to formulate a generalization, description, or rule. (See **Deductive Process.**)

Infer. To arrive at the meaning of a text by reasoning from evidence such as some knowledge of English, knowledge of a first language, or knowledge of the context (linguistic or other physical aspects of the situation). The meaning obtained from a text is the outcome of interaction between the printed page and the reader's cognitive processing capacities or strategies.

Inflection. A change in the form of a word to indicate plurality, possession, etc.

Informant. A native speaker or one with near native ability who may be used as an authentic resource person with relation to his or her language or culture.

Input. The language heard from any source—people talking, a teacher presenting material, television, video, radio, a computer, etc. *Comprehensible input* is a major source of language acquisition or learning.

Intake. The input which is accepted by the learner and processed for storage in short-term or long-term memory. It is accepted because the student is motivated, the affective filter is low, and the input is comprehensible.

Integration. (1) The process of combining related material or elements which belong together. (2) The fusion of different elements into a coherent whole. (3) In discussing individuals, one speaks of a well-adjusted, or well-integrated, personality.

Interaction. The give and take of communication.

Interchange. A conversation of two or more utterances.

Interference. A difficulty or problem in the learning of one habit because of the existence in the learner of a conflicting one, e.g., the difficulty of learning to produce a sound in the target language because it does not exist or exists in another position in the learner's native tongue.

Interlocutors. The participants (speakers and listeners) in a communication act.

Internalize. To understand and learn material so thoroughly that it can be produced at will.

Intervocalic. Between two vowels.

Jack. A box or other piece of equipment for a tape recorder to which additional headphones can be attached.

Juncture. A change in the quality of sounds and in the meaning of an utterance produced by pauses in speech, e.g., nitrate/night rate; I scream/ice cream.

Kernel Sentence. A basic sentence—usually simple, active, declarative, and without modifiers—which can undergo many transformations based on a series of rules. A kernel sentence has two parts or two constituents: a noun phrase (NP) and a verb phrase (VP). (*Base sentence* is used more frequently.)

Kinesics. The study of the nonverbal motions used in communication, e.g., gestures, facial expressions.

Language Acquisition Device (LAD). A theoretical mechanism in the human mind consisting of two parts: (a) the universal rules of all natural languages, and (b) the lower-level rules which permit us to learn how the universal rules are expressed in the language we are learning.

Language Feeling. (*Sprachgefühl*): The intuitive awareness, resulting from intensive practice in the second or foreign language, enabling the learner to recognize and to control production of well-formed sentences.

Langue. The total language system—the code—of the community as compared to an individual's expression (his *parole*). Both terms, *langue* and *parole* originated with Ferdinand De Saussure, a Swiss linguist.

Learning. The process which leads to the acquisition of a new skill or piece of knowledge.

Level. (1) The height to which the voice rises or falls in speaking. In English, for example, we distinguish four pitch levels. (2) The stage of learning—beginning, intermediate, advanced. (3) The degree of achievement toward a goal.

Lexical Combination. Words which co-occur, e.g., *part of*.

Lexicon. The words or vocabulary of the language. (Also Lexis.)

Linguistics. A science which systematically analyzes and describes a language as it is used by its native speakers. There are several branches of linguistic science, e.g., historical, comparative, contrastive, psycholinguistics, sociolinguistics.

Linkert Scale. A values clarification and classification device which is based on agreement or disagreement with an item (value, opinion, fact) on a list.

Longitudinal Studies. In second language acquisition research, studies based on a process-oriented hypothesis. What is studied is the present state of linguistic competence the learner has achieved after a given period of learning or acquisition.

Machine Translation. The equivalent of a text in one language rendered in another language by means of a computer.

Marker. A word or morpheme that helps identify the grammatical function of another word;

e.g.,*'s* added to a singular noun indicates possession; *the* before a word identifies it as a nominal.

Mass Noun: See **Count Noun**.

Master. (1) (verb) To learn thoroughly. (2) (noun) An original recording from which copies can be made.

Metalinguistics. (1) The scientific study of linguistics and its relation to other cultural factors in a society. *Paralinguistics, kinesics, proxemics,* for example, are included in metalinguistics. (2) The study of the language used to talk about language.

Mim-Mem. Mimicry-memorization. A teaching technique in which students imitate a model and then repeat it to the point of memorization.

Minimal Pair. Two words that sound alike except for one phonemic difference, e.g., *bag/back, ship/sheep, bit/pit.*

Model. (1) The perfect or near-perfect production of a sound, word, or utterance given by the teacher or a recording for imitation by the learners. (2) A tentative or hypothetical design or explanation for any phenomenon.

Monitor. To listen to students through an intercommunication device as they record or speak.

Monitor Theory. A theory that states that learners can hear and correct themselves if (a) they know the grammatical or communicative rule, (b) they have time, (c) they have a knowledge of their first language and of the world. (Generally possible with older learners.)

Monostructural Approach. A teaching method in which individual structures are presented one at a time through several examples and not in a dialogue or reading passage.

Morpheme. The smallest meaningful unit of language. It may be "free" (a word such as *girl* which can stand alone) or "bound" (the *s* of *girls* which indicates plurality but which cannot stand alone).

Morphology. The study of the changes in forms of words produced by inflection or derivation.

Morphophonemics. The study of the relationships and changes in phonemes because of their environment or position within a word (a morpheme) or before another word; e.g., in English, the plural morpheme changes its sound depending on the final letter of the word (/z/ in *boys* but /s/ in *books* and iz/in *boxes*).

Multiple-Choice Test. One in which the student is asked to select an answer to a question or problem from among several choices given.

Natural Order Hypothesis. A theory that features of a language are acquired or learned in a relatively fixed order by learners of all ethnic groups.

Notions. (1) *General:* Aspects of matter, space, quantity, time, case and deixis. (2) *Specific:* The vocabulary items—verbs, nouns, adjectives, adverbs—which complete the communicative functions and which can be subsumed under the general notions.

Operant Conditioning. The shaping (reinforcing or extinguishing) of the learner's responses through the forging of a bond between stimulus and response and confirmation of the correct response (termed *reward*).

Organizer. A mechanism in the human mind which classifies and systematizes the language output.

Output. The overt verbal behavior of a learner (what he or she can say or write).

Paradigm. A complete systematic set of the forms of a word or of a verb conjugation, e.g., English: I, me, *my, mine*; Spanish, present of the verb *hablar* (to speak): hablo, hablas, habla, etc.

Paralinguistics. The study of tone of voice, tempo of voice, groans, sighs, and other nonarticulated sounds which convey meaning to a listener.

Parole. The individual speaker's use of language to convey messages.

Passive Knowledge. That which is needed for understanding or recognition only; receptive knowledge as opposed to active knowledge.

Pattern. (1) An arrangement of sounds or words which recurs systematically and is meaningful. (2) The basic design that underlies a sentence, a model, etc.

Pattern Practice. Drills and activities in which the patterns of a language are learned to the point where students can repeat, alter, or respond to them habitually and fluently.

Pause. Another word for Juncture.

Pause Button. In video, a device that permits the "freezing" of a frame.

Peer Teaching. Two or more students helping each other to learn by practicing and engaging in communication activities with each other. (Also Pair(ed) Practice.)

Performance (in generative-transformational theory). (1) The overt verbal behavior of a speaker. (2) An instance of a speaker's competence.

Performance Objective. The degree of learning of an item or a skill which a student is expected to achieve under certain well-defined, clearly specified conditions.

Personalization. Relating dialogues, readings, etc., to the learners' lives and experiential background through questions.

Phatic Function of Language. The ability of a speaker to start, interrupt, or discontinue a conversation.

Phonemics. The systematic study of the meaningful sounds of language.

Phonetics. The study of the sounds of speech—the phonemes and the allophones—and the way they are produced, transmitted, and received by the listener.

Phonotactics. The arrangement of sounds in a language; the study of the restrictions (inappropriate combinations) or arrangements of sounds.

Phrase Structure Rule. One which governs the construction of the two basic parts of utterances: the noun phrase (NP) and the verb phrase (VP) of kernel (or base) sentences.

Pitch. A voice tone which distinguishes meaning.

Pragmatics. The study of the correlation of linguistic forms with situational settings.

Prefabricated Pattern. An utterance which is composed of a learned whole routine and a partly new expression, phrase, or clause.

Process. (1) In language learning or acquisition, the continuing interaction between the internal processing in the brain and the external environment. (2) In writing, the procedure used in composing and in revising.

Product. (1) The learner's verbal performance resulting from the learning process. (2) In writing, the end result of the composing and revising process.

Proficiency Test. One which permits the measurement of a person's knowledge and ability in a foreign language without regard to formal study or text used.

Prognostic Test. One which permits the measurement of hypotheses about a person's possible success in language study. (Also **Aptitude Test**.).

Programmed Learning. The systematic grading and sequencing of language material and its presentation in the smallest possible segments, generally in frames. The material to be learned (the program) is generally placed in a "teaching machine" or in a text.

Prompt. To whisper a word or expression to the learner in order to help him or her produce an utterance; to cue.

Prop. A real object (a flag, a flower, a piece of bread) or any device used in teaching to simulate reality and to elicit student response.

Proxemics. The study of distances maintained by speakers of different languages as they speak to each other or to others.

Psycholinguistics. The scientific study of the relationships between linguistic data and psychological processes.

Recombine. To bring together familiar sentences, dialogues, or reading passages in order to create new dialogues, etc., in which all the elements are familiar to the learners.

Redundancy. The multiple clues in language, some of which could be eliminated without loss of essential information; e.g., in *The boys are wearing their coats*, the /z/ sound, the verb *are*, the possessive *their*, and the /s/ sound in *coats* all indicate plurality.

Reentry. The systematic reuse or reintroduction of words and structures which have been learned with newly acquired language items (in dialogues, readings, etc.) in order to (1) keep them alive in the learners' minds, and (2) demonstrate that a word or pattern can be used in many different situations.

Referent. The actual object or situation in the real world to which a word is related or to which it refers.

Register. The variation in language (in pronunciation, grammar, or vocabulary) as used by persons in different jobs or professions, in different situations (formal or informal), and in different modes (speaking or writing).

Reinforcement. (1) The consolidation or further learning of material. (2) The confirmation or reward which increases the likelihood of a student's giving a correct response again at another time.

Rejoinder. An emphatic response given to a statement or question. The rejoinder may be a formula, another question, or another statement which reiterates or emphasizes the initial utterance.

Reliability. The degree to which a test is consistent in measuring what it is supposed to measure.

Rhetoric. The method and study of the organization of syntactic units into larger patterns of discourse.

Rhythm. The regularity of speech sequences.

Routines. (1) Language learned in whole utterances (e.g., I'm pleased to meet you). (2) A set of customary activities.

Rule. (1) The description of the form, function, and position of a recurring systematic feature of language. (2) In transformation theory, the instructions or directions which account for the existence of kernel (base) sentences (phrase structure rules) and derived sentences (transformation rules).

Scan. To read a passage very quickly in order to find some detail (of a person, an object, or a situation).

Schema Theory. A theory of reading which posits that schemata (which are stored in the mind) must fit with the meaning of the reading material for the material to be comprehensible. *Schemata* are networks of known information, i.e., the learner's background knowledge, previous language acquisition, and knowledge of the structure of English.

Segment. A syllable of a word or a group of words in an utterance.

Segmental Phonemes. The vowels and consonants.

Semantics. The study of word meanings and their effect on communication, interaction, and interpersonal relationships.

Semiotics. The study of the exchange of any messages whatsoever and of the signs which underlie them.

Shape. To lead the learner gradually to a closer approximation of the desired terminal behavior through successive listening and speaking experiences.

Sign. The general term which designates anything which stands for or represents something else.

Situation. (1) The relationship between the elements, events, or things present in the environment and the language used in talking about them, e.g., buying groceries in a market, going to a doctor's office, watching a television program. (2) In communicative theory, the major elements in the social situation which will determine the formality or informality of the conversation: people, place, time, topic.

Situational Teaching. A method in which the new structures or words for presentation and practice are embedded in an authentic conversation or in a narrative event, or in which they are taught in a context of situation.

Skim. To read a passage rapidly in order to find the gist (the main ideas).

Second Language Acquisition (SLA) Theory. A universal process which reflects the properties of the human mind.

Slot. The position of a word or phrase in a sentence which can be occupied by other words or expressions of the same class; e.g., in ''I went to the store,'' the slot *I* can be occupied by *He, Mary, The boys*, etc.

Speech. The oral expression of verbal behavior.

Spiral Approach. A method of presentation in which the same language item or cultural topic is taught in increasingly greater depth at each succeeding level of learning. (Also Cyclical Approach.)

Stimulus. Any signal (manual, oral, visual) to which a person responds or reacts. (Also Cue.)

Stop. A consonant which is made with a momentary stoppage of breath, e.g., /p/, /t/.

Stress. The prominence of syllables or words in speech.

String. A sequence of language items. In transformational theory, the terminal string, for example, is the final sequence of words in an utterance that may have undergone one or more transformations.

Structure. (1) The recurring patterns of language elements as they occur in forms of words and in arrangements of words in utterances. (2) The grammar of the language. (3) A grammatical item that contains more than one word; e.g., *may have gone*. (4) Any organized, systematic item of language.

Structure Drill. An exercise or oral activity in which patterns or structures are practiced.

Structure Word. A synonym for Function Word.

Stylistics. The study of the use of the most appropriate expression available, both connotatively and denotatively, to convey any idea.

Suprasegmental Phonemes. Pronunciation features of pitch, stress, and juncture which co-occur with or are superimposed on the vowels and consonants.

Symbol. A meaningful sign which is consciously produced, e.g., a word or a phonetic symbol.

Syntax. The arrangement of words in utterances and sentences.

System. Sets of recurring combinations and sequences of sounds and words into patterns which signal meaning.

Tagmeme. (1) The slot and its filler. (2) A significant unit of syntax.

Target Language. The second or foreign language that is being learned.

Taxonomic. Pertaining to the description and classification of structures of language.

Teaching Machine. A mechanical device used in some forms of programmed instruction.

Tense. The *formal* categories of verb inflections; e.g., in English, we sometimes speak of the simple present and past tenses only—walk*s*, walk*ed*.

Terminal Behavior. The desired outcome that a learner should achieve in terms of the acquisition of some habit, skill, knowledge, or attitude.

Terminal Contour. The intonation patterns at the end of an utterance. In English, for example, there are three: rising, falling, and sustained.

Top-Down Processing. A theory of reading which posits that, thanks to schemata, the mind can make predictions about what will be read (by looking at the title, an illustration, the first word, etc.). (Also Conceptually Driven Processing.)

Track. (1) A pattern of subject or course organization in a school or school system. For example, in the first year of the secondary school, there may be two language tracks, one for students who have studied English in the elementary school and one for beginners. (2) A stretch or path along a tape on which a recording can be made.

Transaction. A set, rather stereotyped conversation which usually takes place in a specific situation (between banker and client, storekeeper and customer, headwaiter and patron).

Transfer. The ability to use knowledge about a feature of one's native language or of the target language in learning another related feature. (Negative transfer implies the making of false analogies.)

Transfer Rules (in generative-transformational theory). These consist of two parts: (a) the phrase structure that base sentences must have before transfer rules can be applied. (b) the operation or sequence of operations producing a new sentence.

Transformation Theory. A theory of language analysis which assumes (a) that all utterances, the surface structure of the language, are derived from basic sentences—the deep structure of the language—by a series of rules; (b) that all native speakers have competence in recognizing well-formed sentences but cannot necessarily produce them; (c) that language is creative and stimulus-free.

Unconscious Selection. The habitual, fluent use of the correct sound, word form, or word arrangement in free communication.

Usage. The selection by a speaker of a certain language variety, language register, or grammatical structure.

Utterance. A word, a fixed expression, or a sentence said by a speaker which has meaning, and before which and after which there is silence on his or her part.

Validity. The degree to which a test measures what it is supposed to measure.

Variable Competence Model. A model of second language acquisition which posits that learners should be trained to be flexible enough to use any appropriate second language rule already acquired at any point of an interaction when they cannot think of the exact, specific one [cf. Ellis (1986) in Appendix V.]

Variation. (1) A change of some kind. (2) In audio-lingual methodology, the asking of questions on the dialogue itself.

Variety of Language. Changes (phonological, syntactic, or lexical) within the code brought about by such factors as geography (in the case of dialects), social or professional role, situation (formal or informal), and mode (oral or written).

Verbal Behavior. (1) Language. (2) Any manifestation of self-expression and/or communication.

Voiced Sound. A sound made with the vocal cords vibrating, e.g., /b/, vowels.

Voiceless Sound. A sound made while the vocal cords are not vibrating, e.g., /p/.

Appendix V

Bibliography

Agard, F. B., and H. Dunkel. *An Investigation of Second Language Teaching*. Boston: Ginn, 1948.

Alatis, J., H. Altman, and P. Alatis (eds.). *The Second Language Classroom*. New York: Oxford University Press, 1981.

Alexander, L. G. in J. Van Ek. *The Threshold Level*. Oxford: Pergamon Press, 1980.

Altman, H. "Foreign Language Teaching: Focus on the learner," in H. Altman, and C. Vaughan-James (eds.). *Foreign Language Teaching: Meeting Individual Needs*. Oxford: Pergamon Press, 1980.

———. *Individualizing the Foreign Language Classroom*. Rowley, Mass.: Newbury House, 1972.

Arapoff Cramer, N. *The Writing Process*. Rowley, Mass.: Newbury House, 1985.

Asher, J. *Learning Another Language Through Actions: The Complete Teacher's Guidebook*. Calif.: Sky Oaks Productions, 1977.

Bach, E. *An Introduction to Transformational Grammar*. New York: Holt, Rinehart and Winston, 1963.

Bialystok, E. "Some Evidence for the Integrity and Interaction of Two Knowledge Sources," in R. Andersen. *New Dimensions in Second Language Acquisition Research*. Rowley, Mass.: Newbury House, 1982.

Billows, L. *The Techniques of Language Teaching*. London: Longmans Green, 1961.

Block, B., and G. Trager. *Outline of Linguistic Analysis*. Baltimore: Linguistic Society of America, 1942.

Bolinger, D. *Aspects of Language*. New York: Harcourt Brace Jovanovich, 1968.

———. *Meaning and Form*. New York and London: Longman, 1977.

Bratt Paulston, C., *Bilingual Education Theories and Issues*. Rowley, Mass.: Newbury House, 1980.

Bratt Paulston, C., and M. Newton Bruder. *Teaching English as a Second Language: Techniques and Procedures*. Cambridge, Mass.: Winthrop Publishers, 1976.

Brooks, N. *Language and Language Learning*. New York: Harcourt Brace, 1964.

Brown, D. "Affective Factors in Second Language Learning," in J. Alatis, H. Altman, and P. Alatis (eds.) *The Second Language Classroom*. New York: Oxford University Press, 1981.

————. *Principles of Language Learning and Teaching*. Englewood Cliffs, N.J.: Prentice-Hall, 1987.

Brown, G., and G. Yule. *Teaching the Spoken Language*. New York: Cambridge University Press, 1987.

Brumfit, C. J. *Communicative Methodology in Language Teaching: The Roles of Accuracy and Fluency*. Cambridge: Cambridge University Press, 1984.

————, and K. Johnson. *The Communicative Approach to Language Teaching*. Oxford: Oxford University Press, 1979.

Bruner, J. *The Process of Education*. Cambridge, Mass.: Harvard University Press, 1960.

Bung, K. *The Input-Output Relation in Language Behavior*. Strasbourg, France: Council for Cultural Cooperation, Council of Europe, 1973.

Burt, M., and H. Dulay. "Optimal Language Learning Environments," in J. Alatis, H. Altman, and P. Alatis (eds.) *The Second Language Classroom*. New York: Oxford University Press, 1981.

Byrne, D. *Teaching Oral English*. London: Longman, 1976.

————, and S. Rixon. *Communication Games*. London: The British Council, 1979.

Canale, M., and M. Swain. *Theoretical Bases of Communicative Approaches to Second Language Teaching and Testing*. 1980.

Carrell, P. "Some Issues in Studying the Role of Schemata or Background Knowledge in Second Language Comprehension." *TESOL Quarterly*, 1983.

Carroll, J. *Research on Teaching Foreign Languages*. Cambridge, Mass.: Harvard University Press, 1960.

Cazden, C. *Child Language and Education*. New York: Holt, Rinehart and Winston, 1974.

Celce-Murcia, M., and S. Hilles. *Techniques and Resources in Teaching Grammar*. Oxford: Oxford University Press, 1988.

————, and D. Larsen-Freeman. *The Grammar Book*. Rowley, Mass.: Newbury House, 1983.

————, and L. McIntosh. *Teaching English as a Second or Foreign Language*. Rowley, Mass.: Newbury House, 1979.

————, and F. Rosensweig. "Teaching Vocabulary in the ESL Classroom," in M. Celce-Murcia and L. McIntosh (eds.). *Teaching English as a Second or Foreign Language*. Rowley, Mass.: Newbury House, 1979.

Chastain, K. *Developing Second Language Skills: Theory to Practice*. Chicago: Rand McNally, 1976.

Chomsky, N. "A Review of B. F. Skinner's *Verbal Behavior*." *Language*, 1959.

————. *Aspects of the Theory of Syntax*. Cambridge, Mass.: MIT Press, 1965.

————. *Reflections on Language*. New York: Pantheon Books, 1975.

Clark, R. C. *Language Teaching Techniques*. Brattleboro, Vt.: Pro Lingua, 1982.

Close, R. A. *English as a Foreign Language*. London: Allen and Noami, 1981.

Corder, S. P. *The Visual Element in Language Teaching*. London: Longmans Green, 1966.

————. "Error Analysis," in J. Allen and S. Corder (eds.). *The Edinburgh Course in Applied Linguistics*. Oxford: Oxford University Press, 1974.

Cummings, M., and R. Simmons. *The Language of Literature*. Oxford: Pergamon Press, 1983.

Curran, C. A. *Counseling-Learning in Second Languages*. Apple River, Ill.: Apple River Press, 1976.

————. *The Cognitive Client*. East Dubuque, Iowa: Daniel D. Tranel, 1982.

Dacanay, F. R., and D. Bowen. *Techniques and Procedures in Second Language Teaching*. New York: Oceana, 1967.

Danielson, D., and R. Hayden. *Using English: Your Second Language*. Englewood Cliffs, N.J.: Prentice-Hall, 1973.

Davies, A. *Language Testing Symposium: A Psycholinguistic Approach*. London: Oxford University Press, 1968.

Derrick, J. *Teaching English to Immigrants*. London: Longmans Green, 1969.

Dillard, J. *Black English*. New York: Random House, 1972.

Dobson, J. M. *Effective Techniques for English Conversation Groups*. Rowley, Mass.: Newbury House, 1979.

Dorry, G. *Games for Second Language Learning*. New York: McGraw Hill, 1966.

Dulay, H., M. Burt, and S. Krashen (eds.). *Language Two*. New York: Oxford University Press, 1982.

Dunkel, H. *Second Language Learning*. Boston: Ginn, 1948.

Ellis, R. *Classroom Second Language Development*. Oxford: Pergamon Press, 1984.

————. *Understanding Second Language Acquisition*. Oxford: Oxford University Press, 1986.

Fathman, A. "Variables Affecting the Successful Learning of English as a Second Language." *TESOL Quarterly, 1976*.

Felix, S. *Second Language Development*. Gross Gunter Van Verlag, 1980.

Ferguson, C. (ed.). *Contrastive Structure Series*. Chicago: University of Chicago Press, 1960–1965.

————, and D. Slobin, *Studies of Children's Language Development*. New York: Holt, Rinehart and Winston, 1973.

————, and W. A. Stewart. *Linguistic Reading Lists for Teachers of Modern Languages*. Arlington, Va.: Center for Applied Linguistics, 1963.

Fillmore, C. J. "The Case for Case," in E. Bach and R. T. Harms (eds.). *Universals in Linguistic Theory*. New York: Holt, Rinehart and Winston, 1968.

Finocchiaro, M. *Teaching Children Foreign Languages*. New York: McGraw Hill, 1969.

————. *Teaching English as a Second Language*. New York: Harper and Row, 1969.

————, and M. Bonomo. *The Foreign Language Learner*. New York: Regents Publishing Co., 1973.

————, and C. Brumfit. *The Functional-Notional Approach*. New York: Oxford University Press, 1983.

————, and S. Sako. *Foreign Language Testing*. New York: Regents Publishing Co., 1983.

Fishman, J. *Readings in the Sociology of Language*. The Hague: Mouton, 1969.

————. *Bilingual Education: Sociological Perspectives*. Rowley, Mass.: Newbury House, 1976.

Frank, M. *Annotated Bibliography of Materials for English as a Second Language*. New York: National Association of Foreign Student Advisors (NAFSA), 1962.

————. *Modern English*. Englewood Cliffs, N.J.: Prentice-Hall, 1972.

Fries, C. *Teaching and Learning English as a Foreign Language*. Ann Arbor, Mich.: University of Michigan Press, 1948.

————. *The Structure of English*. New York: Harcourt Brace Jovanovich, 1952.

————, and R. Lado. *English Pronunciation*. Ann Arbor, Mich.: University of Michigan Press, 1954.

Gardner, R., and W. Lambert. *Attitudes and Motivation in Second Language Learning*. Rowley, Mass.: Newbury House, 1972.

Gattegno, C. *Teaching Foreign Languages in Schools: The Silent Way*. New York: Educational Solutions, 1972.

Girard, D. *Linguistics and Foreign Language Teaching*. London: Longmans Green, 1972.

Grellet, F. *Developing Reading Skills: A Practical Guide to Reading Comprehension Exercises*. Cambridge: Cambridge University Press, 1981.

Hall, E. T. *The Silent Language*. Garden City, N.Y.: Doubleday, 1959.

———. *The Hidden Dimension*. Garden City, N.Y.: Doubleday/Anchor Books, 1966.

Halliday, M. *Explorations in the Functions of Language*. London: Edward Arnold, 1973.

———, A. McIntosh, and P. Strevens. *The Linguistic Sciences and Language Teaching*. London: Longmans Green, 1964.

Hamp-Lyons, L., and B. Heasley. *Study Writing*. Cambridge: Cambridge University Press, 1987.

Harris, D. *Testing English as a Second Language*. New York: McGraw Hill, 1969.

Hernandez-Chavez, E. "The Development of Semantic Relations in Child Second Language Acquisition," in M. Burt, H. Dulay, and M. Finocchiaro (eds.). *Viewpoints on English as a Second Language*. New York: Regents Publishing Co., 1977.

Hornby, A. S. *A Guide to Patterns and Usage in English*. London: Oxford University Press, 1954.

———. *The Teaching of Structural Words and Phrases, Stages 1–2*. London: Oxford University Press, 1959–1961.

———. *The Teaching of Structural Words and Sentence Patterns*. London: Oxford University Press, 1959–1962.

Hymes, D. *Language in Culture and Society: A Reader in Linguistics and Anthropology*. New York: Harper and Row, 1954.

———. "On Communicative Competence," in *Directions in Sociolinguistics*. Toronto: Holt, Rinehart and Winston, 1970.

Joos, M. *Readings in Linguistics: The Development of Descriptive Linguistics in America*. Chicago: University of Chicago Press, 1966.

———. *The Five Clocks*. New York: Harcourt Brace Jovanovich, 1967.

Kelly, L. *25 Centuries of Language Teaching*. Rowley, Mass.: Newbury House, 1969.

Krashen, S. *Second Language Acquisition and Second Language Learning*. Oxford: Pergamon Press, 1981.

———. *Principles and Practices in Second Language Acquisition*. Oxford: Pergamon Press, 1982.

———, and T. Terrel. *The Natural Approach: Language Acquisition in the Classroom*. Oxford: Pergamon Press, 1983.

Labov, W. *Language in the Inner City*. Philadelphia: University of Pennsylvania, 1972.

Lado R. *Language Teaching*. New York: McGraw Hill, 1964.

———. *Language Testing*. New York: McGraw Hill, 1964.

Larsen-Freeman, D. *Discourse Analysis in Second Language Acquisition Research*. Rowley, Mass.: Newbury House, 1980.

Lawrence, M. *Writing as a Thinking Process*. Ann Arbor, Mich.: University of Michigan Press, 1972.

Lee, W. R. *Language-Teaching Games and Contests*. London: Oxford University Press, 1965.

———, and H. Coppen. *Simple Audio-Visual Aids to Foreign Language Teaching*. London: Oxford University Press, 1964.

Leech, G., and J. Svartvik. *Communicative Grammar of English*. London: Longman, 1975.

Lenneberg, E. *The Biological Foundations of Language*. New York: John Wiley and Sons, 1967.

218 Bibliography

Lightbown, P. "Exploring Relationships Between Developmental and Instructional Sequences in L2 Acquisition," in H. Seliger and M. Long (eds.). *Classroom Oriented Research*. Rowley, Mass.: Newbury House, 1983.

Littlewood, W. *Communicative Language Teaching*. New York: Cambridge University Press, 1981.

———. *Foreign and Second Language Learning*. New York: Cambridge University Press, 1987.

Long, K. *The Sentence and Its Parts*. Chicago: University of Chicago Press, 1961.

Long, M. "Inside the Black Box: Methodological Issues in Classroom Research on Language Learning." *Language Learning*, 1980.

Lozanov, G. *Suggestology and Outlines of Suggestopedy*. New York: Gordon and Breach, 1978.

Lyons, J. *Introduction to Theoretical Linguistics*. New York: Cambridge University Press, 1969.

Mackey, F. *Language Teaching Analysis*. London: Longman, 1965; Bloomington, Ind.: University of Indiana Press, 1970.

Madsen, H., and D. Bowen. *Adaptation in Language Teaching*. Rowley, Mass.: Newbury House, 1978.

———. *Techniques in Testing*. New York: Oxford University Press, 1983.

Malamon-Thomas, A. *Classroom Interaction*. New York: Oxford University Press, 1987.

Maley, A., and A. Duff. *Drama Techniques in Language Learning*. Cambridge: Cambridge University Press, 1982.

———, and F. Grellet. *The Mind's Eye*. New York: Cambridge University Press, 1987.

Malinowski, B. *A Scientific Theory of Culture and Other Essays*. New York: Oxford University Press, 1960.

Malkoc, A. M. *TESOL Bibliography: Abstracts of ERIC Publications and Research Reports*. Washington, D.C.: Georgetown University Press, 1971.

Marckwardt, A. *Linguistics and the Teaching of English*. Bloomington, Ind.: University of Indiana Press, 1966.

———, and R. Quirk. *A Common Language*. New York: Modern Language A Association, 1964.

Marcussen, Lillian Hatch, and E. Hatch. *Second Language Acquisition*. Rowley, Mass.: Newbury House, 1978.

Maslow, A. *Motivation*, 2nd Ed. New York: Harper and Row, 1970.

McArthur, T. *A Foundation Course for Language Teachers*. New York: Cambridge University Press, 1987.

McIntosh, A., and M. Halliday (eds.). *Patterns of Language: Papers in General, Descriptive and Applied Linguistics*. London: Longmans Green, 1966.

McRae, J. *Words on Words: How to Write a Commentary on a Passage of Literary Prose*. Naples, Italy: Loffredi, 1988.

Mead, M. *Continuity in Cultural Evolution*. New Haven: Yale University Press, 1964.

Moskowitz, G. *Caring and Sharing in the Foreign Language Classroom*. Rowley, Mass.: Newbury House, 1978.

Oller, J. W., Jr., and P. A. Richard-Amato. *Methods That Work*. Rowley, Mass.: Newbury House, 1983.

———, and J. C. Richards. *Focus on the Learner*. Rowley, Mass.: Newbury House, 1973.

Omaggio, A. C. *Teaching Language in Context: Proficiency-Oriented Instruction*. Boston: Heinle and Heinle, 1986.

Osgood, C., and T. Sebeok. *Psycholinguistics: A Survey of Theory and Research Problems.* Bloomington, Ind.: University of Indiana Press, 1965.

Pei, M. *Glossary of Linguistic Terminology.* New York: Doubleday, 1966.

Piaget, J. *Readings in the Psychology of Cognition.* New York: Holt, Rinehart and Winston, 1974.

Praninskas, F. *Rapid Review of English Grammar.* Englewood Cliffs, N.J.: Prentice-Hall, 1975.

Postovsky, V. *The Effects of Delay in Oral Practice.* Berkeley, Calif.: University of California, 1970.

Prator, C., and Robinett, B. J. *A Manual of American English Pronunciation.* New York: Holt, Rinehart and Winston, 1972.

Quirk, R., and S. Greenbaum. *A Concise Grammar of Contemporary English.* New York: Harcourt Brace Jovanovich, 1973.

Raimes, A. *Focus on Composition.* New York: Oxford University Press, 1978.

————. *Identifying the Needs of Adults Learning a Foreign Language.* Oxford: Pergamon Press, 1980.

————. *Techniques in Teaching Writing.* New York: Oxford University Press, 1983.

Revell, J. *Teaching Techniques for Communicative English.* London: MacMillan, 1979.

Richards, J. *Error Analysis: Perspectives in Second Language Learning.* London: Longman, 1974.

————. *The Context of Language Teaching.* Cambridge: Cambridge University Press, 1985.

————, and M. Poliquin. *English Through Songs.* Rowley, Mass.: Newbury House, 1973.

————, and T. S. Rodgers. *Approaches and Methods in Language Teaching.* New York: Cambridge University Press, 1987.

Rivers, W. M. *The Psychologist and the Foreign Language Teacher.* Chicago: University of Chicago Press, 1964.

————. *Speaking in Many Tongues.* Rowley, Mass.: Newbury House, 1972.

————. *Teaching Foreign Language Skills.* Chicago: University of Chicago Press, 1981.

————. *Communicating Naturally in a Second Language: Theory and Practice in Language Teaching.* New York: Cambridge University Press, 1983.

————. *Interactive Language Teaching.* New York: Cambridge University Press, 1987.

————, and M. S. Temperley. *A Practical Guide to the Teaching of English as a Second or Foreign Language.* New York: Oxford University Press, 1978.

Rixon, S. *Developing Listening Skills.* London: MacMillan, 1986.

Robinett, B. W. *Teaching English to Speakers of Other Languages: Substance and Techniques.* New York: McGraw-Hill, 1979.

Sage, H. *Incorporating Literature in ESL Instruction.* Englewood Cliffs, N.J.: Prentice-Hall, 1987.

Savignon, S. *Communicative Competence: Theory and Classroom Practice Texts and Contexts in Second Language Learning.* Reading, Mass.: Addison-Wesley, 1983.

Scarcella, R., and S. D. Krashen. *Research in Second Language Acquisition.* Rowley, Mass.: Newbury House, 1980.

Scherer, A., and M. Wertheimer. *A Psycholinguistic Experiment in Foreign Language Teaching.* New York: McGraw Hill, 1964.

Schumann, J. H., and N. Stenson. *New Frontiers in Second Language Learning.* Rowley, Mass.: Newbury House, 1978.

————. "Second Language Acquisition Research: Getting a More Global Look at the

Learner," in H. Brown (ed.). *Papers in Second Language Acquisition, Language Learning*, Special Issue, 1976.

Sebeok, T. *Current Trends in Linguistics*. The Hague: Mouton, 1968.

Seelye, N. *Teaching Culture*. Skokie, Ill.: National Textbook Co., 1974.

Seliger, H., and M. Long. *Classroom Oriented Research in Second Language Acquisition*. Rowley, Mass.: Newbury House, 1983.

Sharwood-Smith, M. *Consciousness-Raising and the Second Language Learner*. Applied Linguistics, 1981.

Sinclair, J., and D. Brazil. *Teacher Talk*. Oxford: Oxford University Press, 1982.

————, and M. Coulthard. *Towards an Analysis of Discourse*. Oxford: Oxford University Press, 1975.

Skinner, B. *Verbal Behavior*. New York: Appleton, 1957.

————. *The Technology of Teaching*. New York: Appleton-Century-Crofts, 1968.

Spolsky, B. *The Language Education of Minority Children*. Rowley, Mass.: Newbury House, 1972.

Stern, H. H. *Languages and the Young Child*. London: Oxford University Press, 1969.

————. *Fundamental Concepts of Language Teaching*. London: Oxford University Press, 1983.

Stevick, E. *Helping People Learn English*. Nashville, Tenn.: Abingdon Press, 1957.

————. *A Workbook in Language Teaching*. Nashville, Tenn.: Abingdon Press, 1964.

————. *Adapting and Writing Language Lessons*. Washington, D.C.: Foreign Service Institute, 1971.

————. *Memory, Meaning and Method*. Rowley, Mass.: Newbury House, 1976.

————. *Teaching Languages: A Way and Ways*. Rowley, Mass.: Newbury House, 1980.

————. *Images and Options in the Language Classroom*. New York: Cambridge University Press, 1986.

Strevens, P. *Aural Aids in Language Teaching*. London: Longmans Green, 1958.

————. "Theoretical Model of the Language Learning/Teaching Process," in P. Strevens (ed.). *New Orientation in the Teaching of English*. London: Oxford University Press, 1977.

Stryker, S. *Teaching American English*. Rowley, Mass.: Newbury House, 1972.

Talansky, S. B. *The Art of Teaching English as a Foreign Language*. Ancona, Italy: Casa Editrice Nuove Ricerche, 1986.

Tarone, E., M. Swain, and A. Fathman. "Some Limitations to the Classroom Applications of Current Second Language Acquisition Research." *TESOL Quarterly*, 1976.

Taylor, A. *357 Songs We Love to Sing*. Minneapolis, Minn.: Schmitt, Hall and McCreary, 1972.

Trager, G., and H. Smith. *An Outline of English Structure*. Washington, D.C.: American Council of Learned Societies, 1957.

Trim, J. *Draft Outlines of a European Unit-Credit System for Modern Languages Learning by Adults*. Oxford: Pergamon Press, 1980.

Ur, P. *Discussions That Work: Task-Centered Fluency Practice*. Cambridge: Cambridge University Press, 1987.

Valdes, J. *Culture Bound: Bridging the Cultural Gap in Language Teaching*. New York: Cambridge University Press, 1986.

Valette, R. *Modern Language Testing*. New York: Harcourt Brace Jovanovich, 1967.

Van Ek, J. *The Threshold Level for Modern Language Learning in Schools*. London: Longman, 1976.

Vygotsky, L. S. *Mind in Society: The Development of Higher Psychological Processes*. Cambridge, Mass.: Harvard University Press, 1978.

Wardhaugh, R. *The Contexts of Language*. Rowley, Mass.: Newbury House, 1978.

Wells, G. "Becoming a Communicator," in G. Wells (ed.). *Learning Through Interaction*. Cambridge: Cambridge University Press, 1981.

Wenden, A., and J. Rubin. *Learner Strategies in Language Learning*. London: Prentice Hall International, 1987.

Widdowson, H. *Language Teaching Texts*. London: Oxford University Press, 1971.

———. *Teaching Language as Communication*. London: Oxford University Press, 1978.

———. *The Teaching of Rhetoric to Students of Science and Technology*. CILT Reports and Papers, 1981.

Wilkins, D. *Linguistics in Language Teaching*. London: Arnold, 1972.

———. *Notional Syllabuses: A Taxonomy and Its Relevance to Foreign Language Curriculum Development*. London: Oxford University Press, 1977.

Winitz, H., and J. Reeds. *Rapid Acquisition of a Foreign Language*. IRAL21 12:4, 1973.

Wode, H. "Operating Principles and Universals in L1, L2 and FLT," in D. Nehls (ed.). *Studies in Language Acquisition*. Julius Groos Verlag, 1980.

Wolfram, D., and R. Fasold. *The Study of Social Dialects in American English*. Englewood Cliffs, N.J.: Prentice-Hall, 1974.

Wright, A. *1000 Pictures for Teachers to Copy*. Reading, Mass.: Addison-Wesley, 1985.

———, D. Betteridge, and M. Buckby. *Games for Language Learning*. Cambridge: Cambridge University Press, 1984.

Wright, T. *Roles of Teachers and Learners*. Oxford: Oxford University Press, 1987.

Yalden, J. *Principles of Course Design for Language Teaching*. Cambridge: Cambridge University Press, 1987.

Yorio, Carlos. "Conventionalized Language Forms and the Development of Communicative Competence." *TESOL Quarterly*, 1980.

Appendix VI

Some Additional Resources

Agencies and Associations

American Council of Teachers of Foreign Languages (ACTFL). 60 Fifth Ave., New York, N.Y.

Association of Teachers of English to Speakers of Other Languages (TESOL). Georgetown University, Washington, D.C.

Binational Centers. Many countries; schools jointly sponsored by the United States and ministries of education in the host country.

British Council. State House, London, England.

Center for Applied Linguistics (CAL). 1118 22 St. N.W., Washington, D.C.

Education Section of ministries of education, of migration offices, and of private educational and social agencies.

English Teaching Division. United States Information Service, Washington, D.C.

Modern Language Association (MLA). 60 Fifth Avenue, New York, N.Y.

National Association of Foreign Student Advisors. 809 United Nations Plaza, New York, N.Y.

National Council of Teachers of English. Champaign, Ill.

Nuffield Foundation. Leeds, England.

UNESCO. United Nations Plaza, New York, N.Y. (also Belgium).

U.S. Department of Health, Education and Welfare. (DHEW). Washington, D.C.

U.S. Office of Education (USOE). Washington, D.C.

Periodic Collections, Monographs, and Reports

Annual Bibliography on Teaching Foreign Languages. New York: MLA.

Britannica Review of Foreign Language Education. Chicago: Encyclopedia Britannica (published yearly).

Council for Cultural Cooperation. Strasbourg, France: Council of Europe.

ERIC Clearinghouse on Linguistics. Arlington, Va.: CAL.
ERIC Focus Reports on Foreign Language Teaching. New York: ACTFL.
Georgetown Round Table Monographs. Washington, D.C.: Georgetown University.
Language Research in Progress. Arlington, Va.: CAL.
Northeast Conference Reports. New York: MLA (reports available from 1954).
Research in Education. U.S. Government Printing Office. Washington, D.C.

Periodicals and Journals

Anthropological Linguistics. University of Indiana, Bloomington, Ind.
Archiv für das Studium der Neuren Sprachen und Literaturen. Braunschweig, Germany.
Audio-Visual Aids and Teaching of Languages. Antwerp, Belgium.
Audio-Visual Language Journal. Hertfordshire, England.
Babel. Australian Federation of Modern Language Teachers Association, Melbourne, Australia.
Cahiers Ferdinand de Saussure: Revue de Linguistique Générale. Geneva, Switzerland.
Canadian Journal of Linguistics. Toronto, Canada.
Canadian Modern Language Review. Ontario Modern Language Teachers Association, Toronto, Canada.
Classical Journal. Ohio State University, Columbus, Ohio.
Contact. Fédération Internationale des Professeurs de Langues Vivantes, Berne, Switzerland.
English—A New Language. Commonwealth Office of Education, Sydney, Australia.
The English Journal. National Council of Teachers of English, Champaign, Ill.
English Language Teaching. IATEFL, Middlesex, England.
English Teaching Abstracts. British Council, London, England.
English Teaching Forum. USIA, Washington, D.C.
English Teaching Guidance. Ministry of Education, Tel Aviv, Israel.
English Teaching News. British Council, London, England.
Foreign Languages in School. Moscow, USSR.
Français dans le Monde. Paris, France.
French Review. American Association of Teachers of French, Baltimore, Md.
German Quarterly. American Association of Teachers of German, Cincinnati, Ohio.
Glottodidactica. Poznan, Poland.
The Grade Teacher. Darien, Conn.
Hispania. American Association of Teachers of Spanish and Portuguese, Washington, D.C.
The Instructor. Owen Publishing Company, Dansville Park, N.Y.
International Journal of American Linguistics. University of Indiana, Bloomington, Ind.
International Journal of Applied Linguistics in Language Teaching. IRAL, Heidelberg, Germany.
Italica. American Association of Teachers of Italian, Evanston, Ill.
Journal of English as a Second Language. American Language Institute, New York University, New York, N.Y.
Language. Linguistic Society of America, University of Texas, Austin, Texas.
Language and Language Behavior Abstracts (LLBA). University of Michigan, Ann Arbor, Mich.

Language Learning: A Journal of Applied Linguistics. 1522 Rackham Building, Ann Arbor, Mich.

Modern Language Journal. Curtis Reed Plaza, Menasha, Wis.

Modern Language: Journal of the Modern Language Association of the United Kingdom. London, England.

NAFSA Newsletter. NAFSA (National Association of Foreign Student Advisors), United Nations Plaza, New York, N.Y.

Publications of the Modern Language Association of America (PMLA). Modern Language Association, 60 Fifth Avenue, New York, NY.

Rassegna italiana di linguistica applicata. Rome, Italy.

Revista de Educación. Madrid, Spain.

Russian Review. The Hoover Institution. Stanford, Calif.

School and Society. 1860 Broadway, New York.

TESOL Newsletter. TESOL, 1118 22 Street N.W., Washington, D.C.

TESOL Quarterly. TESOL, 1118 22 Street N.W., Washington, D.C.

Index

Index